ITALIAN
NEIGHBOURS

*An Englishman
in Verona*

TIM PARKS

Minerva

A Minerva Paperback
ITALIAN NEIGHBOURS

First published in Great Britain 1992
by William Heinemann Limited
First published in paperback 1993
by Mandarin Paperbacks
This Minerva edition published 1994
by Mandarin Paperbacks
an imprint of Reed Consumer Books Limited
Michelin House, 81 Fulham Road, London sw3 6rb
and Auckland, Melbourne, Singapore and Toronto

Reprinted 1994

A CIP catalogue record for this title
is available from the British Library
ISBN 0 7493 1102 9

Printed and bound in Great Britain
by Cox & Wyman Ltd, Reading, Berks

Italian Neighbours

Tim Parks is the author of six novels, including *Tongues of Flame* (winner of the Somerset Maugham and Betty Trask Awards), *Loving Roger* (winner of the John Llewellyn Rhys Prize) and most recently *Goodness*. He has lived in Italy since 1981 and is married with two children. Apart from his writing, he also works as a teacher and translator.

Author's Note

I often find it useful, or at least amusing, to think of a book in terms of a gesture, a mood, a posture. In which case the gesture of this book might be that of a busy but inexpert fellow dashing about the narrow confines of his territory waving a net on the end of a long stick. It's not a butterfly net, by the looks of it. It's altogether too big for that, huge in fact. But it might be a will-o'-the-wisp net. Which would explain the extremely fine silk mesh, the random way it is being waved. And if we were to ask this frantic fellow what particular species of will-o'-the-wisp he is after? He stops, out of breath, surprised at our interest. Well, some of the most common, he pants: national character, a sense of place, the feeling people, place and weather generate. And how is he getting on? He shrugs, pouts, as if to say, this is a mug's game if ever there was one. Will-o'-the-wisps – you know – the thing is, even when you do catch one for a moment you have a terrible job recognising them, and then when you pin them on the pages of your book they immediately lose all colour and shape. Anyway, he is spending most of his time picking truisms, clichés and caricatures out of his net. Not to mention the mere grit and chaff the air is full of. You leave him to get on with it. He rushes off, apparently at random. And it seems that in his desperation he's beginning to wield his net quite wildly, and perhaps in not altogether legitimate fashion, sweeping backwards in time when he ought to go forwards, allowing the fine fabric to fill with all kinds of things from moments years apart, and places, even dimensions, far from contiguous. You shake your head. Whatever it is that finally gets catalogued in his book, obviously this is not a man you'll be able to trust on such imponderables as documentary authenticity.

1

Afa

How to forget the day we arrived in Montecchio? How even to begin to describe the weather to someone who has not been in the Veneto in July? For the weather must surely have played its part in how things went.

We're not talking about heat really. Or that's only part of the problem. The temperature is maybe only 31°C or 32, which is not impossibly hot. One has managed with 35 and more on beaches down south or in the mountains. But there is no sunshine with this heat today, no blue sky, no colour, no air. Above you – and it doesn't seem very far above you either – is a uniform, oppressive, at once damp and gritty greyness, the sun only a suspicion somewhere, a blond thumbprint, a smudge. Nor is there the slightest inkling that this strange, simmering, spongy atmosphere is going to roll itself up into some kind of raincloud or liberating storm. There's not a breath, not a whisper of wind.

You don't notice it perhaps in the town, but as you leave Verona, heading east, you suddenly become aware how miserable visibility is. The hills immediately to the north whose cherry blossom you enjoyed so much in spring, the toothy peaks of the Alps beyond which were so dramatic in sharp and slanting winter light, have all disappeared. Perhaps you're not seeing more than a couple of kilometres. And if – and God forbid – you were to turn south into the *bassa padana* itself, Po-bound across the open plain, you might well find, beyond Nogarole Rocca, towards Mantua, a sort of brilliant grey heat fog, so dense the world will seem a haze and the other cars ghosts, and the vines and fruit trees and towering maize and tobacco plants one vast steaming minestrone of a landscape . . .

But we are going to Montecchio, which, like Verona itself, lies at the foot of those first now invisible hills that mark the beginning of the long climb up to the Alps. And, curiously, it is the Alps, you are always told, which are one of the guilty parties as far as this weather is concerned. But only in this sense: that they shut out the merciful winds that might otherwise blow away everything that makes the atmosphere in the plain so unpleasant: the slow accumulation of exhaust fumes, the exhalations of a thousand pig- and chicken-factories, and the abundant insecticides that hover and mingle in the stale air over what otherwise, or in other weather, would be scenes of exquisite beauty.

The local name for the whole phenomenon is *afa* – or *lo smog* (pronounced zzzmog). You pick your shirt away from armpits and feel uncomfortable about the crotch. The only thing close to it in British terms perhaps is a packed Friday afternoon rush hour on bus or tube when the *Standard* has taken up half its front page to tell you WHAT A SIZZLER!

But, just at the moment, we are travelling behind the rusty white Fiat 127 of our future landlady, our *padrona di casa*. We are going to see and hopefully move into a 110-square-metre flat in the outlying village of Montecchio. Hence our own car, an ageing tangerine Passat, is loaded to the stops with all our worldly belongings; the boot is held down by shotcord over piles of boxes, the handlebar of one of our bicycles is creeping down the windscreen.

Across the toneless, almost invisible countryside, the narrow road is flanked by low cement walls, deep flood-emergency dikes, dusty poplars, cypresses, vines. We pass an occasional peasant figure, broad-butted on his puttering *motorino*, helmetless, cigarette in the corner of his mouth. Or it might be a woman, shopping-bag between fat knees, kerchief tight on grey hair, monumental somehow despite precarious movement, the face so grimly set. Other vehicles our cautious guide chooses to overtake are a tractor with an ageing dog balancing on the mudguard and a three-wheeled *furgoncino*, a sort of motorised wheelbarrow with tiny cabin, handlebar drive and a pile of scrap metal rattling perilously behind. Meanwhile, we ourselves are overtaken by bikes so white and fast my wing mirror doesn't appear to register them, space-suited riders flashing into the distance, and then, of course, the usual chase of black or metallic Mercedes, Alfas, Lancias, BMWs. It was a traffic mix, a social mix, with which we were to become familiar.

Perhaps ten minutes out of town, without any noticeable change of speed, we find we are in a built-up area again;

first a loose alignment of stuccoed houses, then the broad open space of Montecchio's main, Montecchio's only real piazza: small shops, tall cedars in two patches of scrubby green, a petrol pump with a weigh-in for trucks, a war memorial. All at once, the buildings close in, the road narrows drastically, the pavement on each side rises to a metre above ground level. Stout legs and slim are barely a foot from the passenger window. And still the traffic doesn't change speed. We emerge, cross a bridge, wind left past the glaring heterogeneity of a huge new red-brick church, then more bridges, ditches and streams, until, just before the road climbs out of the village and into the hills, our would-be *padrona* indicates left and we are in Via Colombare.

Narrow, perhaps two hundred metres long, and straight as straight, Via Colombare achieves an exquisite confusion of invading suburbia and peasant tradition. It is where *furgoncino* and Mercedes both come home to lunch. Closely packed along either side, the houses are all different: two, three or four storeys, one facing this way, one that, some centuries old, handsome or poverty-stricken, others new, crude or lavish; one pink-stuccoed, one blue, one green, many with just bare, pitted cement the same grim colour as today's unpromising sky. There may be a new Alfa 75 drawn up outside one door, and a decrepit straw-hatted grandfather on rickety chair parked outside the next. To add to the sense of emblematic collision, from the far end of the street a painted Madonna gazes from her shrine in the wall of a cherry orchard, right along the flat ribbon of patchy tarmac to where a derelict bottling factory is due for redevelopment opposite.

There is no pavement in Via Colombare. The front doors

4

of most of the older, poorer houses thus open directly on to the hot asphalt. Their owners have to remember to keep their window shutters tied back in case a truck (presumably lost) should carry them away (one day it was an old stone balcony that went). And where the newer houses of urban arrivals or peasant farmers made good are set back from the road, or perhaps there is a garden, the welcome breathing space that might result is lost because of the obsession with tall and elaborate iron railings as an indicator of wealth. Likewise, gates must be tall and iron and complicated and, where possible, rendered all the more impressive by the addition of little brick and stucco shelters with terracotta-tile roofs.

It was by these gates, as we parked the car, and by the humbler doorways with their fly curtains, as we climbed out, that the street's inhabitants had begun, if not quite to gather, then at least to appear: a heavy woman with the alibi of a broom, a man not quite intent on forcing his dog into the boot of his car, others with no more excuse than the walls or railings they were leaning on. And it was impossible not to get the feeling that they were there to watch us. Not in any way suspiciously, nor with hostility. But with curiosity, yes. With definite and considerable interest.

Well, we felt uncomfortable enough with the heat, the humidity. It was possible we looked out of sorts. And, of course, we were aware by now that Italians don't drive bright orange cars (or bright yellow or green cars for that matter) and that the owners of such cars are looked upon with a certain amount of condescension and immediately understood to be Germans, an epithet more or less synonymous with bad taste. Then despite our new Verona plates we still had that old GB sticker on the back, and so could be, what, from *Gibilterra* it has often been suggested. Yes, we were used to all this; in a mild, light-hearted kind of way perhaps we even cultivated it, for it is fun to be foreign, at least for a year or two. But however far out in the country we were, an orange car and an air of disorientation and discomfort were not usually enough to get ten or fifteen people hanging around their doors in the glaring heat to watch us. And so soon after lunch, too. Did they know something we didn't? Were they expecting a show?

Our future *padrona* was nervous, clumsily pushing the wrong key into the gate of what was certainly the most modern building on the street: newish lime-green stucco with a rough, *graffiato* finish, huge, broad, quite superfluous Californian eaves, double-glazed glass front door, large terrace balconies to each of the four flats. She made no comment on the watching faces around us; they did not surprise her. Was it safe to assume that what they knew, she knew too? And why had she insisted, so uncharacteristically for an Italian, on arranging our meeting at a time when most people were resting, shutters half drawn, dazed by the combination of heavy lunch and humid heat?

Quite unprompted now, and in a nervous attempt to be offhand, this dry, thin-faced, intelligent woman with her small bright brown eyes was telling us about some gynaecological problem she had. She'd been to the clinic again this morning. All the tests doctors made one do nowadays. The time, the expense. Especially when one more or less had to go privately if one was to get any decent service. But who could afford to risk the unnameable diseases? You know how it is? Her hand was shaking. She

6

was having terrible trouble with her bunch of keys, forcing quite improbable versions into the lock on the gate.

My wife and I exchanged glances, looked about us. The sun did not so much lie along the street like a white-hot poker, as it would do later in August and September; it was more that the whole scene, the scarred asphalt, the flaking stone or cement of the walls, the gardens, the vines, the dusty ivies, were fizzing with light. Everything glared.

'*Eccoci!*' the gate snapped open. And at that precise moment Lucilla appeared on a balcony above us and began to shout, or rather to yell, to shriek, to scream.

Lucilla was, is, a short, squat woman, big-breasted, fat, more than round-faced, tinted hair thinning almost to baldness, teeth with the quality of bones, set apart from each other and slightly protruding. Certainly the general impression she gave us that first day in Montecchio was not improved by the fact that every feature was contorted with rage.

This, then, was what the inhabitants of Via Colombare had been waiting for. The tubby woman danced and screamed on her balcony. Her voice filled the air in the narrow street. She pointed down at us, waving her arm as if to hurl anathema and excommunication.

I had been in Italy just over a year at the time. I lay no claims to being a linguist, but I think I had reached the point where I understood perhaps 80 per cent of what was spoken directly to me, and say 50 per cent (far more than enough) of what was merely said in my presence. But that afternoon I could identify not one syllable of what Signora Lucilla was so urgently bawling.

I turned to Rita for help. She understood very little more than me. This was not apparently the local dialect. Which was reassuring. On the balcony above us the little woman continued to be galvanised by rage. A quite extraordinary energy. As if determined to spit out her teeth at us by dint of shrieking.

'*Pazza*', Signora Marta said firmly. 'Crazy.' She was refusing to look up and acknowledge the tirade. '*Completamente pazza*. It's the *afa.*' By great good luck she got the key to the glass front door first time and we were inside; there were creamy marble stairs, a feeling akin to coolness, tropical plants, a reduction in the noise level, but absolutely no time to lose. Up we panted past the two ground-floor flats on the first landing with their funereal, polished-wood doors and round, brass knobs; on we rushed to the second landing where an identical pair of doors again faced each other like diametrically opposed choices in some masonic trial. Our *padrona* knew to go left. Out came the keys again amidst growing nervousness. Ah, *finalmente*! But no, there was still the security lock. And Lucilla simply exploded from the door opposite.

Later I came to think of Lucilla's story as something that in England would be exclusively the stuff of nineteenth-century novels – child labour and deprivation, uncertain inheritance, deathbed fawning, wills burnt or buried and others with forged signatures or clauses added under duress with the complicity of generously bribed physicians – a world where money was not sensibly regulated by the likes of pension funds and insurance policies. I remember planning a novel around Lucilla, but then thought nobody would believe it, they'd think I'd been reading too much Dickens, was stealing passages from *Middlemarch*. Hence, in describing now the scene that followed, it seems natural to use expressions like, 'her bosom heaved', for heave it did, and greatly; or, 'eyes and cheeks were blown out with apoplexy', for blown out they most certainly were. Smaller even than I had imagined, and bigger breasted, Lucilla stamped a high-heeled foot as if to strike sparks from the marble. Her heavy jowls quivered. The blue print dress stretched and strained about her. Tears of rage rolled down her cheeks. And now we began to understand something. Her shouting had resolved itself into a simple chant of, '*è mio, è mio, l'appartamento è mio*! The flat is mine! Mine, mine, mine!' She grabbed the other woman and shook her. She spat. As for ourselves, it was as if we hadn't existed. Which was just as well . . .

Still fumbling with her keys – I wished she would give them to me – Signora Marta at last lost her nerve. So far she had been playing cool city woman to this ill-bred, peasant savagery. Now she too began to shout. 'You need a doctor, *signora*, a *psichiatra*!' And in her eagerness to get away from the unpleasant scene, she yanked quite viciously at the key in the security lock and it snapped in her hands.

Silence. Surprise. Then Lucilla was saying, '*Grazie Gesù, grazie!*' Behind her back, after swiftly making the sign of the cross, her hands seemed to be trying to loosen off some girdle or brassiere. Her face was purple: '*Maria Santissima, grazie!*' The key had broken. We couldn't get in. It was a sign from God. It was proof of her claim to ownership. She was weeping for joy. Signora Marta led us in a hasty retreat down the stairs. As we drove away the onlookers were already converging on the house for news of how the battle had gone.

2
Iella

Over *espresso* in a bar back in Verona, Signora Marta endeavoured to reassure us. That ignorant old witch had run the cleaning company for which Marta's uncle – Patuzzi – had done the accounts. When the company was sold off, Lucilla, her brother Giosuè and sister-in-law Vittorina had built the *palazzina* in Via Colombare together with Patuzzi so that they could all retire happily together. Lucilla's daughter had been supposed to move into the fourth flat but hadn't wanted to be near her mother. Signora Marta pouted thin lips and tapped a city nose, as if to say, 'and we know why, don't we?' In any event, Lucilla had somehow got it into her head that the whole *palazzina* had been built with her money, that is the company's money, and that all flats would revert to her or her heirs on the death of the occupant. 'Can you imagine anything so crazy?' Uncle Patuzzi had died a year ago. His wife, Anna Rosa, Marta's aunt, had hung on in the flat a year longer, but was ill, infirm and constantly harangued by an ever more threatening Lucilla with whom she had never *andata d'accordo*, being herself from an altogether different social class. Now the old lady, *poveretta*, had gone into a home, mainly to escape Lucilla, and she, Signora Marta, as future heir and present administrator, needed to make some money out of the place, if only, as we would surely appreciate, to pay the various bills and taxes. No sooner were we actually in the flat than Lucilla would accept the situation, this afternoon's outburst being anyway mainly due to this abysmal weather which could play havoc with anyone's nerves.

Well, Rita and I had spent most of our life together looking for rented accommodation. We had searched twice in Boston, three times in London, and this was our second time in Italy. We knew that finding a place is tough and that the more generous and idealistic the tenancy laws are, the tougher it becomes. Italy's laws are idealistic in the extreme, with a sort of permanent freeze on evictions, since no political party seems ready to face the flak of unfreezing the situation (the same might be said of almost every area of Italian politics). What's more, we had no place to stay. So it was agreed that no sooner had the locksmith done his job – and Signora Marta had a friend who had another friend who knew something about locks – than we would try again under cover of darkness.

Thus it was. Poor Lucilla must have been in bed, or deafened by her television. Signora Marta had her keys carefully labelled. Barely a minute after the cars had been parked, their doors clicked quietly shut, we were already tiptoeing into the flat. Under a 40-watt bulb, Marta made us sign something on the kitchen table; to the effect that we promised to leave in exactly one year's time or at any moment thereafter when she should so desire. Of course, such a contract could have no legal validity since wise Signora Marta had no intention of declaring us as tenants and getting caught for tax on her rent. But as you discover after a while, Italians lay great store by the signing of pieces of paper, *'documenti'* they insist on calling them. There is a certain ritual attached to the practice, a warding off of evil spirits, and an appeal to the notion of honour which, people feel, should take precedence over legal quibbling, if only because it is generally more convenient to keep the government out of things.

Satisfied, but still nervous, Signora Marta gathered up her piece of paper. Here was the bank account number to pay the rent to: at the Banca Popolare di Verona in Piazza Nogara. Three hundred thousand Lire. Apparently, she didn't have time to show us the place. If we had any problems finding anything we could call her on the phone. The furnishings, she could guarantee – and she made the gesture of someone in a hurry – were excellent. Her uncle and aunt had been people of considerable culture, well educated, much travelled. We would find books and art works that were *estremamente interessanti*. If there was anything left in the drawers or cupboards we could store it in the *solaio*, the loft, upstairs. The key was on the bunch. *'Va bene?'* This thin, nervous woman took more than a cursory look through the Judas hole in the door, drew a deep breath, whispered *arrivederci* and scuttled off down the stairs.

So far we had barely looked about us. Now we explored. And discovered that none of the light bulbs in the flat were any more than 40 watts, so that even the grotesque five-armed chandelier in the *salotto* dripping with globules of smoky glass cast only a dim glow of sad pomp. For such a cultured man Uncle Patuzzi had been doing remarkably little reading of an evening.

Still, minor shortcomings of this variety could easily be remedied, we thought. Likewise the array of department store Madonnas, Sacred Hearts, Sant'Antonios and clumsy bric-à-brac crucifixions that stared down from every wall could be removed and stored away with minimum effort. And the orange-and-green floor tiles did have a smooth, clean, cool feel to them; the window fittings were, by London standards, quite luxurious, while the bathroom, with walls tiled almost to the ceiling, hardwood loo seat and handsome creamy beige bidet and bath, was palatial. Certainly, when one remembered the bedsits and miniflats of Acton and Willesden, this was a very well-appointed place indeed.

But the furniture . . . Well, we had seen it elsewhere, so it was not entirely unexpected. But depressing all the same. So many Italians, even young Italians, will move into the most modern buildings, light and airy with attractive ceramics and fittings, only to clutter the space with heavy coffin-quality furniture which affects the antique and noble but achieves only the cumbersome and uncleanable, casting sad shadows into the bargain. Thus, a dark-stained console with twisting candlestick legs was shedding neat piles of sawdust to let us know the wood-worm were at work. Veneer was blistering on a mammoth bookcase with surely anachronous frosted glass doors, while above the sofa a teak-framed mirror with cracked silvering found 40-watt reflections of a darkly noble dinner-table opposite. Venturing as far as the bedroom, and rather disconcerted now, we found great, square, black-varnished head– and footboards supporting a sagging boat shape between, reminiscent of the bed in a school-of-Veronese *Death of the Virgin* I had recently seen in a local church. On opening dusty chests, dark wardrobes, deep drawers, we discovered that all without exception were full to overflowing with the worn-out possessions of thirty years ago.

In need of air, we rolled up plastic slat shutters and walked out on to the main terrace balcony into the luminous, breathless heat of the evening. Across the street, in front of an older peasant house with fine pink stucco, a group of people our own age were laughing, drinking, smoking and playing table tennis under a fluorescent tube whirring with moths, strung up between two tall cypresses. In the street, despite the hour, their numerous children kicked a football amongst the cars, including our own, bicycles still on top, strips of chrome hanging off the sides. We sat on the arms of an old armchair that Uncle or Aunty Patuzzi had abandoned out here to make a home for spiders and provide the stuff of birds' nests. The sharp tock-tocking of the ping-pong ball, the laughter of adults and children, the background whirring of crickets, was not unpleasant. And would have been pleasanter still with a glass of chilled white wine in our hands. That was something to look forward to. Walking to the far end of the balcony, we saw a young man manoeuvring his sober blue Lancia into a makeshift garage of corrugated iron and breeze block. Then came the strains of the news programme from perhaps three or four open windows. What time was it, eleven o'clock? At midnight we could expect the first fresh stirring of the air. And we intended to be naked on the bed for that.

This has always been one of the pleasures of high summer here. You have been uncomfortably sticky all day. Maybe you've showered twice, tried shorts, long cotton trousers, T-shirts, tank tops, exchanged shoes for tennis shoes, tennis shoes for sandals, sandals for bare feet, had the fan on top speed blowing your papers about while you're typing, sucked ice cubes, put your legs in a bucket of cold water, etc., etc., and nothing has worked. The heat seems to come from inside you. Comfort is unimaginable.

Naturally, you feel irritable. Towards evening, you look at the sky, listen to distant thunder, watch the heat lightning playing over low hills, and you know that it won't rain; so often the elements put on this show just to tease. Going to bed you must decide: the open windows and the *zanzare*, the mosquitoes, or the closed windows and the heat. Inevitably, you opt for the mosquitoes, because in the end, at least around Verona, there aren't that many.

You lie there naked. The idea of any superfluous contact with your body in the form of a sheet or pyjamas is unthinkable. Through a kind of breathy intimacy the summer darkness has, you listen to chatter, facetious variety shows, card games and music from other open windows; because nobody in the entire neighbourhood is asleep, nobody would dream of installing air-conditioning so as to be able to turn in at the normal time (and even mosquito nets are rare). Everybody is waiting for it to happen. Until at last, around midnight or shortly afterwards, like some good spirit suddenly moving across the face of the earth, or the touch of a lover's finger dipped in cool water, the air stirs, it shifts, it breathes, and the notion of freshness becomes imaginable again. Almost immediately the sounds fade, the TVs snap off, the children cease to shriek and chatter, Via Colombare is falling asleep.

It was an hour or so later on this particular night that Vega began to bark. I am not exaggerating when I say of Vega that I have never heard another dog sound so deeply disturbed, so much an *anima in pena*, a tormented soul. She bayed, wailed, was at once furious and desperate. I remember asking Rita which circle of the *Inferno* we might be in.

The third or fourth time the beast woke up, I went out on to the tiny balcony of our bedroom at the back of the house away from the street. On a raised terrace not five yards away, the other side of a narrow canyon of garden between, a big golden labrador strained a long chain to paw at flaking shutters barring the back door of an old peasant house. It howled rather than barked, perhaps moaned rather than howled. And as I watched, enjoying the now cool night air on my skin, somebody threw something at the creature from an upper window, food perhaps, for the dog was immediately scrabbling excitedly among the terrace sweepings between a Cinquecento and an Alfetta.

Back in bed, the apparent relief of silence was shortlived. The insidious whine of a *zanzara* hovered just above our pillows. Up in a flash, light on, a dusty accountancy magazine of Patuzzi's grabbed from the bedside table, within a minute I'd reduced the thing to a bright red spot of blood on the greying tempera wall. 'Can AIDS be passed

on by mosquitoes?' the local paper had recently been
alarming us.

'I wonder, you know,' I asked, coming back to bed, 'I
wonder if the yups and artsy guys and retired professors
checking through estate agents' lists of farmhouses in
Tuscany have been adequately filled in on these details.'
My wife, who always seems ready for questions of this
kind, remarked that first the weather was never this
unpleasantly sultry in Tuscany, second that local dialects
there were all more or less comprehensible, since they
formed the basis of modern Italian, and third, and most
convincingly, that anybody who could afford to buy a
farmhouse in Tuscany need not have somebody else's
hunting dog breathing down their necks, and would
doubtless have screen windows fitted before moving in. As
far as we were concerned, however, she continued, there
was just the small problem that we were not so fortunately
placed *vis-à-vis* our bank accounts and, furthermore, that
there were so many Brits in Tuscany that our linguistic
skills would not be in the kind of demand that might allow
us to pay a hefty rent.

'Plus the fact', she added, '*che tu porti iella*. You bring bad
luck.'

Only months later, when I took the liberty of saying the
same thing to a business acquaintance, did I appreciate that
such an accusation is one of the worst things an Italian can
say to somebody. Had I known, we would doubtless have
argued long into the night.

3
Pasticceria Maggia

Am I giving the impression that I don't like the Veneto? It's not true. I love it. I'm going to tell you some wonderful things about it. When I've finished, I hope you'll be wishing you'd been here too, at least for a little while. But like any place that's become home, I hate it too. And, of course, you can't separate the things you love and hate: you can't say, let's move to so and so where they have the *cappuccini*, the wines, the *lasagna*, the marvellous peaches, the handsome people in handsome clothes, the fine buildings, the close-knit, friendly secretiveness of village life, but not, please, the howling maltreated hunting dogs, the spoilt adolescents on their *motorini*, the hopeless postal service, the *afa*. You can't do it. It's a package deal.

In any event, the morning after our unnerving arrival,

we set off to find the village bar/*pasticceria* and console ourselves with the pleasanter side of the arrangement, make ourselves known, see the lie of the land. And for anyone moving to Italy, this is a habit I really can't recommend too warmly: frequent your local bar, and if possible bar/*pasticceria*; frequent it assiduously, decorously, even religiously.

Timing is important. In general, if you want to order a *cappuccino* with *brioche* you should try to arrive before ten-thirty. Of course, you could still order the same things later, but this would be a declaration of your foreignness. And while Italians usually seem to like foreigners, the foreigners they like most are the ones who know the score, the ones who have caved in and agreed that the Italian way of doing things is the best. For this is a proud and profoundly conservative people, as careful observation of ordering at the bar will confirm. And a tightly knit one too. How is it that they all instinctively sense, without even glancing at stylish watches, that such and such a time is the moment to switch to their *aperitivi*? How they chuckle and grin when a German orders a *cappuccino* rather than an *espresso* after lunch, pouring that milk on to an already full stomach. And here's a curious detail: *espresso* is always OK, twenty-four hours a day, even *corretto* (i.e., with *grappa*), but *cappuccino* has a very definite time slot: 8–10.30 a.m. Trivia? No, good training. When the full complexity of these nuances becomes apparent – because the *digestivo*, the *gingerino*, the *prosecco* all have their right times and contexts too – you will be less surprised by the labyrinthine process of, say, switching your driving licence to an Italian one or sorting out your position *vis-à-vis* the health system. There is an order to all things; follow it, even when it borders on the superstitious and ritualistic.

Warning. If the first sip of your *cappuccino* tells you that long-life milk is being used, change bar before you have invested too much time there. Use of UHT milk (all too frequent alas) indicates that either you are far far out in the sticks where the urbane delights of the *cappuccino* have never really been understood, or that this is a bar where most people (men) are ordering *grappa* or wine, or if they are ordering coffee are putting *grappa* and wine in it, not milk. A typical confirmation that you are in this variety of bar might be that the *barista* replies to your Italian, whether competent or hesitant, in defiantly incomprehensible dialect, quite probably revealing that dental work and oral hygiene are not high on the list of personal priorities. No matter how characteristic you may find this UHT bar, how picturesque its old wooden chairs, dusty pergola, sports trophies, sentimental paintings hung askew, and weather-beaten old characters arguing volubly over games of *briscola*, the fact is that, ultimately, you have no business here, you will never be accepted however many times you come. You are only making these doubtless very wholesome people feel slightly uncomfortable.

Another scene which is definitely to be avoided is the bar where you are invited first to pay at the till, then present your receipt to the, in this case smartly dressed, even uniformed *barista* behind his polished pink granite bar under a row of fashionable halogen lights. Reasons? First because this is probably a bar where if you want to sit down you will have to pay for waiter service, and hence, having picked up your coffee and taken it to your seat, you will be scolded, perhaps quite severely, and invited to pay a surcharge. Payment for seating is of course perfectly understandable in the busy city centre, but not really on if you plan to be in that bar as frequently as I'm suggesting. But the second and more important reason is because this is not the sort of bar where the same people come and relax every day and can thus, as weeks and months pass by, be placed and identified and become part of your life. No, this is a busy bar. A business bar. A tourist bar. And we are not interested in any of those.

I cannot claim to being widely travelled, but I have lived in London, Cambridge, Boston, spent fairly long periods in Switzerland, in New York, holidayed in most of Western Europe. You can draw your own conclusions. In any event, I'm now going to stick my neck out and say that I honestly know of nowhere, nowhere, where the whole experience of ordering and consuming coffee and a pastry is, *or could be*, more pleasant than in Pasticceria Maggia, Piazza Buccari, Montecchio. And we selected it from five or six other candidates that very first Sunday. Obviously, we had a nose for these things by now.

You enter through a glass door polished only seconds before you arrived, display windows to either side frothing with colourful goodies, since Italians will always favour the most extravagant packages, however miserly the contents, and are always ready to renew their long love affair with crinkly Cellophane and foil, ribbons, bows and tinsel flourishes of every kind. Opposite you, as you adjust to a pleasant but not excessive dimming of light, is a long bar with attractive curved corner, polished wood to the front and yellow travertine on top. Behind and above is the typical array of bottles, mainly *amari*, *digestivi*, distillations of this and that (artichokes, rhubarb), things you have never heard of and most probably will never learn to like; to the left is the seating area, just a handful of tables, to the

21

right a great glass counter with four tiers of small and dainty biscuits, cakes and pastries.

Needless to say, the whole arrangement has a cleanliness, smoothness of line, sureness of touch unthinkable in England, but without the antiseptic feel of the same thing in Switzerland, the self-consciousness of anything that is not a fast-food chain in the States. Tense as you may well be after negotiating that main street where the zebra faded years ago, depressed perhaps by a broken fountain full of litter, you can hardly help wondering, as you push in through the door, at the way this same people so infallibly reproduces these two starkly contrasting environments: anarchy without, ceremony within.

But, now we're here, by all means let the ceremony begin. You close the door on the busy, dangerous world outside, glance around. The girl serving is small, dark, pixily attractive, and loves to be looked at. So look. And take a seat. The first times we went to Pasticceria Maggia I remember experiencing a sniff of anxiety over the question of seating: was there space for us? Later one realises that part of the civilisation, the magic of the place is that there always seems to be just enough space for everyone who wants to sit. Good. You settle into a comfortably cushioned chair. The simple red tablecloths are pleasant without creating the impression that you must be paying for them in some way or other. The *cappuccino* (and this is so important) is absolutely right: dark strong coffee at the bottom, thick creamy foam above, with, on request, the *cappuccio*, or hat of bitter cocoa sprinkled on top. Add just a dusting of sugar, use your spoon to draw up a little coffee and mix it with the foam. Now spoon up the frothy sweetened milk between bites of *brioche* and relax.

To spin things out, it's a good idea to try and get hold of one of the newspapers the bar is legally obliged to buy for its customers. Don't worry if the thick pink *Gazzetta dello Sport*, by far the most widely sold daily in Italy, seems a little daunting at first. Sports writing is almost the only journalism with any verve to it here (and in lots of other places for that matter) and the Sunday edition will have the first division results from England even if it never quite stretches to cricket. After a while you learn not to be ashamed of a residual interest in the home country.

On another table – wait until somebody kindly passes it to you – is *L'Arena*, Verona's local newspaper. Since they are talking about the agricultural fair, a headline proudly announces that the city is *L'ombelico verde d'Europa* – the Green Belly Button of the EC. Well, there are the two scrubby patches of green outside the window in Piazza Buccari . . . The fact that a member of the local government is under investigation for corruption barely gets ten column centimetres, for this is his party's newspaper. Turning a page, yesterday's dead stare at you from identity-card photographs – you can look for the features of some hated employer – while advertisements opposite offer tickets for tonight's *Aida* at the Arena, Shakespeare at the Teatro Romano, ten or twelve channels of TV viewing.

Why am I advising you to do all this? Because, quite apart from its simply seeming the height of relaxation and civilisation, it is impossible to be a regular customer here at Pasticceria Maggia, to soak up the chit-chat around you, to be sweetly served and smiled at by that pretty *barista*, to browse through the local scandals in the paper, watch bicycle races passing by amidst honking and cheers across the street, without gradually beginning to feel that you are getting into the spirit of things.

People begin to nod to you, beginning disconcertingly with the child-size village idiot in his deerstalker cap. But you will gain respect by putting up with his badgering. Smile, show no embarrassment. Say: *Salve, Moreno, tutto bene*? He's a nice boy in the end. And here's an invitation to teach your doctor's struggling daughter English, a request that can be politely turned down having discussed at length the inadequacies of the education system (the *Arena* will keep you informed). On weekday mornings around ten you can score points by greeting the post-office workers coming in for their long coffee break. These are not your favourite people when they refuse to look up at you from behind their murky little windows and then start weighing your postcards and forgetting whether Britain is part of the EC. Now you can enjoy perhaps glancing at your watch and smiling too brightly as they lean on the bar and discuss what shopping they have to do. Frustratingly, they are unperturbed. They even seem friendly, as if the bar were a place of truce. Perhaps they will serve you faster if they see you here a lot. Or, when those British football oo-lee-gans commit one of their regular atrocities, you can agree with local youngsters poring over the strident *Gazzetta* that your fellow countrymen are a degenerate lot, although pointing out in their defence that the performance of the national team, at least until Gazza came, has often been almost an incitement to insurrection (nothing more welcome to Italians than gently running down *la perfida Albione*, they feel extraordinarily competitive in our regard).

As the months pass and you continue to sit and sup, you

will doubtless be approached by the ex-priest, Lorenzo, now converted to ecology and admirably determined to save Montecchio's famous ditches. He will ask you to sign something and you will sign it. In the corner, old men are muttering over Verona's relegation prospects; soon you will be able to talk about that too. After Mass on Sunday mornings (did I mention the tiny crucifix on the wall above the liquor?) it will be the eight widows who put two tables together and confabulate in low voices, forming, in winter, a wall of fur coats. Even they will begin to smile at you after a year or so, perhaps wondering how long your own wife will outlast you.

Maybe you spot your butcher, your greengrocer, your dentist. Somebody asks you if you can do a translation for them. They run a picture-frame company. No invoice required. For heaven's sake. Somebody walks over to mention a friend who has failed his exam at the university a couple of times and needs a helping hand. 'Perhaps you'll remember the name if it's you doing his oral.' 'Well, I'm afraid I shouldn't really . . .' 'Virgilio, he's called. Virgilio Gandini.' Somebody else is having trouble with the American instruction manual to the sprinkler system for his lawn. And that somebody knows another somebody who could fix the wobbly bearings on your car . . .

It would be a foolish resident of Montecchio who did not at least occasionally pop into Pasticceria Maggia, a short-sighted newcomer who did not invest in at least a couple of years' worth of *cappuccini* . . .

Coming out on that first occasion, the morning after the evening before, I remember we almost ran into two grinning young *carabinieri* sauntering in in their beautiful uniforms with the scarlet-striped trousers and white breast straps. Something that might have been an elongated black beer-can swung from a handsome belt, complete with trigger. A tall, dark girl appeared from the kitchen holding high two trays of *cannoli* and various other pastries; there were smiles, some relaxed flirtation. The *barista* minced. They ordered their *cappuccini*. Cigarettes were lit. One crouched down to chat to a little child, asked predictably: What is your name, where do you live? Nobody seemed at all concerned by the submachine-gun the other was fingering as he spooned sugar over his foam.

Outside, we found their small, dark blue 850cc Fiat van parked in the middle of the small road, blocking anyone who wanted to get by. A radio could be heard calling them with some urgency. Should we go back in to tell them? But no. They are having their *cappuccino*. They only have a few minutes before it's *aperitivo* time. They wouldn't want to be disturbed.

4
Laghetto Squarà

With all that unpleasant unpacking and sorting out awaiting us back at the flat, we might well have chosen to make a detour before returning to Via Colombare that morning. Anything to stave off the evil day. We would thus have discovered how, following the line of the hills coming down from the north, the village of Montecchio, grey-green with dust and heat, is crossed, crisscrossed, by perhaps a score of small, lively streams bubbling swiftly through stone and grass and following a complex system of sluices which divert the water to feed neglected sheep dips, duckponds, irrigation ditches and great flat scouring slabs at the bottom of broken steps where the occasional older woman can still be seen scrubbing her husband's underwear with a soapstick. The through road from

Verona thus corners sharply left, right and left again, as it gropes for the two key bridges that will allow it to continue on its way to the outlying village of Olivè. With all the dips and curves it takes in the process, the sudden widenings and narrowings, the canyon-high kerbs followed by treacherous gutters and unexpected cambers, this chameleon strip of tarmac confers upon the village a splendid sense of the haphazard *ad hoc*, as if the asphalt had been put down in thick fog to reach the scene of some emergency, or, more likely, festival.

Geography, we discovered, is immediately mystified in Montecchio. Paths cut this way and that. One watercourse flows over, beside, under another. House, factory, farm, supermarket, all stand next to each other, although higgledy-piggledy, or are even built one inside the shell of another. The most obvious routes are blocked by dikes or long stone walls. Apparently parallel streets mysteriously lose all contact with each other. So that for the first few weeks one feels a sense of admiration, even bewilderment at seeing how confidently and, above all, how fast, cars shoot through streets where, due to the lack of pavements, so many corners are blind. Such things as bollards are unknown of course, and certainly undesired. Only a memory of a white line haunts the thoroughfares like some sermon heard and ignored long before; with the result that the sharp bends and corners of the main street are viciously cut by motorists and cyclists alike, especially during siesta time when it is not generally supposed that anybody could be coming the other way.

Tyres screech between the narrow walls of a bridge and into the tight bend immediately afterwards. A Vespa swerves: the little boy sitting in front of his father has grabbed the handlebars. Wrists precariously interlocked, a fourteen-year-old on his *motorino* pulls a younger girl on her bicycle up the slope of a dike, finding time to rev and buzz his buzzer as he does so. Somehow, beneath it all, the sleepy, underlying, village serenity persists, is always there, but there to be constantly violated by this indomitable Dionysiac principle on wheels. Here comes a moped reared up for fifty metres on its back wheel, overtaken by a Porsche in second at forty, roaring past the new church straight into the vicious turn by the chemist's. So that if Via Olivè was not in fact laid in a fog or a drunken stupor, one can only presume that it was conceived as a practice track for apprentice race drivers, stunt artists and other would-be suicides. All of which inevitably takes its toll of those heedless elderly cyclists in trilby and shirtsleeves, head-scarf and blouse, who wind and wobble about one-handed as they clutch walking-stick, fishing-rod or shopping-bag. As so often in Italy, the picturesque is combined with a sharp edge of danger.

The first bridge, around which cars will be loosely parked for butcher, barber and cobbler, takes you over a dry flood-overflow ditch. Perhaps five metres deep, seven wide, and straight as a die for miles, this unfortunately necessary piece of engineering slices the village in half with a ribbon of brambly scrub, Coke-cans, bottles and other discarded trophies of summer nights. As we were to discover later, the fact that such a considerable obstacle has still only been bridged to one end of the village, is a matter of smouldering political recrimination in Montecchio. For us, that first morning, it merely meant that the bar was perhaps five minutes further away than it need have been.

Having crossed the ditch, you follow the road past the

new church, past a single AGIP petrol pump, perfectly at home beside a handsome stone arch, and arrive at the second bridge. More attractive than the first, this spans a tiny river, the Fibbio, which flows beneath windows and balconies, linking ponds where men stand fishing under NO FISHING signs, taking the mountain rains southwards toward the Adige, the Po, the Adriatic.

Returning from the bar that morning, we doubtless turned left here to follow the stream a little way to its source, since this was also the direction for Via Colombare. And so would have made our second delightful discovery of the morning: at the bottom of a little dead-end, not two hundred yards from our new flat, a great battered water-wheel was thrashing away in magnificent dereliction. The discovery was all the more welcome when we found that, standing on a little bridge a few yards downstream of the wheel, the air was mercifully cooler, sparkling with bright droplets, damp and breezy.

Did we go on to the Laghetto Squarà that morning? I imagine we did. The little path behind the wheel would have been too inviting to ignore with anything more than an hour before lunch. It's stony underfoot. There are tall, sagging fences to protect an extravaganza of peppers, aubergines, young tomato plants. Water is everywhere: tiny streams gurgling through the vegetable patches, the small river rushing at the millwheel, and to the right, through a Roman arch framing rusty silos, a stagnant pond with stone surrounds which presumably once had some industrial purpose. There are big blue dragonflies and livid green surface weeds. A scooter buzzes urgently at a blind corner, forcing one to step smartly aside, and then the path emerges into the open space of Laghetto Squarà.

What happens here is that spring water rising beneath an abandoned seventeenth-century church flows out under its rotting door and bubbles across the path into a small square lake, the *laghetto*. There are tall plane and poplar trees around it, a stone embankment this side, and grassy banks the other, with three or four sluice gates. Moving to the edge, the glass clearness of the water allows you to look down two or three metres on to abandoned Roman building stones, pollution-fed weeds and that characteristic assortment of junk that people all over the world feel obliged to throw into attractive expanses of water: old tyres, a shoe, electrical appliances.

It's sad. Despite the obvious attraction of Laghetto Squarà, nothing has been composed or finished, nothing appears to be tended or even cleaned. For this is the public sector, not the private commercial world of the bar. Indeed, it's difficult to imagine the *comune*, the local government, having spent anything on the place in the last ten years, aside from paying someone to prune the surrounding trees with extraordinary ruthlessness (because paid, we later discovered, in the form of firewood procured).

Yet precisely because of this neglect, the *laghetto* hangs on to a quality it might lose with transformation into some modern notion of the recreational picturesque; it retains its weathered, rather haphazard air of simply, naturally being there. You sit by the waterside on a big square stone fished out from the bottom some years ago; there are faded Roman inscriptions on its bumpy surface, a date, a few letters suggesting the name of an emperor. Spring water chuckles over the shale path to your left; the hills are behind you; the lake, the busy village and the plain in front. 'So,' you think, 'this is the water table, I am at the foot of the Alps.' Kids throw themselves into the lake in their underwear. Girls scream, protesting they don't want to be pushed. And maybe they don't. It's a little more comfortable here than back in the dusty streets. A lizard basks just a few inches from your foot, reminding you how long you've been sitting still. Montecchio, you feel, may turn out to be OK.

5

Fantasmi

It took us two long, hot days. We made friends at Brandoli, the local supermarket, where three trips were required to accumulate the necessary boxes, and we moved a whole culture from Flat 3 up into the suffocating *solaio* below the roof.

Should we have paid more attention to what we were moving? Would I know more about Italy if I had read all the various diaries and letters with attention? Perhaps so. But old bric-à-brac, old clothes, old medicines, old shoes, old files, accounts, newspapers, rags, toiletries, shopping lists, votive items, paperbacks, military hats, jewellery boxes, camp cooking equipment and tins upon tins of assorted nuts, bolts and nails, have a very bad effect on my morale. Where another might find each item numinous

33

with meaning, I feel overwhelmed by a sense of insignificance. I think of mountains and mountains of such relics multiplied by every household in every corner of the world – varying, of course, from country to country, each with its own cultural matrix, its own peculiar make-up, implying this value and that, but in the end just debris, life's parings waiting to be thrown out – and all I want to do is to see the back of it all as fast as possible. I'd never make it in archaeology or anthropology. Thus, what I did save from our supermarket boxes for a moment's examination, and what my memory and my wife's now offer me in the way of details of that marathon clean-up, can only be scraps, clues, hints to the character, life and times of Umberto Patuzzi – or '*il professore*' as we were later to come to think of him – and of his still vegetating wife, Maria Rosa. Had we known how intriguing these people were to become for us, we might have paid more attention.

Signora Marta had said her aunt and uncle were well travelled and, indeed, the gigantic frosted glass and peeling veneer cupboard in the *salotto* was stacked with sufficient tourist brochures to keep an agency going for a couple of months in high season: except that these brochures dated back ten, twenty, even forty years. The oldest, in alphabetically ordered piles, for the most part extolled cheap hotels in the local mountains or on the nearby Adriatic coast, with fragile brown-and-white photographs giving ample evidence of the fifties building spree. Tuscany, Elba, the Abruzzi, Rome and Sicily followed close behind, like pieces in a rapidly expanding and now colourful jigsaw – Technicolor seas and gaudy local delicacies – until, with the sixties boom, mass prosperity and the Italians' love affair with the *automobile*, here came the first price lists for hotels in Austria, Switzerland, Yugoslavia. Pile after pile of them. The most recent and lavishly seductive exhibits featured the Azores, the Bahamas, pensioners' package trips to Florida.

Clearly there was material for a couple of Ph.D.s in this cupboard but, nevertheless, straight into our Brandoli boxes it all went. We were in a hurry. An essay on holiday destinations as an expression of Italian economic development over the last three decades was not what we had in mind. Except that here, beneath the brochures, was a photograph album. Well, who can resist at least glancing at photographs?

Such was Patuzzi's love of the road and his motor car, he must have had the habit of getting someone, presumably Maria Rosa, to snap him by exotic road signs (as others might want to record their presence at the top of mountains). So here he is, in black and white, full head of virile hair brushed back, thin aquiline, intelligent nose, arriving in Trento with stout climbing boots round his neck and a knapsack on his shoulders; he has the confident, satisfied look on his face of someone who has just been admired for making an intelligent remark, or at the very least has eaten a good lunch. Nineteen thirty-seven, says the spidery hand. And here he is again, in colour now, balding, but still sporty, in wool trousers and green anorak, by a sign that tells us 'Wien'. We flick through page after page of these things: mountain villages, hotel billboards, *autostrada* exits; until finally, most recently and most extraordinarily, here is a much older, weathered, bent Patuzzi, leaning on a stick, by black lettering on a white road sign announcing 'Praha', with, beside him, and even more extraordinarily, a very recognisable Lucilla.

That does put a new slant on things. More a ménage than a condominium perhaps? Could she even be right about ownership of the flat? Or am I jumping the gun?

Further back in the cupboard are some collectors' items from the war days: an army hat, a school textbook ('Describe your feelings – of admiration and gratitude – on contemplating a photograph of *il Duce*'), and a stack of the macabre *Signal* magazines: tabloid-size, in German with Italian translations, these offer comic-strip propaganda, mainly directed against – well, against *us*. '*Bombe sull'Inghilterra!*' one enthusiastic piece is entitled. Is this, I sometimes wonder, why the young men in the bar still feel such rivalry? And what had friend Patuzzi done in the war apart from reading such heady stuff (later we learned that Lucilla had been begging for bread on the streets of Vicenza).

Further back still (I said the cupboard was huge) was a rather more harmless (and more numerous) collection of magazines going under the enigmatic title of *NAT*. A moment's close attention to the inside cover revealed that these letters stood for *NUOVA ALTA TENSIONE*, and it took only a few seconds' leafing through them to appreciate that such tension was presumably meant to be created in the lower abdominal area by late fifties and early sixties pin-ups of Brigitte Bardot, Jane Fonda, Sophia Loren and a host of lesser names, photos of such breathtaking touched-up tameness you wondered how people managed after all the bomb-toggling excitement of wartime. Was Patuzzi slipping them in between his accountancy journals as he walked out of the *tabaccheria*? Did he read harmless gossip about bathing beauties between toiling over accounts on the great ugly desk in the second bedroom which clearly had a longer history than this house? At what point had Lucilla come in, if she had? Beneath a photo of a tiny, delicate-featured girl from the south, a caption was still telling us twenty-five years later that Mariangela Rainaldi, a devout Catholic, presently worked as a party hostess but was eager to become a film star.

In the drawer of Patuzzi's bedside table we found a long shoehorn, a catechism, an *Alpini* hat (the famous Italian mountain regiment), a long expired tube of haemorrhoid cream, an oval, silver-framed photo of a solemn Maria Rosa, and a long piece of thick leather with a handgrip at one end and a heavy ball of lead tied to the other. What on earth for?

But there was a problem with rubbish now. Not that we felt we could throw away anything precious, like the diaries full of additions and subtractions in figures of eight and nine digits, the replies to letters Maria Rosa's brother must have sent to a number of marriage bureaux in Paris – no, everything that should be preserved for prying eyes more patient than our own would be preserved. All the same, there was much in the way of old toothbrushes and toiletries from the early seventies that would be missed by no one. Who needed to know that *il professore* had cleaned his teeth with *Pasta del capitano*?

Unable to locate anything inside or outside the flat that remotely resembled a dustbin, we eventually tiptoed downstairs to make ourselves known to the Visentini in the flat below Lucilla's (the one that had been meant for her daughter). Presumably they would be able to tell us what the score was.

We knocked lightly on the door. A voice asked who we might be, for nobody will ever open in Italy until identity is declared. Security, even in the remotest villages, is at New York standards. We explained. Came the sound of a heavy lock turning over once, twice, three times, and the door opened. A wispy, attractive little woman in a pink tracksuit stood before us and immediately insisted we come in.

Well, we were in the same country, the same village, the same building even, in a flat that in structural terms was a straight mirror image of our own, and yet on stepping into *casa Visentini* we were immediately in a different world. Everything here was modern, pleasantly styled, clean as a pin, with a light touch to the ornaments, the lithographs on the walls, the low, modern, comfortable sofa. If there was, perhaps, just one thing in common with our own accommodation, and with so many other homes I have been into in the Veneto, it was in the desire for a certain formality, a certain achieved composition in every room, ritualistic and ceremonial. Cosy is not a word one would normally apply to an Italian interior, nor would the owners be proud to hear their furnishings thus described. The briefest glance at the Visentini's flat showed that the whole domestic environment had been most painstakingly arranged, nothing left to chance, nothing haphazard. Everywhere lines met and diverged in clean, carefully calculated, stylish angles. The exact opposite of the world outside.

And at first Orietta and Giampaolo were as guarded and rigidly polite as their furniture was attractive and composed. Yes, we were invited in, and with kindness. Indeed they insisted we come in. For this was the right thing. But it was not clear what we were to talk about. They did not want to be drawn immediately on the – for us – burning issues of a hostile Lucilla and a howling dog. Giampaolo in particular was poker-faced. The rubbish, he explained, was usually placed in a large, shared, plastic dustbin which was then put outside the gate for collection every morning. However, Lucilla had removed this bin on our arrival, making it abundantly clear she did not want us to enjoy the use of it.

The Visentini offered no comment on this state of affairs. Presumably, we must procure a bin of our own.

I then asked about the garage which Signora Marta had mentioned. Tall and serious, but handsome too, and with something boyish about him somewhere, Giampaolo led me downstairs to a semi-basement where, turning right at the bottom of the stairs, a very big area the size of a whole flat served as the shared condominium garage. I was immediately impressed by the positively licked cleanness of the smoothly finished red-brick tiles that had been chosen for the flooring: no oil stains, barely visible tyre marks. Attractive as it was, this simply didn't seem necessary for a garage.

Four parking spaces had been marked out between cement pillars. To the far side was Giampaolo's gleaming white twin-carburettor Giulietta, just in front of us a minuscule Fiat 126, again white. The other two places were empty.

I asked which was my space. Giampaolo said this one on our right was Flat 1's and so Vittorina's (Lucilla's sister-in-law), and the space to the left of the Giulietta at the far end was Flat 3's, our own. *Però*, he warned, neither space had been used since the death of the male members of those households: Umberto Patuzzi and Giosuè Zambon. This was a question of respect. He showed me the small crucifixes on the pillars beside the spaces. Lucilla, he said, was a superstitious person, but not ultimately an unpleasant one. It was merely a question of time.

I remarked that if using the garage meant war with Lucilla, forget it, it didn't matter, my car had little body-work worth saving. This did not bring a smile, and in retrospect it occurs to me how foolish such jokiness is amidst a nation of car worshippers. A man who has spent six months of his *stipendio* buying an Alfa Romeo twin-carburettor Giulietta which he hardly ever uses, does not want to hear that others are quite happy to get by with a ten-year-old rusting Passat. And bright orange at that.

Before returning to the women upstairs, Giampaolo made a point of showing me the communal *taverna*.

A *taverna* is a large basement or semi-basement room situated beneath a modern *villetta*, *palazzina*, or small condominium of central or northern Italy, and it is dedi-cated to partying. It must have a large, preferably enor-mous fireplace, suitable for barbecuing; a selection of strictly labelless wines, alpine-style pine furniture, one long banqueting table, an area with sink for washing dishes, and perhaps a stereo. On the walls, as was the case in Via Colombare, decorations should include old posters showing views of the mountains or the country, some hunting trophies (here, remarkably, a surely fake cheetah) and such things as old swords or shot-guns. In Via Colombare there were Patuzzi's wooden skis from perhaps forty years ago.

It should be said that old houses do not have *taverne*. Only new ones. For the *taverna* is the contemporary Italian's dream of the past, an exercise in urban adaptation and nostalgia. That is to say, this big below-ground party room attempts to recreate, for the modern flat-dweller in his cramped condominium, the feeling of those huge old country kitchens with their abundance of game, *polenta* and local wine which still take up such a large space in the national consciousness. Thus, in many a *taverna*, often beneath the most uninspiring prefabricated structures, you will find that the occupants have bought an authentic old *pietra serena* fireplace to install in the wall, or, if they cannot afford the real thing, then at least a decent imitation, with an impressive array of black iron fire-tending implements. Tables likewise tend to be old or to look old and you must have at least one ornate high-backed hard wooden chair which no one ever sits on.

When a couple of condominium families get together to invite their friends to eat here, on the Bank-holiday evening of *ferragosto* perhaps (15 August), or on 25 April, *la festa della Liberazione*, they expect these furnishings, particularly the splintery pine benches and fake oil-lamp light fittings, to induce a mood at once of merriment and traditional wholesomeness, the rightness of family and friends enjoying the fruits of their labours around the common hearth. As if for the space of an evening, the office worker, or shopkeeper, or pharmaceutical salesman could enjoy the healthy repose of the *contadino* after the grape harvest; as if, like some Jungian subconscious, the *taverna* could be used to store away a primitive past and all its richness.

My own experience is that, like so many dreams, the *taverna* is better in the dreamer's imagination than in the realisation. Happier the Veronese choosing his fireplace and barbecuing instruments, than the same irritated fellow trying to enjoy them. You go to a *taverna* party in a damp basement, unheated and un-aired since the last binge, and quite possibly you will catch your death despite the most stifling weather above ground. The chimney doesn't draw properly because it is rarely used. You eat off a miscellany of plates, survivors of other dinner services once used upstairs; you drink from dusty glasses that no amount of rinsing will clean, perhaps because there is no hot water in the basement sink. Items of cutlery are found to be missing. Your knife doesn't cut very well. Conversation booms about the bare cement walls. After about an hour or so, just when the wine and barbecuing are beginning to take the chill off the place, the condominium dog-in-the-manger comes downstairs to complain that the noise is making it impossible for him to follow the latest episode of some favourite *telenovela*, i.e., a recycling of *Dallas*, *Dynasty* or whatever. He is reassured, amidst much contrition and invitation to join in (for this is by definition a wholesome party), then promptly forgotten, though remaining perhaps as a nagging subconscious irritation.

The food begins to arrive. You eat the flesh and sometimes it seems the bones and feathers too of blackbirds and small pigeons, crushing, as instructed, Maltesersized heads between your molars so as to suck out the brains inside. Which are indeed toothsome. But pitifully small. While all around the table people are trying too hard to be jolly.

Out come the *carabinieri* jokes (right angles boiling at 90° and so on), the shaggy dog stories of bureaucratic odysseys ('so when I went back for the third time he says that since my birth certificate was from another province and dated prior to 1959, the whole procedure should have been done by post with the office in Rimini . . .'). There is much loud guffawing, head shaking, glass filling. 'No, you must have another *uccellino*. You must. They're *squisiti* and I've already cooked it now.' The thing falls on your plate with a definite resemblance to those hapless little corpses one finds on wet pavements in spring. Accordion music strikes out from the stereo. Six couples launch themselves into traditional dances in six square metres. Loud giggles. Somebody burns themself on a hot poker left sticking out of the hearth, etc. etc.

The *taverna* seems to induce this behaviour, this determination to be festive at all costs. Indeed, almost any *taverna* party has the flavour of those New Year's Eves when you simply can't feel there is anything to celebrate and wish you had stayed at home. But then my wife constantly tells me I'm a *gufo*, an owl, a spoilsport. She thoroughly enjoys these occasions. In my defence, I would merely say that, whatever the surroundings, I always love the wine, I can even tell with my eyes closed more or less which of the local varieties I'm drinking, and if only we could be having it in well-ventilated accommodation upstairs with some tortellini *al dente*, followed perhaps by a plate of finely sliced rare horsemeat and a *tiramisù* straight from the fridge, I would be in heaven.

Throwing open the iron door, drawing me to the threshold to gaze inside, Giampaolo Visentini was obviously a *taverna* fan. Perhaps for him the *taverna* represented some unthinkable loosening up, or an occasion when the more difficult social skills could be replaced by simple prowess with the barbecuing fork. In any event, showing me the gloomy place (I remember antlers and crossed ski poles on thin whitewash) he began to betray the first signs of life and enthusiasm. Did I like barbecuing? Did I like grilled aubergine? And *bruschetta* (toasted bread with olive oil and garlic)? I said, yes, yes I did. And was I interested in bottling my own wine? The people in his company always clubbed together to bring a truck-load of casks from a particularly good vineyard in Friuli. If I would like to split a cask of Cabernet or *prosecco* with him I should let him know in good time. We could buy in October and bottle next spring. The price was low and the quality excellent. I said to count me in at once, I was always ready to give something a try. By the time we were climbing the stairs again there was a feeling we might just make it as neighbours.

Then, running the gauntlet of Lucilla's door to get back through our own, we heard our phone ringing for the first time. Signora Marta, perhaps, having forgotten to tell us where the serious books and spare light bulbs were kept. Or one of the numerous schools and agencies we had immediately passed the number on to.

'*C'è il dottor Patuzzi?*' a confident older man's voice asked.

I froze.

'*Parla Giordano. Una questione di documenti.*'

'But Patuzzi's dead. He's been dead two years and more.'

'But his name's in the phone book,' this voice objected.

'He's dead,' I said.

'*Ah. In quel caso non insisto.*' And the phone went, well, dead.

Rita said: 'It's if they say, "Patuzzi speaking", you should start worrying.'

But somehow it seemed that when you had just cleaned all of a man's junk out and read a few of his letters and seen his well-thumbed girly magazines and his boyhood skis and a crucifix by his parking space, then *fantasmi* were not an unreasonable proposition.

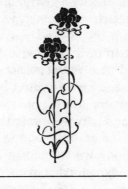

6
Residenza

It would have been some weeks later we tried to change that entry in the phone book. We phoned SIP, the telephone company and were told that in order to have our names in the phone book with that number we would need a recent certificate of *residenza in bollo* (that is with a few thousand Lire's worth of special stamps on it) and signed renunciation of the number by Patuzzi, or his heir. The *contratto* for the phone would then be shifted, for a small charge, into our name and the bills would be addressed to us.

By the standards I have grown used to, this seemed something of a breeze. A check at our local *comune*, a pleasant enough little office with the inevitable crucifix, an impressive collection of rubberstamps and a large

45

computer on line to the city registry, provided the information that for certificates of residency we would need either proof of ownership of the said flat as first home, or a written statement from the owner that we were tenants there. This should be on *carta bollata* – legal paper with, again, a few thousand Lire's worth of stamps on it.

So we rang Singora Marta. She was very polite but unable to understand why we wanted to change the name, 'referring to the number in the phone book'. Couldn't we simply tell everybody we wanted to phone us what our number was? We explained that there might be people who wanted to track us down for work. We were *liberi professionisti*. But if, she objected, they knew of our names, then they could ask the people they'd heard of us from. *Non è vero*? People who would surely have our telephone number or know someone who had it. Telephone directories were thus demonstrated to be entirely useless.

No, she added, the point was, it would be extravagant if we were only staying for a year. Because when we were gone we would of course renounce the number, so as not to be listed under it any more and have bills for it in our names, at which point she could if she chose have the line disconnected, but then God knew how long it might take to get it reconnected and how much that would cost. The result being that she would most probably have to take the number on in her own name (rather than Patuzzi's). And since she already had a phone number, this number (Via Colombare's) would be registered as a second home phone, meaning much higher basic bills even if she made no calls.

So many conversations in Italy follow these serpentine paths, with new laws and regulations constantly raising their ugly heads to turn the most obvious ways forward into dead ends. With the creeping sense of paranoia that results, you occasionally find that people have been imagining rules that don't actually exist, simply because they seem to be the kind of thing the government would invent to make life more difficult and hence probably has. Was it really true, for example, that Marta would be obliged to register the number in her name. Couldn't she register it in a child's or grandmother's? Or was it that if she did that they would then have to switch their *residenza* to Via Colombare with all the problems that entailed?

I proceeded cautiously: when we left the flat, I said, if she asked us to leave it that is, and we rather hoped she wouldn't because we liked it here, then this would presumably be because she had decided to sell it, or had found someone else to live in it, and in either case the new occupant would want to take over the phone, wouldn't they?

'Not if they already have one in their own name elsewhere,' she came back. 'Or if they want to retain residency in another province.'

Who could have thought of this before starting the phone call? Then, when I had already given up and offered a cool *arrivederci*, she suggested by way of an olive branch: 'I don't mind writing to say that you live there, though, if you need to have *residenza* for other purposes.'

How explain the elusive yet all-important significance of 'residency' to a Brit who merely lives where he lives and acts accordingly? Can we hazard a definition? Residency means that the state now recognises that you live where you live, or say you live (for example, in the province of X at such-and-such an address) and henceforth will distinguish you from all the people who live in another province, or country, or who do, yes, live in X but whom the state does not recognise as living where they live (in X), either because those people want to be recognised as living elsewhere (where they don't live) and have managed by some wangle to achieve this, or because they can't get hold of some precious *documento* that would allow them to demonstrate that they do in fact live where they live (in X), and must thus continue to be recognised as living where they no longer live (in Y or Z, for example).

But does it actually matter? Well, yes. Once the state recognises that one lives where one lives, there are all kinds of benefits: the right to register your car in the area (otherwise you will have to travel to Y or Z to register it); the right to register with a local doctor; the right to apply for all kinds of local state jobs; the right to have access to certain services and benefits; the right to pay lower phone and utility bills; the right to vote; and, most importantly for us, a 2 per cent reduction on the amount of income tax withheld at source on free-lance services.

'*Va bene*,' I told Signora Marta, if she could write such a letter we would be very happy. '*La ringrazio*.'

But I was puzzled. She hadn't wanted a formal rent contract. I had half suspected that this was why she hadn't wanted the phone number in our name: she didn't want it to be in any way official that we lived here. And now, on the contrary, here she was offering to help us get residence. A calculated risk? Generosity?

'The flat,' Rita suggested, 'is officially owned by Maria Rosa, who is gaga in a nursing home. How is anybody to know that we are paying into Marta's account?'

Still . . . Life is complicated. In any event the drift seems to be that the government makes well-meaning but complicated laws and people very sensibly get smart and get round them. For example, there was this business Marta had mentioned that second homes carry much higher utility bills – a popular tax-the-rich measure. However, it is quite common in Italy for the middle and even lower-middle classes to rent their real home in the city where they work and possess a small holiday flat (second home) by the sea, by one of the lakes, or in the mountains. Result: many people register themselves or their wives or children as resident in the holiday home, so as to avoid higher bills. This in turn will create all kinds of other problems. On election day, the registered residents will have to travel a couple of hundred miles to go and vote in some place whose local politics they know nothing about. So they don't vote, you object. But, in Italy, if one doesn't vote three times in succession, one loses certain rights . . . etc. etc. Bureaucracy is a huge tangle of sticky string in which every attempt to loosen one knot tightens another.

And checks, or *accertamenti*, to make sure that each citizen is contributing his length of string to this tangle, are quite common. A few weeks after moving into Via Colombare, I went out on the balcony to see who had buzzed our bell and found a seriously fat man in uniform sitting on a moped with big dispatch boxes. Montecchio's local *vigile*. Taking some papers out of one of these boxes, he asked me something. I asked him if he could please speak Italian. He politely switched from dialect to something more comprehensible, upon which it emerged that he had been asking me whether I lived where quite obviously I was living (wearing pyjamas, a piece of toast in my hand). I said I did. He then asked if he could come and see. And in my kitchen he explained at length about the *tassa sui rifiuti*, the rubbish-collection tax. This apparently was paid, not by the owner or even renter of a property, but by the head of the household actually living there *whether or not resident* – that is, they wanted the money and red tape was not a problem (similarly, it is perfectly normal for a foreigner to file an income-tax return without having a work permit). The person in question was me, I said. I would pay. He scratched his head, cocked it to one side, eyed me carefully from his tubby face. *'Bon,'* he said.

The *vigile* then wrote something amazingly painstakingly on his sheet of paper. While he worked, I noticed how clean his uniform was, how well-ironed his shirt, how white the little pouch on his belt. It was another day of sultry heat. Despite the weight of flesh beneath all these clothes and accessories, he was not sweating.

He asked my name. Then asked me to spell it. Fair enough. We got through Parks quite rapidly, and were speeding through Timothy (Torino Imola Monza Otranto – I say it in my sleep sometimes) when we ran up against the age-old problem of Y which does not exist in the Italian alphabet. 'Hotel, Epsilon.' I finished. He hesitated, raised his head, blew out his cheeks and narrowed his eyes. What was epsilon? 'Epsilon,' I said, 'is a letter.' *'Ah sì?'* he said. It was clear that he was used to having his leg pulled, and so had developed these mannerisms – the suspicion, the slow questioning, the stare – to make himself seem less gullible.

Having studied me for a sufficient length of time, he decided I was not the type, said: *'Sì, Sì, sì, d'accordo,'* and scribbled something down, I didn't dare to ask him what. But then I had the idea of pulling out my English driving licence and offering it, *'per una verifica'*. Offended, he waved it away.

'Residenza?' he now enquired, for even if it had no bearing on my paying this tax or not it was important to write it down. Three or four times.

I was applying for it, I said.

'Stato di famiglia?' (a document describing relationships within the family – who is the mother, the father, the head of the household, who the breadwinner, who dependent).

I was waiting for my marriage certificate to arrive from England.

'Profession?' For everybody must be classified according to their profession.

I told him teacher. Rather flatteringly he wrote down *Professore*.

Then just as he was leaving I made the foolish mistake of remarking that we didn't have this residency business in England.

Again he was clearly concerned that he was being made fun of. There was the same cocking of the head, the puzzlement. He was one of those fat people who are terribly graceful, nimble almost, very aware of their bulk. He turned on his heel away from the door in almost a dance step, pushed back his cap and lowered himself on to a seat at my kitchen table. This was a serious matter.

How was it possible, he asked, for us not to have residency?

We didn't.

So what do you do? When you move.

You move, I said.

And the registration plates on the car?

You leave them as they are.

And your identity card?

There are no identity cards.

And the doctor?

You go and register at the nearest surgery.

He clearly didn't believe me. It couldn't be that easy. Not that I was lying. But I must be ingenuous. There was so much I hadn't understood. He was wondering how he could prove this to me. He had prickly, Latin black hair cut short under his cap and he scratched at it slowly, tugged at the tubby lobe of an ear. Then he had me.

How, he asked, would the post work?

In what sense?

How would they know where to bring it to, when you moved?

I tried to be equable, offhand. Somebody wrote your address on an envelope, affixed a stamp of the appropriate denomination and the postal service would hopefully take it to that address and ask no questions.

The man got up and left in polite disgust. Obviously it was not a country for *vigili*.

I was not surprised a few weeks later when the first refuse bill arrived addressed to Parks Thimothj. As for the phone, if you open Verona's very handsome telephone directory, you will still to this day find the name of Umberto Patuzzi covering up for whoever is enjoying the pleasure of SIP's services at Via Colombare 10, Flat 3. Doubtless the gas bills are still in his name too. And the electricity bills, despite the curious fact that these actually include the modest charge of 7,000 Lire a year for the votive light over his grave . . . (second home?).

7
L'animale domestico

July. Dog-days. The heat that is, and Vega.

We had settled down in the flat, bought a few 100-watt bulbs, only to realise what an attraction they were to the moths and mosquitoes. We had got used to the tock-tock of midnight ping-pong from across the street, discovered that something of a breeze could be created by opening all the windows of the flat simultaneously and waggling one of the communicating doors, eaten our way through mountains of water-melons (to every season its antidote), and dedicated a shelf of the fridge to bowls of sliced peaches swimming in Valpolicella.

We had even made our first tentative peace with Lucilla, offered our help around the house should she ever need it, assured her we would take no part in the court case pending in which Marta and Maria Rosa were to be accused of having dashed to *il Professore*'s bank security box only moments after his heart attack and burnt the will naming Lucilla as his sole heir.

'But who was *il professore*?'

'Why Umberto! Patuzzi! A wiser man never lived. A real *professore*.'

As I had been for the *vigile*.

'*Un uomo squisito*. His death was such a terrible blow.' Tears had a way of forming rapidly in Lucilla's veiny eyes. We shook our heads. And our assiduousness and sympathy (genuine, actually) had its reward in the reappearance, on about day ten, of the communal dustbin and the prospect of talks about one of those sacred spaces in the garage. Downstairs in the flat beneath our own (and hence opposite the Visentini) the more timid, perhaps dour Vittorina seemed ready to follow whatever lead her volcanic sister-in-law would suggest. All, or much, was coming right.

There was just the problem that night after night our sleep was ruined by the howls of Vega scrabbling at his master's shuttered door, while towards mid-afternoon, as I shifted from buttock to buttock in front of Patuzzi's huge desk, translating papers for an international conference on the decline of opera, it was impossible not to notice a slight odour of dog faeces rising from the small patch of ground where the creature was kept imprisoned. I mentioned this on the stairs one day to Giampaolo. His surprising reaction was to phone the local *carabinieri* immediately. They came out very promptly, confirmed that there was a potential health hazard and warned the one-armed, fiercely eye-browed Signor Negretti that he'd better clean up his dog's act.

Negretti came out on to the terrace with his two teenage boys and hosed down the grassy area below where the dog was sometimes chained, sometimes free to roam for four or five metres in any direction. He hosed it for perhaps ten or fifteen minutes, directed a last squirt at the shambling, excited dog itself, then went indoors. After which all was left as presumably it always had been.

Animals. Did I mention in the opening pages about somebody bundling a dog into the back of a car? Quite a normal sight on Via Colombare. The car will be a well-worn, dull green Fiat 128, the *contadino*'s car *par excellence*; the man will be wearing rubber boots and a straw hat with the name of the tractor company on its band. He will drive off with admirable caution, although without buckling his safety belt, if he has one. As the car passes you, muffled barking may be heard, or the thumping of the pointer's tail against the petrol tank.

But perhaps a better way into the relationship between Italians and animals might be to consider the normal translation of the English word 'pet'. The Italian expression is: *'animale domestico'*. *'Il cane è un animale domestico.'*

Well, in English one might feasibly say to one's girl-friend, boyfriend, wife, husband, son, daughter – 'What a pet you are!' meaning, what a delightful, friendly, cuddly bundle of fun, pleasure and loyal friendship around the cosy hearth. And of course we have the fine word 'petting', which I have so often tried to explain to puzzled students. But could one, in Italian, say to one's mate: *'Che animale domestico che sei!'* No, this would be inadvisable. For it would mean, first that they were *merely* an animal, as distinguished from the more elevated, thinking, speaking and shotgun-toting *Homo sapiens*, and second that they were submissive, knew their place, didn't bother anybody and barked only when supposed to. Even throwing in palliative adjectives – '*che bell'animale domestico . . . che animale domestico carino*' – would not help in the least, since these could only be perceived as irony, thus adding insult to injury.

In short, Italians think differently about their pets/ *animali domestici*. In 99 per cent of cases they keep them outside; they do not like them coming into their houses and would not dream of having them sleep say, at the foot of their beds. The idea of one's child being licked all over by a dog, as I was as a boy, would be unthinkably horrible to the modern Veronese mother (perhaps very reasonably so). But there is also something obsessive and exaggerated in this aversion, something which may have to do with the fact that it wasn't so very long ago that many families in the country around Montecchio had goats in the kitchen and the cow stall opening on to the sitting-room for warmth. Proximity to any but the most expensive 'luxury' animals has become a sign of social backwardness. And hunting dogs like Vega are a mere utility. You don't want them prancing into the house with their wet paws and dirty backsides. You use them when you go off shooting so they can bring back the *uccellini* which you eat in your *taverna* in nostalgic revelry at the joys of country life which you have wisely left behind. Otherwise you keep them chained in the yard.

Outside our window, Vega barked, howled, moaned deep into the night. With that extraordinary insistence dogs sometimes have. Bark, bark, bark, bark, for hours on end. What were we to do about it?

'Poison the thing,' a student suggested at once.

Poison. For weeks, months, it was to become an obsession. We noticed stories in the paper reporting dog
poisonings. They seemed quite common. Almost the done
thing. Somebody in a place called Bussolengo had killed
more than twenty in a single evening. Well, we needn't go
that far. And I read Sciascia's novel, *A ciascuno il suo*, where
he mentions a whole Sicilian tradition of dog poisonings, a
sort of low-order vendetta between rival huntsmen.

We considered rat poison. And bought some. We
studied the dosages. Twenty or thirty pellets in a meatball
should be enough. But what if a child were to pick it up?
Occasionally the Negretti had guests with small children
who were left to ramble about the defecated garden area. A
student whose father was a vet cheerfully suggested the
easier solution of a sponge soaked in meat juice.
Apparently, the sponge expands enormously in the
animal's gut, blocking intestines and eventually leading to
death. He knew people who had found this method very
effective. Well, we had a small sponge in the bathroom
which overlooked Vega's little patch. Part of the Patuzzi
heritage. Nothing would be easier.

We observed the animal's eating habits. She seemed
perfectly used to having her food tossed at her from
considerable distances. She was instinctively friendly,
running to her master or his sons in the hope of a pat,
which very occasionally, grudgingly, she got. Although
sometimes it was kicks. On a sort of dry run, we tossed her
a biscuit from the bathroom window. Immediately it was
snapped up and appreciated.

'The only problem with the sponge', my knowledgeable
student explained at another lesson, 'is that the creature
will die in unspeakable agony, and you'll have to hear her

howling like mad. Probably for a couple of days. Although of course it will be worth it in the end.'

We couldn't do it. At night, startled from sleep by bloodcurdling howls, we would feel that we could. I might go to the bathroom and squeeze the yellow sponge in my hand, feel how it contracted and expanded, sense how easy it would be, laden with the weight of the meat juice, to chuck it the three or four metres over the fence to the howling dog. But something prevented us. And we developed the alibi that it wasn't the animal's fault, it was the master's, and we would kill the master if only such things were feasible. As a poor substitute for serious action we took to phoning *casa Negretti* whenever the dog woke us. After a couple of nights they left the phone off the hook.

We talked to our neighbours about it. The Visentini weren't badly affected because they lived at the other side of the building and had installed elaborate double glazing. But the subject did allow for our first real contact with Vittorina. No sooner had we mentioned the dog than she was telling us how, when her husband had been dying the previous July, he had been unable to sleep because of the creature and she had begged Rocco Negretti to do something about it, to no avail. They were *gentaccia*, filth, no fate was bad enough for them. She burst into tears, remembering her husband's suffering and we were able to offer her coffee in our flat, where she amazed us by remarking that she had never been in here before. No, she and Lucilla had been good friends with *il professore*, but the hateful Maria Rosa was a city woman and believed herself above them. They had never been invited into the flat. *Il professore* had always taken his coffee at Lucilla's. While Maria Rosa did the shopping.

Vittorina was in her late sixties, big boned, only slightly overweight. With great dark rings about her eyes, she was obviously morose by nature, a lover of candlelit churches, superstition, mystery and gossip. But when she laughed it was with sudden heartiness and enthusiasm, a sort of profound natural health. She would go and tell Lucilla, she said, what nice people we were, because her sister-in-law was mad not wanting us to use *il professore*'s parking place after *il professore* had treated her so badly.

This was good progress, and terribly interesting of course (should we ask Vittorina about the photo taken near Prague), but it didn't solve the problem of Vega.

Until one Sunday we would wake at dawn to the celebratory crackle of gunfire. The hunting season had begun, the hunting season that litters the paths with spent cartridges and deposits as much lead on the national territory as all the Fiats, Alfa Romeos and Mercedes put together. And although we had never seen so much as a wild rabbit on our Montecchio walks, the surrounding hills echoed with sharp reports all morning. *Uccellini*, pigeons, purpose-bred pheasants were presumably tumbling from the sky. And Vega was quiet that night, having had some exercise at last.

8
Stile cimitero

August is a better month than July in the Veneto. The days are still scorchingly hot but, after a series of dramatic thunderstorms bringing hailstones as big as marbles and prompting radio and newspaper discussions as to whether farmers could ever have had all the crops they are claiming compensation for, the humidity finally fades like a bad dream; the days are drier and clearer and the welcome dusk comes that bit earlier.

It's a good time to take walks. The countryside assumes its dusty green long-suffering summer look: matt colours under sizzling light. The vines are thicker now, their shoots knotting swiftly across the system of wires between one row of posts and the next, completely shading the ground below. You can walk beneath them under a panoply of leaves through vineyard after vineyard up the valley toward the village of Mizzole, your hair brushing against berries that are just beginning to swell. In the scented green light a wealth of insect life goes about its business: you see extraordinary, bright yellow spiders spinning their threads fast from tendril to tendril. And through the still air and intense heat, you gradually become aware of a great silent seething all around, urgent and secretive, as if the whole world were concentrated on growth, growth, growth. One tends to fall silent oneself crossing vineyards on hot summer days. The plants don't want to be disturbed. There is so much still to be done before September.

On the plain to the south, the corn is already in and the *contadini* are burning the dusty stubble with a cavalier disregard for fire hazards. On the hill above us *il conte* (as most rich landowners seem to be known) loses an acre of woodland and there are whisperings of arson. Climbing a steep slope of stunted trees and scrub we find two men running around a large burnt area trying to stamp down flames every time they flare up: here, there, behind them, in front. The smoke has a pleasant smell and is thin and lazy in the shimmering air. The men's task seems hopeless, but, no, they say, they don't need help. We climb on and find the count's huge house, mansion rather: an ochre stucco, austere façade with travertine sills and plinths. Looking through the ironwork of the old gate we count six expensive cars. Rita reflects that Mussolini's round-up of iron for the war effort generally seems to have passed over the gates of the rich, while the *contadini* shelled out their saucepans. I feel we could do with another war effort to get rid of the thousands of kilometres of superfluous ironwork sprouting up in modern suburbia.

The radio begins to speak of drought and, in this our first year in Montecchio, the regional government ordered us to stop watering our gardens. Weeks passed. The ban was not lifted. But there was little sign of deterioration in the swelling tomatoes, aubergines and peppers which flourished in every vegetable patch. For the fat *vigile* entrusted with the business of enforcing the regulation, the same who had come to see if I was living where I was living, was not to be seen beyond six in the evening, while watering began more or less with the arrival of fresh air around midnight: old men and women pushing their hoses quietly between thick clods, the more arrogant new arrivals leaving it to their timers to turn on sprinkler systems under the stars. One thing the Italian politician perceives in a way his ingenuous English counterpart does not, is that it is the enforcement of a law which is unpopular, not the law itself, which is patently a good thing and the right response to whatever problem it is supposed to be solving. Just as it is right for the Pope to insist on chastity, as long as one is left to do as one pleases. In the model anarchic society, to which Italy frequently approximates, there will be rules without end whose value will never be questioned. And under this excellent cover everybody will live as he sees fit.

In the minty night air the water hissed. The aubergines plumped out with their dark mauve of secret flesh. Practised fingers tied up the pepper plants and fat salad tomatoes were left to ripen on stone windowsills. Growth was almost audible.

So that at number 10, poor Vittorina was perhaps the only person in all Montecchio who, out of some misguided sense of guilt or civic duty, actually bothered to carry out her dishwater in buckets and chuck it over our vegetable patch. With the result that one would find strands of spaghetti draped over the *radicchio rosso*, or a few bones of *baccalà* in amongst the parsley.

Giampaolo came out with a red colander, looked at the ground, frowned, went back in empty-handed.

Every condominium is galvanised by a sort of magnetic field of attractions and repulsions. Nowhere could these be more strongly and urgently felt at Via Colombare 10 than in attitudes to the large square communal garden to one side of the house. The truth is that the modern Italian has problems with his garden. He is not at ease with it yet as the Englishman is. Behind him he has centuries of a peasant culture which ended, if it has ended, not a hundred years ago, but yesterday. For him the ground means crops, the vines, the towering corn plants, tobacco, fruit trees, tomatoes. Quite simply, he has this in his blood. And there are many who buy or build huge villas on the slopes just outside Montecchio, with a swimming pool on the terrace, gymnasium in the basement and the most ornamental iron fence imaginable all around, and can then think of nothing to do with the garden but turn it into a vast cabbage and spinach patch, producing more than they could ever hope to eat or even give away. Out of a sort of nostalgia one assumes, or inertia, or lack of imagination.

On the other hand, there are those who feel ashamed of their peasant roots and see the garden as a means of expressing their arrival in the stylish world of office jobs, high tech and magazine-inspired domestic environments. In which case they attempt to reconstruct the traditional ornamental garden of the Italian aristocracy: dwarf cypresses, oleanders, religious statuettes and tiny stone paths, spiced up perhaps with a variety of exotic plants some garden centre is passing off as fashionable and which haven't a hope of surviving the cold Veneto winter. Once everything is planted and growing, such people don't play in their gardens as an English family might. They tend them, brush them and sweep them like some never-to-be-used front room, the way other people are forever cleaning cars they never take out of their garages. Until, with the sombre smell of the cypresses and a curious stony stasis of upright trees and crisscross flagging, the status-symbol garden begins to look like a little cemetery without the graves (but waiting for those of its owners perhaps). And house after house along Via Colombare, garden after garden, decorous little cemeteries alternate with vigorous pea and cabbage patches as each *capofamiglia* declares his particular response to the profound change that has taken place, the loss of that old obviousness that the land was for food which you needed to survive.

Vegetable garden, cemetery; chained dogs in the first, a Siamese cat perhaps in the second; nervous animals in uncertain patches of green marooned by the lava flow from the city as it solidifies day by day in streets and wrought-iron fences. The tall tall fences of Montecchio, *la fortuna del fabbro*, the blacksmith's jackpot. Nowhere, nowhere does one find that happy, relaxed, cosy, *ad hoc* floweriness of the suburban English garden. It must be one of the only areas of domestic civilisation where the British win hands down.

Lucilla and Vittorina were nostalgic for a peasant past. Understandably. They wanted those tomatoes and *peperoni*, lettuce and *radicchio rosso* too. But Lucilla was fat and lazy. And a little ashamed. She drew the line at vines, for example, and was famous for having torn down with her own hands an attractive *filare* that Vittorina's husband had set up. What's more, if there was a vegetable patch, it must be away from the road, secluded from the casual glance of passers-by. After all, the house itself was so stylish with its pretentious Californian eaves, *graffiato* finish, and big terrace balconies, gave such an impression of having arrived, it would be a crime to disabuse the passer-by with some humble salad crop.

So a thin strip of land away from the road and immediately beneath the wall of Negretti's house and terrace turned out to be the only place for productive cultivation. This annoyed Vittorina, who did the lion's share of work in the garden and got some real sense of recreation from it. It annoyed her because the ground below Negretti's three-storey windowless wall got no sunshine, little rain and was full of snails, indeed teeming with them. They bred in the unkept clutter and cracked cement of Negretti's terrace and then slithered down three metres of damp brickwork in the night to stake out number 10's lettuces and peas. So Vittorina would far rather have had a sunny patch over towards the road, to feel the sun warm on her back in the early morning as she tied up her tomatoes. She didn't care about the impression this would give to the neighbours, as she didn't care about being seen carrying out her dirty dishwater; she had none of Lucilla's obsession with social status.

But a difference of opinion between Vittorina and Lucilla was easily resolved. Lucilla stamped her small, fat high-heeled foot and, aside from a little dark muttering of a saint's name here and the Virgin's there, Vittorina inevitably succumbed. Along with her peasant's attachment to salad and vegetables, she also had the peasant's age-old submission, to master and bad weather. With her never perfectly plucked moustache and fierce temper, Lucilla resembled both.

No, the real problem with the garden in Via Colombare was that of integrating the old ladies' earthy mix of nostalgia and shame with the younger Visentini's more sophisticated, media-based, urban vision: an English lawn, shady trees, and, yes, a vegetable patch (because Giampaolo is a gourmet and fresh greens are tastier), but run along ecological, natural-food lines (because Giampaolo, like any modern man, is also something of a Green). Thus Vittorina not only had to work the communal vegetable patch under the tall bare wall of Negretti's grim house but, to add to her troubles, she wasn't allowed to poison the quite multitudinous snails. It all came out in the food, her younger neighbour scared her. We would all die of cancer.

And that was one battle Giampaolo won. Indeed, whenever Vittorina took up a position on something it was always clear she was going to lose. A bulky, heavy-breathing woman, she prayed a great deal, had Masses said for her husband, visited the cemetery almost daily and subscribed to such periodicals as *I miracoli di Sant'Antonio* and *La salvezza*. Her face had a morose wisdom which would occasionally light up in genuine friendliness. One suspected she was already resigned to losing the quarrels of this world, banking on the next. A pushover for the persuasive, courteous and always well-informed Giampaolo.

However, since Giampaolo only rented his flat, whereas the others owned, when it came to getting trees or bushes for the garden proper, Lucilla insisted on choosing and locating them herself (Giampaolo was quick to disclaim responsibility). The result was one of the very saddest collections of dwarf cypresses and ornamental mutants imaginable, unhealthy things picked up in sales and planted apparently at random across two hundred square metres of dry lawn. A funereal tone was everywhere apparent and, indeed, it occurred to us that Lucilla had probably never been into a garden that wasn't a cemetery. There were no gardens in her poverty-stricken youth and most of her life had been spent operating an industrial cleaning business from a small suburban flat. Whereas the early death of her husband and various relatives had made her all too familiar with cemeteries.

To her credit, Lucilla was aware that something was wrong with the garden at number 10, aware that this gloomy assortment of dull evergreens was not really what she was after. In the hope of achieving some improbable rightness, she would thus, Giampaolo explained, move the trees about year after year, dig one up, shift it a metre or two this way, dig up another, swop it with yet another, put this one in the shade, move that one out of it, and so on and so forth, so that the weary plants became sadder and sadder while the business of mowing the lawn in Via Colombare now involved a dizzy weaving back and forth through the lost labour of Lucilla's search for harmony.

And of course the lawn had to be mowed regularly. Giampaolo was strict about this. Regularly and very low. Because it had to be an *English* lawn, as the Italians imagine English lawns to be, an extension, that is, of the meticulous formal elegance of the Visentini's flat, licked clean from top to bottom day in day out with sacrificial anality. Yes, Giampaolo said at our first condominium meeting when

my duties were outlined, the lawn had to be mowed twice
or three times a week from spring through autumn and the
cuttings had to be gathered with a rake and piled on a
compost heap in the most hidden corner of the garden
where shameful things like compost heaps are piled. It
should be said here, in Giampaolo's defence, that most
surrounding gardeners of the cemetery variety just had
their grass taken away by the refuse men, and this was the
easy solution that Lucilla, if not Vittorina, would undoubtedly have plumped for. But being a Green,
Giampaolo rightly insisted that grass was a limited re-
source to be husbanded and utilised – along the snail-
infested wall . . .

Never has good neighbourliness been more onerous, as,
with the two ladies unable to handle the mower and no one
willing to pay for a gardener, I was enlisted into the ritual
twice-weekly mowing. And daily watering. For the lawn
had to be watered assiduously throughout the hot
summer, and most particularly it had to be watered at the
front of the house where the terrace balconies of the two
lower flats were only a metre or so above quite a few square
metres of grass below, depriving the grass of water, but not
light, since a low slanting sun shafted in of an evening to
shrivel the poor plants up.

How we mowed and mowed that lawn. And how many
hours I was to spend distractedly pointing a hose pipe at
those doomed patches of grass beneath the balconies,
which were so important of course, being amongst the
most visible, through iron railings, from the dusty street.
To make matters worse it was assumed that, being English,
I would naturally know a great deal about lawns and my
advice, as we settled in, would frequently be sought on dry

patches, ringmoulds, moss, etc., as if such knowledge were carried in the genes. I thus got used to observing a genuine sense of disappointment when it was discovered that I knew nothing, but nothing about lawns. And what's more (to my shame now, actually) showed every sign of not greatly caring.

Giampaolo: 'What kind of fertiliser do you think we should put on the lawn toward the end of summer?'

Me, with a shake of the head: 'The cheapest.'

'Do you think we should leave the cut grass down this time, or rake it up?'

'Oh, let's leave it. Good idea.' But my enthusiasm was too evident, and very soon it was understood that my opinion could be ignored, and that I wouldn't even mind if it were not solicited. Which was a relief. And to salve any conscience I might have had, I reflected that at least I was doing my neighbours the favour of demonstrating the hollowness of national stereotypes.

9
La stagione è finita

Sometimes when I wasn't actually called upon to partici-
pate in the garden, I would watch the others from the big
window in our *salotto*. For, ironically, ours was the only flat
with a good upper-storey view of the garden. I thus
observed that, while the old ladies followed the seasons,
Giampaolo went by the book. Or rather, it wasn't quite the
seasons Lucilla and Vittorina followed, but the rigid set of
proverbs and rules a thousand years of peasant culture
offered them. Some of which they themselves, having
spent their adult lives in industrial cleaning, remembered
only approximately. I recall in mid-September going out
into the garden for a couple of tomatoes (just reward for all
that mowing), to discover to my amazement that not only
were there none left, but the plants themselves had gone,

disappeared, been uprooted, the ground already forked over and raked.

'When Lucilla decides the season's over, she tears them up,' Orietta told me. Her voice was still completely neutral as it had been at all our early meetings. But now a half-smile played about the lips, suggesting the possibility of future confidences. 'She's pulled up the peppers too and the aubergines. It's the same every year.'

'But they were still growing.'

'Lucilla thought the season was over.'

Lucilla was an extreme, indeed manic case, but it has to be remembered that this is the country where, if you go swimming any time after September, even if the temperature is in the sweltering upper thirties, you will be looked on with surprise. *La stagione è finita*. The season is over.

Giampaolo, on the contrary, to plant a row of peas, brought out the encyclopaedia he was buying piecemeal and at considerable price. This would be at the weekend, since he had a regular office job. He laid the appropriate volume on a dry patch of ground and was careful not to touch it with earthy hands: if I happened to be around I would turn the pages for him and read. The spacing between one seed and another? Five centimetres. The depth of the hole? Three centimetres. Soil preparation . . . Brought up the last child of five in Venice, he knew nothing of the earth, but being a modern man he believed that information could be had from books. We planted the peas together. We did everything the book said. Most of them never came up. And the few that did were eaten overnight by the rampant snails.

The ladies sniggered. As indeed Giampaolo sniggered when they tore up tomato plants that still had a good couple of kilos in them. Lucilla would stop you on the stairs: 'Have Signor Giampaolo's carrots come up?' With that same half-smile around the corners of her lips, Orietta would say: 'Now they've pulled up the pepper plants.'

And yet . . . Giampaolo had considerable respect for the local peasant culture, because books teach this too. Parsley and spinach should be planted with a new moon, a lawn sown with a full moon, still wines bottled with a waning moon, etc. etc. And the old ladies in their turn had more than a sneaking admiration for anybody who could genuinely read a book and find something out. After all, it was Giampaolo who fixed their boilers when they burst, adjusted their cars and appliances, even if his peas never came up and the bulbs he planted didn't flower. In the garden, everybody watched each other in a delicious tension to see whose culture would prove the most effective. And in this respect the situation was typical of the small handkerchief of Italy I live in. There is such a collison of ancient ideas and new. Which will win? In a way it was not unlike Elija and the worshippers of Baal waiting to see whose sacrifice would burst into flames.

And in the meantime we were all watched by old Lovato, our neighbour on the Via Colombare side, whose tiny garden bordered on our own. Bald, towering, broad-shouldered, Lovato was one of the old guard, a never-say-die, pea-cabbage-tomato-and-pepper man, a retired farmer. His gaze, looking over the wall at our sad orna-mental garden, was one of genuine puzzlement, turning to pity and just a hint of derision when his eye fell upon our miserable vegetable patch. In his own few poky metres he produced a quite prodigious abundance of vegetables in the way only the small farmer knows how: working the ground furiously and using obscene amounts of fertiliser, weedkiller, and pesticide. The snails must have felt sick if ever the faintest breeze blew from his direction.

Stolid, solid and quite unashamed of a businesslike shamble of pots, canes and cuttings all about him, Lovato watched. Through wire netting. For, above the waist-high dividing wall, he had unaccountably erected a fence reaching up a good three metres and lethally barbed on top, although sagging and rusting. I say unaccountably for intrusion from the direction of Via Colombare 10 was surely unlikely. But it was interesting that neither Giampaolo nor the old ladies found anything strange about his wanting to guard his property so determinedly. If an Englishman's house is his castle, an Italian's is his bunker. There is this obsession with self-defence: railings, remote-controlled gates, security cameras, bulletproof windows, armoured front doors . . . No, from the Via Colombare point of view, Lovato's attitude was understandable. But it absolutely must not be at the expense of the ornamental quality of number 10's garden. Railings, yes; rusty wire, no.

Lucilla and Vittorina had years ago asked Lovato to remove this *vergogna* (one is tempted to translate this as 'eyesore', but literally the word means 'shame', which is what they felt Lovato should feel). Lovato refused. Giampaolo more diplomatically referred to the fence as '*antiestetico*'. Lovato played deaf. He would not take the thing down. At which Giampaolo had suggested that the ladies buy a hedge which would grow up and cover it all. Yes, all three metres high of it, thus protecting the aesthetic qualities of number 10's cemetery. The hedge was duly planted. This had apparently infuriated Lovato, who claimed it would eventually rob all light from his small

73

patch, although it's possible he was equally concerned about losing his pensioner's view of our miserable garden (which must have provided considerable entertainment). He would go to court, he said. There was a law about blocking other people's light. Giampaolo politely remarked that his ramshackle garage of breeze block and corrugated iron located to one end of the fence had surely not been erected with the appropriate building permission. Since this was where Lovato's son-in-law kept the Lancia Prisma of which the whole family was rightly proud, it seemed unlikely they would be willing to pull it down just in order to embark on uncertain litigation against number 10. When Rita and I arrived in Via Colombare the hedge was a metre high with everything still to play for.

To straighten out your topography then, we have the threatening hedge and nosy Lovato diametrically opposite the northern (and lateral) wall of the condominium which includes our living-room window where I sometimes stand beneath the elaborate, if dim, chandelier to look out on the world. To my left (and west) as I look out, is the long ironwork railing along Via Colombare, and to my right (never forgetting the mobile triffids in the garden between of course) Negretti's tall windowless wall. And here's a curiosity. Negretti's wall has a cinema screen on it, a huge rectangle of white, for before number 10 was built the present garden area had been a cinema. Yes, rural Montecchio had once had a cinema, albeit tiny. Now of course the screen was no more than cracking white paint surrounded by broken brickwork where the cinema had been demolished and Negretti's wall reinforced. Not a little of Negretti's intransigence with his dog, we discovered, his almost relishing the disturbance it caused, was the

74

result of his having wished to buy the cinema himself, only to be outbid by these two old ladies, who then ignored building regulations to stick their own *palazzina* rather too close to his. In revenge he refused to do anything about the unsightly wall, the yellowing screen, the broken bricks. Lucilla and Vittorina offered to go halves to have it stuccoed, but Negretti, like Lovato, refused. And the more they showed that the wall bothered them, the more stubborn he would be. The ornamentality of number 10's garden was thus irretrievably compromised; for whereas Lovato's fence might one day be covered by that hedge, no ivy could really get a grip on the smooth white of that cinema screen. As for myself, wandering around in stifling heat, hosepipe in hand, doing my bit for the lawn, the snail-sad lettuce, the scorched earth beneath the terraces, I would look up at the screen and wish with all my heart that the cinema could have remained.

10

Il palo della cuccagna

Montecchio mornings late September. Seven o'clock. The tiles under bare feet are beginning to feel more than pleasantly cool. You go through to the kitchen, heave up the heavy plastic roll-down shutter, all the rage in the late seventies, but spurned now in the general return to natural materials. You have to be careful not to pull too hard or the thing will roll away through the slit and into its little box above the French window, to be retrieved only after hours of fiddling. On the outside, the plastic is peppered with holes where the wind hurled big hailstones in an August storm.

You step out on to the balcony, air fresh and glass clear. Number 10 is exactly half-way along the street. In a lacquered morning light you see the Madonnina in her niche with fake flowers a hundred metres away to the right, the derelict bottle factory the same distance to the left. Opposite, above the houses, rise two more, rather nobler nineteenth-century mills, likewise derelict, one with an attractive design of little pillars and arches just beneath the cornice some six floors up. Both buildings have been listed, their empty windows staring, innards gutted. And behind these again rises a low ridge of hills pushing south into the plain, with *Il castello di Montecchio* on top: a square tower, a wall, a taller tower, a wall, a third tower the same height as the first: Austrian defences. The Communist Party want to turn it into a sports and community centre. The Christian Democrats don't seem to be able to find the money, or the enthusiasm. At present, amid banks of blackberries going to waste, it's used only by the so-called *emarginati*: drug addicts, homosexuals, immigrants.

But what a splendid sight on a bright morning, with the larks still twittering high in the air, the most delicate fleecy clouds (*pecorelle* the Italians call them, little sheep) curdling in milky blue above, and the light green horizontal flow of the ridge beautifully pointed up by the sombre verticality of cypresses winding serpentine towards the sharp silhouette of the castle.

Down in the street, the old man who lives opposite slithers off his muddy bike. Giobatta Marini. Pushing eighty, hunched, flat-footed, fishing gear slung over his shoulder, he has his dawn catch in a plastic bag under his arm. The stout wife, who bore him all those table-tennis playing children, comes out in apron and slippers to meet her patriarch and whisk away the fish. An early lizard creeps between railings along the wall. And, leaning on the cool marble of the parapet, still in your pyjamas, you breathe deeply, as your father used to whenever he got a chance to be out in the country. 'How marvellous, what air!'

A boy in overalls, with bedraggled hair and pasty face, roars by on an ancient and deliberately unsilenced *motorino*. Leaving a cloud of oily blue behind. Well, OK. It's all part of the happy scene, not unpleasant really and he does boast the name of Raffaello. At the end of the street he revs quite violently – a bit of frustration, unsatisfied libido to burn up. Fair enough. He works in the mechanic's at the corner. But now he's turned the thing off, the cloud of exhaust has dispersed, and you can relax again, breathe in this beauty, and breathe deep: aah!

Until, quite suddenly, the whole marvellous morning is corrupted, tainted, transformed, by the most unpleasant smell.

It's sudden and overwhelming. One moment you didn't notice it, the next the whole picturesque scene – castle, fisherman, Madonnina – has become a deception, an enamel over something that reeks.

Words and smells don't go well together, but perhaps I could describe it as a corpse smell, a smell of something wrong, an abusive, acrid, clogging smell, and certainly a smell that one shouldn't be smelling at seven o'clock in the morning in a village in northern Italy. The chemical factory in the small industrial estate is letting off the fumes from its storage tanks. Go in, close the door and all the other windows too. Look at the fine morning through the glass you really ought to clean. And get the *espresso* pot on to drown that stench.

The following morning, if the pressure is suddenly low and fine mercurial clouds are thickening over the *castello*, it could well be a chicken-dung smell rolling down from the factory farms which have taken over the surrounding hills as the *contadini* beat their long retreat. An all-pervading smell which may last half the morning.

And the next day, if we imagine a rare breeze is flowing from the north after rainfall, it will be the smell of intensive pig farming further up the valley. Is this the worst? Or should pride of place go to the synthetic-fabric factory to the south whose methylated fumes, thank heaven, come only with the sirocco? But they're all bad. They all add to that constant threat of encroachment which typifies these villages. They all have to do with making money fast on territory which is cheap because it's being abandoned, territory which once provided a living, and little more. Unless perhaps a culture.

The evenings are more pleasurable. There are no particular smells. Your wineglasses are perched on the marble parapet of the balcony while from Patuzzi's abandoned armchair you watch huge moths whirr about the streetlights hanging from wires which run zigzag between the houses. The sound of Giampaolo's stubborn hose hisses from under the balconies, the old ladies call to each other up and down the stairs over the babble of their televisions: 'Cilla!' 'Rina!' Tock tock tock goes the Marini tribe's pingpong. And a blackbird whistles quite beautifully at twilight. Over a period of a couple of months we get to know his call. We stand on the balcony and whistle. There is a pause, perhaps a minute. To tease you. Then he whistles back. And again. And again. 'Lest you should think he never could recapture . . .' but that was a thrush of course. The blackbird whistles, we answer him. It's upsetting to discover later that he sings so well because Giobatta has blinded him. For on the mornings he doesn't go fishing, old Marini will take the creature out into the country in its tiny cage, to attract other birds to the muzzle of his shotgun.

Perhaps it shouldn't be upsetting. This kind of thing has always gone on. This is the old way. Why am I so squeamish? Yet whenever I whistle to the bird now I can't help imagining the moment of its blinding, and I both want and don't want to know how it was done.

Giobatta, of course, is short for Giovanni Battista. When a friend of mine recently took his child to be baptised and said, 'Giovanni', the priest immediately came back, 'Evangelista or Battista?' There was no other choice. You would have thought with his namesake ending up the way he did, Giobatta might have been a shade more mindful about taking sharp instruments to creatures.

Night falls. But the gently swinging lights keep the street quite bright. In the glow, little girls are playing something like hopscotch. There is no bedtime here. They dodge about their chalk squares and shrill and argue. Comes the sound of clashing gears and a car scatters them, driving recklessly fast in the narrow space. Their parents playing ping-pong under the pergola do not seem concerned. A red light goes on above the Madonnina. Or perhaps it is always on but only noticeable in the dark. From the window below we can hear the ladies giggling together over their television. Comes the portentous sound of the pips. A woman's voice announces that it is 10.04 precisely, then the strain of the tune introducing the evening news programme. It is an endearing characteristic of Italian broadcasting that they are not overly concerned about starting programmes on the hour.

One Sunday, after a morning of particularly unpleasant smells, we walked to Montecchio's industrial estate to check the situation out. It lies just the other side of the cherry orchard behind the Madonnina. Sadly, the orchard is closed off by a ten-foot-high dry-stone wall some hundreds of years old. You skirt around this barrier and go by way of the bus terminus, where the driver is enjoying a few minutes in a bar before his return trip to Verona (*termini* always coincide with bars, which is as it should be). The road here is straight and narrow with tall ivy-bitten walls either side. A first iron gate on the right leads into an avenue of cypresses and the cemetery. Then, after a large tarred area, which trucks could presumably park in but never do, you turn into the industrial estate.

And are immediately surprised. For what you see is: attractive villa, followed by long low prefab; then, salubrious three-storey *palazzina*, followed by grubby factory; then, green-stuccoed terrace with cascading geraniums, followed by woodyard; and again, lavishly funereal garden, chemical plant; gnomed patio with barbecue, print-works; and on and on: expensive house, business, expensive house, business, expensive house, business for three hundred metres. All the local *padroni* live here with their factories and factory smells. How can we complain when they get the worst of it? Circulars from the Communist Party will later explain that the land was more or less given away allowing *imprenditori* to build cheap villas for themselves, their children, their grandchildren. 'Not a single job more was created,' they protest. Perhaps erroneously.

But as industrial areas go, and when the early morning smell of lucrative enterprise has subsided, this is not an unpleasant place. Well-dressed families are eating ice creams on balconies. There's a sound of chatter and children. A fat man in fashionable tracksuit is clearing up his toasting forks. The chained guard-dogs are asleep in the shade.

Then on our way home we stumbled upon *il palo della cuccagna*. In passing I might say that everything I have discovered in Montecchio I have stumbled on. It seems in keeping with the spirit of the place. And perhaps it was only because we saw them both on the same day that it occurred to me that this amusing celebration was not entirely unconnected with the mentality that produced the industrial zone.

We had planned to walk back a different way so that we could lounge on the Roman stones by Laghetto Squarà for a while, something that was becoming a favourite pastime: just sitting and watching, in the heat, by the water, with the sound of the spring gurgling across pebbles from under the broken church door. But the banks of the *laghetto* were packed this afternoon. A hundred and more people were shouting and cheering. As we approached, the cheering grew louder and louder, then a great splash. And more cheers, or jeers, before somebody called a name on a megaphone.

We climbed up on a stone. Into a drain hole in the bank, the trunk of a fir tree, perhaps twenty metres long, had been fixed so that it stretched out horizontally just above the water, supported half-way by a spike driven into the lake bottom. A small red flag fluttered right at the end where the pole was no more than four or five inches thick. On the bank, above the base of the trunk, stood a small gaggle of boys and men in swimming costume, shivering under towels. Beside them, on a high stool, sat the umpire.

The umpire calls out a name. The boy who serves me my *prosciutto crudo* in Brandoli's, the supermarket, lets himself down gingerly over the weedy stone on to the base of the pole, and begins to walk. All he has to do is reach the other end of the pole and grab the flag. This feat will transport him into the land of Cockaigne, that is, he will get a reward. In the event, despite the thickness of the pole at its base, he manages no more than three metres.

Because the whole pole has been thickly greased with soap.

There are about fifteen contestants and they go again and again in turns, slipping and slithering clownishly on the soap. If you refuse to go when it's your turn, you're out. And since the water rises right here from under the hills, it is not exactly warm. An older man, in his sixties perhaps, is shivering violently as he lifts his stomach on to the bank. A muscly exhibitionist clutches his crotch. There's a clammy weed in his hair. At each attempt, each contestant dissolves a little more of the soap, and then for four turns each is allowed to carry a handful of sand which he spreads in front of his feet. Thus some kind of progress is made, pushing further and further towards the flag, amidst the screams of girlfriends and mothers, and the chuckling of those men wise enough to appreciate that this is definitely a spectator sport.

It's interesting (and rather a shame) that no girls are competing.

At the end of the day (and we stay two hours and more), since it would be impossible to provide the winner with the real cockaigne of *palazzina* and family business beside, the prize, finally awarded to the lad who delivers bread from one of the village's bakeries, is 150,000 Lire's worth of

83

petrol from our local petrol pump. As a vision of plenty, it says much perhaps. Though this archaic festival is obviously timed to coincide with the harvest.

11
Bepi

Orietta Visentini says that in twenty odd years she has never really been accepted in Montecchio. For she was born in Peschiera, on the southern shores of Lake Garda, forty kilometres away. People's friends here are their childhood friends, their family. Orietta sighs. They don't even know how to make friends, because they have never had to do so, and anyway, they can't imagine anybody being without their own circle.

What hope for me then?

Very little. I step off the bus outside the derelict bottle factory and walk down Via Colombare. I nod to people: to the grappa-scented car mechanic in his overalls whose work overflows on to the narrow street; to ancient be-capped Giobatta, the hunter and fisher, but working on his

vines today along a sagging fence; I nod again to the
slightly mongoloid-looking woman in black who puts her
father out on a chair by the doorstep in the morning,
squashes his straw hat on his head, and brings him in in the
evening (surprisingly their dingy house, which opens
directly on to the street, has an expensive aquarium in the
window of a bare room with large table, wooden chairs,
stone floor and nothing else). I salute the portly, heavy-
jowled man in the light suit who finds climbing out of his
Alfa 75 something of an effort, the more casual fellow who
sells insurance in a Fiat 126, the stout, vigorous woman
who every morning takes a twig brush to sweep the dust
from the road outside her house and push it over toward
her neighbour's. My greetings, which after all follow the
traditional Italian style and which all these people exchange with each other every time they cross paths – *Buon
giorno signora, buon giorno signore* – are met at first with
embarrassment, perhaps even suspicion, since clearly I am
part of that world which encroaches; later with returned
nods, muttered courtesies. And perhaps that is quite
enough. Only in the greengrocer's does a loud voice reply:
"'ello, sir, 'ow are you!' And it is Bepi. My first friend in
Montecchio.

I suppose Bepi fits into that class of Italians who are eager
to know foreigners. One has to be careful not to be
collected by these people. It's a group Giampaolo Visentini
belongs to in a rather different, more sophisticated way.
Not that these people have in any sense ceased to believe in
the supremacy of Italian cooking, Italian wine, Italian style,
and so forth, just that they are sensitive to a certain
provincialism, eager to be associated with anything that
lies outside their narrow circle. Perhaps they have been

frustrated: Giampaolo by the stifling promotion proce-
dures in the monolithic company he works for, Bepi by the
obstacles put in the way of anybody without contacts who
wishes to get a licence for a lucrative shop. Both feel they
have ideas bigger than the narrow mentality of the people
around them. But, interestingly, they don't feel this
provincialism could be overcome by going to Rome, as a
man stifled in Barnsley might head for Birmingham or
London. On the contrary, Rome would be even worse, the
locals would already have staked the place out for themselves. No, they look to the fairness and openmindedness
of the efficient nations further north. Extraordinarily, they
believe Britain to be such a nation. And can never
understand what on earth I am doing here in Montecchio.

From behind his stone-topped counter, Bepi pumps my
hand. He is 'very 'appy' to have an Englishman in his shop.
He smiles broadly, he's my own age or thereabouts, but
physically a much more impressive specimen: hugely
solid, with thick shoulder-length curly hair, and such a
look of eagerness about him, such a presence. Green green
eyes. He sticks a couple of kiwis into my bag and doesn't
want to be paid for them. *Per carità*!

As I turn to go, the priest walks in, Don Guido. I am thus
able to witness the whole scene. In his black cassock, the
priest stands there sniffing the air, a short, droll, old-woman
of a man. He sniffs and sniffs, snub nose upturned as the
other customers go about with their little plastic baskets
picking up artichokes, peppers and what have you from the
boxes around the wall. Then he lifts his shoulders sharply up
and down in a gesture of impatience. The cassock has a
shiny, worn look to it. 'Something smells rotten in here,' he
announces out loud and with almost a threat in his voice.

Quite unperturbed giving or taking change, Bepi replies, 'Must be the carrion flesh of the last person to walk in.' '*Carogna*' is a common insult. At which the priest calmly proceeds with his shopping.

I never managed to get to the bottom of this dispute between our greengrocer and priest, a quarrel made attractive by its combination of intense animosity and total lack of consequence. And perhaps that is the essence of the Latin quarrel, at least on this level. It is almost enjoyed for its own sake. There is no feeling of any need to make up or resolve things, because no harm is being done. The priest came every day, ritual insults were exchanged, fruit and vegetables selected, money handed over, and that was that.

In a place like Montecchio, the indigenous population are, as Orietta had said, almost impenetrable. Because self-sufficient. Thus, being a newcomer and peripheral to village life, one inevitably gets to know other peripherals, people who like yourself have been washed up here, because at some particular moment this was where the current flowed, and the place turned out to be convenient. Bepi had tried for years to get a licence to open a supermarket – anywhere in the Province of Verona would do – until finally they allowed him to rent the downstairs of an unprepossessing old house on the outskirts of Montecchio – for a greengrocery.

Invited to dinner, he sits down, legs wide apart on his seat, his powerful body straining his clothes, and immediately, before I've even poured an *aperitivo*, announces: the man I call father in the shop is not my father.

In a country where reserve and formality are usually excessive on these occasions, it is certainly a dramatic opening. And embarrassing. He proceeds to tell us that he is the illegitimate child of a woman whose family threw her out. Not wanting her baby, his mother left him with a childless sister and her husband: the man he calls father and who helps in the shop.

He then goes on to tell us how, poverty-stricken, the family sold their house in Rivoli and came to live in a meagre flat in one of the downmarket residential areas of Verona. But he swore to buy back that house for the family to demonstrate that he was more than just an illegitimate child. And last year he finally did so.

If Bepi's abrupt, reductive autobiography is disconcerting, the obsession with family and home comes as no surprise. When an Italian leaves a place it's almost always with the intention of returning victorious and vindicated. Even if he believes that place to be hopelessly provincial.

How had he made his money? Bepi laughs. He taps a finger on his temples. All in here, he says, all in here. He tells the picaresque story of his entrepreneurial career. You know they're always saying Italian wine has no added sugar? Yes. And it's illegal to add sugar to wine in Italy? Yes. Well, I drove the truck that took the sugar to all the wine producers from Vicenza to Verona. At night of course. There are no police about at night. They only work office hours. He grins, he is very pleased with himself. For this was an act of *furbizia*, of cunning, and it paid very well. Spent all the money setting up a restaurant with a friend, near the main road to the lake, a big restaurant, for coach parties and the like. The mistake was doing it with somebody else. The friend couldn't see reason. Didn't have it up here. Bepi taps his forehead again. They went bust. There followed two or three other restaurants, then

finally the licence for the shop. He had wanted a supermarket, but local shopkeepers always gang together and
bother their political contacts to make sure no new licences
are given. This is common practice, they have the politicians in their pockets, or they *are* the politicians. But Bepi
will beat them at their own game in the end. Yes, he will.
Sooner or later he'll have the knife by the handle . . .

As so often in conversations here, one notes this
assumption of a fundamental lawlessness. The law is only
one of the arms the individual uses in his essentially
lawless struggle. Bepi talked at length about various court
cases he was engaged in: with the phone company about
stupidly high bills, with a neighbour about his (Bepi's) dog
kennels, with INPS, the national-insurance people, about
unpaid contributions for the girls in his shop, and there
were others too which I forget now. Far from any desire to
reform or change the situation, Bepi seemed pleased to
have these various fights going on and not at all concerned
he might lose them. As Negretti had seemed pleased when
Visentini called the police about the stench of dog filth
rising from his garden, as Lucilla was galvanised by her
fight with Signora Marta. It is a bellicosity one finds hard to
take at first, but which constant contact with other people,
and above all the authorities, gradually tends to make more
comprehensible, and even attractive. If there is an
anarchical tradition here, there are certainly reasons for it.

Towards nine o'clock, his dinner barely over, Bepi
simply falls asleep in the middle of a conversation on
Patuzzi's cheap synthetic couch, one of the only modern
items of furniture in the flat. The chandelier now has five
small 60-watt bulbs casting sharper shadows from the
fancy mouldings on the bookcase. But Bepi snores just the

same. When we wake him he looks at his watch. *Diamine*, he has to drive thirty kilometres to Rivoli now to feed his dogs. Fifteen of them. Tomorrow he will be up at five to get to the vegetable market and pick up stuff for the shop, then in the evening he teaches a gym class at the abandoned church by Laghetto Squarà which he rents from Don Guido (the source of their quarrel perhaps?). Yes, he teaches gym on Mondays and Wednesdays, karate on Tuesdays and Thursdays. Do we want to come?

How can I say that after a day's teaching and translating I'm not sure if I'll have the energy?

12

L'uomo rinascimentale

We go out running with Bepi. He gathers about fifteen young people by the abandoned church beside the *laghetto*. Most of the group are girls, more than one with their eyes on Bepi. Off we trot out into the country, up the valley towards Mizzole. The evening air is cool. We run by the cherry orchards, leaves limp with a first suspicion of autumn. We run past the first long, low poultry farm. The stench is unbelievable. And on an empty box by the side of the road, I read: 'BEST CANADIAN CHURKEY EGGS – SEALED CONTAINER – FOR INCUBATION FOLLOW INSTRUCTIONS.'

Jogging (or 'footing' as the Italians unaccountably call it) along tractor paths, we pass through a large vineyard, the purple fruit almost ripe around our ears. Here, beneath the

L'uomo rinascimentale

dense foliage, Bepi stops for some exercises, barking out orders with an unmistakeably authoritarian ring to his voice. *Flessioni!* And he's down on his stomach doing press ups. *Addominali!* He's on his back doing sit-ups, hands behind his head, legs bent at the knee. *Dorsali!* Over on our stomachs again. Such a desire for leadership! He flogs us. Showing off his macho dynamism. It's endearing. The girls titter, most of them making only token efforts. Footing again, we pass through a delightful old wine-stuccoed farm. There's an ancient well in the garden with stone top and swallows mustering for departure on the roof of the barn. Panting now, we run on through the picturesque village of Mizzole with the golden onion dome on its church. Posters tell us about pollution from pig farming, courses in secretarial skills, the imminent grape festival and the most recent deaths: Magnagatto Marta: ninety-two *anni*, much missed by her family. Graffiti on the stone walls, however, is mainly directed against a group of southerners from Reggio Calabria who have formed a cooperative and plan to build themselves some *villette a schiera* – terraced houses (a brand new fashion in Italy): '*Benvenuto a Reggio Mizzole*', has been scrawled over a road sign. Italians have a gift for grafitti. In the central square by the war memorial we read: 'Long live the government, long live taxes, long live the South . . . or no?' The work of the local separatists. Opposite, a sign over one of the village's two bars announces: Real American Cocktails, by Gianni.

We arrive back puffing and panting. Bepi wants to do some more exercises, but I've had enough. Perhaps anyway he is only waiting to see which groupie will hang on the longest. A process of natural selection. Walking

93

home, past the millwheel, past a Roman arch, under which heavy trucks pass to two huge silage containers in a small yard, we reflect that if he votes at all, Bepi probably votes MSI, the not very reformed fascists.

Another evening we drop by the gym where he is teaching karate to a mixed group of all ages. Italians take their sport very seriously. Black belt tight round his waist, Bepi barks out commands in what we presume is Japanese, his body squatting low, making the impressive ritual movements with concentration etched on his features. 'All here,' he tells us afterwards, 'all here,' and he taps his forehead.

A few weeks later we are invited to the house Bepi has repurchased and is now renovating up in Rivoli. He drives us west through Verona and then strikes off north up the Valpolicella. It's *vendemmia* time, the grape harvest. The Alfettas and BMWs fret and fume behind tractors inching along with their cartloads of grapes; it's important that the fruit doesn't get too knocked about, so they're taking the road as slow as they can. The air is heavy with an extremely pleasant drunken smell, an almost tangible sweet stickiness. Midges swarm in quite unbelievable numbers. Storms and clouds of them. These *vendemmia* days, you find yourself breathing midges the way the whale simply swallows his plankton as he swims along.

We arrive in Rivoli, perched high on the hills above the Adige, site of one of Napoleon's famous victories. Bepi turns his grocery van into a narrow track, bumping steeply down. At the end, the old peasant house that has focused his enterprising mind for so long is unprepossessing: a humble two-storey rectangle divided into two small dwellings with chickens pecking about outside. Buying it back can have had only symbolic value. Especially seeing as Bepi doesn't want to live here himself, and can't even get on with the ancient grandmother he has installed there. On our arrival they exchange fierce insults, much as he did with the priest.

The grounds are large though, perhaps thirty or forty acres sloping steeply downward away from the house. Once laboriously terraced and cultivated, they are neglected now, like so much of this countryside. The vines are overgrown, the support walls crumbling, so that here and there a terrace has collapsed, showing how chalky white the soil is beneath. Bepi takes us down to his dog kennels, a low concrete building a good fifty metres long and full of big, black, barking dogs. Our host, apparently – he tells us himself – is the foremost breeder of Belgian Shepherds in the Veneto, if not in Italy. His neighbour, despite being out of sight and earshot of the dogs, has started a court case about the kennels because he is resentful that Bepi outbid him for possession of the house. The same old story. Bepi thus stands accused of having built them without planning permission. In typically belligerent fashion Bepi has turned the case on its head, sueing the local authorities for being so slow over granting permission that he was 'forced' to go ahead without in order to accommodate his business.

He releases a couple of dogs and lets them come with us. Disconcertingly, as we walk along, he barks at them in German. I ask him which language he prefers for his girlfriends. With touching honesty he tells us he hasn't as yet found the language that girls respond to best. I assure him it is not English.

Before going in for lunch, he takes us up to a ridge at the edge of the property where we have a breathtaking view northward up the Valpolicella to the Alps, their rocky peaks barely visible for the haze. Deep deep below in the valley a huge irrigation canal leaves the River Adige and disappears into a tunnel under the hill. Disused marble quarries now converted into mushroom farms are dotted all about. The vista is vast, open, inspiring. I remark rather banally that it seems out of this world, *fuori del mondo*. To which, quite naturally, Bepi replies that, yes, UFOs (Oofoes as the Italians call them) used to visit here quite often, but have now ceased to do so, ever since people became too violent. The Veneto, he says, along with parts of Russia, boasts the highest frequencies of UFO sightings in the world. He used to see the lights himself further up the valley. I feel it isn't the moment to say that the Veneto also shares with Russia one of the highest consumptions of alcohol in the world.

Returning to the house we find Bepi's delightful 'father', Vittorio, who has come out to the country for the day with his wife. Strong, squat, of great girth and irrepressibly merry, Vittorio is just the kind of jolly chap one tends to see interviewed in the local paper after a UFO sighting. Now he presides over the big wooden table in the kitchen, where he has lined up five or six bottles of wine and seems intent on opening all of them at once. Meanwhile, his wife, Gina, buxom, retiring and embarrassed about her poor Italian, has prepared the most wonderful lasagna from scratch. Oceans of it.

We sit down. Vittorio begins to describe the qualities of each of his bottles at considerable length. Since he speaks only dialect and, unlike his wife, isn't at all embarrassed about it, I can't understand. I pick up half of a jolly joke about a dog that only went for dead birds. 'Don't let him come near me then,' is the punchline. Bird in Italian also means John Thomas.

Midday. The abundant lasagna. The labelless wine bottles. The smoke from an unnecessary fire in the huge limestone grate. Big thick steaks, which of course Bepi gets through a friend of a friend who would never give him anything but *roba buona* – good stuff. Then *tiramisù*, again abundant, creamy, calorie-rich, cholesterol-rich, splendid. Alongside a treacly Recioto. And, finally, a score of different grappas to choose from after, or with, your *espresso*. Vittorio makes the grappa himself, with what's left after making the wine, flavouring it with such things as lemons, peaches, oranges, even coffee. The different brews are arrayed before us in the kind of tall, greasy, nameless bottles one expects to find in the garage with a couple of inches of brake fluid in the bottom. I try two or three and make a toast to the UFOs.

Going back in his greengrocer's van, Bepi tells me that what he'd like to do is study theology. The Church and the Masons still hold on to many of the deepest secrets of this world; only the initiated will ever be allowed to know anything worth knowing. He has applied to join a lodge and is studying the cabbala in the evening when he can stay awake. Vaguely it occurs to me that this is all part of the P2 mentality. And I wonder if Bepi isn't the closest I am ever likely to get to a Renaissance man.

13
Troppo gentile

To be earthquake-proof, modern Italian buildings are legally required to be constructed around a reinforced concrete frame. In the event of tremors, the whole structure should thus shift as one unit, rather than crumbling into its separate parts. And, indeed, as one walks about the outskirts of Montecchio and on into the surrounding hills, builders are eagerly pouring cement into columns of roughly nailed planks, in a hurry to get things done before the November rains.

Concrete the columns and the beams, where shortly before were olive trees; concrete the roofs, too, of these new *palazzine* and *case a schiera*; and likewise concrete the floors, all wires and plumbing laid forever inaccessible in the cement. Gaunt frames take over a vineyard. Up go the walls between one beam and the next. The roof is then topped with terracotta, the living-space inside tiled with ceramics: sombre colours and smaller tiles in the seventies, brighter gloss-finish colours and much larger tiles in the eighties.

It makes for some rather curious acoustics. With no wood, you are saved the creaking board, the moaning stair. If you want to sneak in to check on a sleeping baby, or, God forbid, sneak out on wife or husband, there is no danger of the floor betraying you. In stockinged feet you are soundless. On the other hand, a hard object dropped on that ceramic-on-concrete floor, even a coin, will be heard in every room in the building, volume and intensity depending on the vicinity to a loadbearing beam or column. Patent leather soles clicking across the tiles will thus click across all the floors and ceilings of the condominium. A lavatory flushing in the dead of night is an explosion, an act of terrorism. And if you should take a drill to the wall and, after penetrating the plaster, happen upon one of those steel-reinforced columns, then all over the building, from *taverna* to *solaio*, it will seem that the eventuality for which the structure was designed is in full swing. The air vibrates. Soundwaves oppress the ear. It is as if one were caught inside a guitar with some naughty Brobdingnagian child incessantly twanging the bass string.

We did experience a couple of small quakes in Via Colombare. The *palazzina* shuddered and sang. Patuzzi's wineglasses tinkled on their shelves. Apparently, columns of trucks were passing in the night, or ships' engines starting up in the basement.

Lying down to sleep of an October evening, thankful that we can now close the windows against the TVs, accordions and ping-pong of the velvety dark outside, we hear instead an unmistakeable fierce trickling, coming, well, presumably from below us. At eleven-thirty every night. Trickle trickle trickle, dribble dribble, drop, drop, stop. We hold our breath. But there is no explosion of flushing, for unspoken condominium etiquette requires that the toilets *tacciono* – fall silent – after eleven o'clock. It's a special kind of intimacy this concrete brings.

Trying to sleep again after being woken by Vega in the early hours, I begin to hear footsteps going back and forth in our *solaio* under the roof above. This is alarming. Slow heavy footsteps, back and forth, back and forth, above our heads. Rita confirms, they definitely come from our *solaio*, supposedly an empty attic. And in the dead of night one believes in *fantasmi*. Vega has been moaning rather than barking this evening, howling and wailing at the moon.

I get up, pull on a pair of trousers, then slippers against the cold tiles, and go out of the flat and up the stairs. Where I slip and fall on the highly polished marble. This particular flight to the roof is rarely used, but Lucilla waxes it regularly just the same. Everything must always be just so, a mausoleum odour. Cursing and rueful, I reach the iron door of the *solaio*, open it, and then remember I still haven't put a light bulb in. At which point the timed landing light goes out. I grope for the switch, but don't know where it is on this floor. So I go into the *solaio* blind.

I stare, waiting for my pupils to dilate, recognising a smell of geranium cuttings and thick dust. A dark, softly shifting light, filtering from the attic's one window, finally enables me to see the shadows of untidily piled boxes, an ancient bed, a crucifix, a pair of bellows unaccountably left on the windowsill, and rows and rows of *il professore's* old climbing boots. None of them moving, thank God. I cock my head. No sound.

But back downstairs, the footsteps go on and on above us.

Talking to Orietta, the quiet repository of all condominium gossip, we discover that Lucilla suffers from insomnia. The footsteps are hers, the ventriloquist building sends the sound where it will.

Orietta is loosening up. She is losing her suspicion of my Englishness. She recognises the advantage of having other non-Montecchiesi to make friends with. Giampaolo, she tells us, has frequently complained about those footsteps. Getting up in the night, it seems, Lucilla will put on her fur coat, partly against the cold, partly because she likes her fur coat; she finds its luxury comforting, its monied smell reassuring. But since she is small and bought the coat long, she puts her heels on so as not to have it trail on the floor. And paces up and down.

Another night it is the squeal of heavy furniture being scraped above our heads. Bumps and banging. Thud, scrape, squeal. Yes, Lucilla tells us brightly on the stairs, she decided to rearrange the sitting-room, do we want to come and see it?

Please would we come and see it?

Perhaps we would take a little drink with her? She has some *Lacryma Christi*.

Or perhaps we would like to have a piece of her *pastafrolla*?

Surely, if she isn't disturbing us, we would like to come and see her new curtains, eat her shortbread? Also, if we could explain something in the instruction book to her steam iron . . .

There is a scene in Fellini's film, *La voce della luna*, where a local politician, fallen upon hard times, is seen returning to his dreary flat in an old *palazzotto* in some tiny town of the Po valley. But every time he climbs the stairs and approaches his door, whether it be two in the afternoon or two in the morning, four ancient neighbours will appear at the door opposite and, like awful decaying sirens, try to lure him into their flat to share some old-fashioned dainty: a thimbleful of some sweet forgotten liqueur, a morsel of traditional crumbliness. Their faces are pictures of decrepit flattery and seduction. Close to obscenity. The furniture, dingily glimpsed behind them, is sombre and coffin-inspired with candlesticks in abundance, photographs of dead relatives on lace doilies. 'Would a small glass of sherry be to your liking, your honour? Would a small slice of *pan di spagna*, councillor, be acceptable as our humble offering?' Their veiny hands are outstretched in supplication. Which is immediately perceived as a trap, as if a whole culture were refusing to lie down in its grave, but were rising ghoulish to eat our contemporary flesh. Horrified and furious, the man manages to escape into his room, slams and bolts the door behind him. But already the four leathery faces are down by the keyhole. 'Would your honour be so kind as to take a glass of brandy with some humble folk . . .' They haunt his dreams. He sees their faces floating outside his window at night with the moon behind, luring him back into some archaic, provincial Italy of polished woodwork and thickly smoking candlewax, flattery, favours, back-stabbing.

Such, for me, were Lucilla's insistent invitations. So that I almost looked back with regret on her ravings from the balcony, her confiscation of the dustbin. Those days when I at least knew where I stood.

Barely has she got us inside her polished door – *troppo*

gentile, too kind, *Signor Tino* (she never registered the name Tim) – than she is leaning out into the stairwell calling down to Vittorina. She has a direct intercom connection with Vittorina's flat, but prefers to call down the stairwell, if only to remind all residents in the condominium of her existence. 'Rina! Rina! Come and have something to drink with *i signori inglesi*.' Is she calling up reinforcements? Or just increasing the size of her audience?

We walk in, and promptly slither on imitation animal-skin rugs strewn over the usual lethally waxed floor. Lucilla is clearly nostalgic for her cleaning days. The year before we arrived, she slipped on the rug in the entrance and broke her hip. But this has not deterred her. I all but come a cropper on the synthetic white hairy thing between low glass table and imitation leather sofa. Vittorina, who has now appeared in a nightgown, hair thinner than ever, frowns with the air of one who is wiser than the person she is used to being bossed about by. And indeed, she doesn't even try to remove her moustache as Lucilla does. A vanity beneath her.

We are shown round the flat. The walls are simple whitewash, as in almost every Italian house. The furniture is what a local Veronese would laughingly describe as *stile Bovolone*, Bovolone being an industrial settlement twenty kilometres away in the foggy *bassa* where scores of busy companies produce clunky replicas of antique furniture. A Louis XIV dresser, bright and new, features prominently in the entrance way. There is a Renaissance chest in polished pine, and Lucilla's is the first home, aside from paying visits to Waltham Abbey and Hatfield House, where I have seen a bed with a canopy curtain affair over the headboard, here upholstered in electric nylon pink. The room is about ten by twelve.

Il professore was a great man, she begins impulsively, having put little red glasses of *gingerino* in our hands. A great man. Of culture. She speaks in fierce dialect. I strain my ears to distinguish the words, my mind to understand. It is not unlike trying to make out a strange landscape through thick fog. Was that a house or a tree, a tail light or shop neon? And we are going so fast. My head starts to ache. Still, at the end of an hour or so of non-stop haranguing, I do manage to discern the following salient landmarks, if only because Lucilla goes round and round them so insistently, not unlike Pooh Bear following his own tracks in the snow: so, *il professore*, that is, Patuzzi, had written a will and put it in his deposit box in the bank (half of Montecchio seems to have a deposit box at the bank). He then died quite suddenly, of a heart attack, breathing his last on the ambulance stretcher right outside her door, *poveretto* (obligatory epithet for describing the dear departed). And what a fright for her! *Comunque*, the will had clearly stated that the wife would have use of the property only until her death, after which it would pass to her, Lucilla. Such an exquisite man, *il professore*. As had been agreed of course. Because it was her money, her money had paid for the *palazzina*. She had worked her fingers to the bone all her life. So cultured. We would have admired him immensely. But no sooner had he passed away than Signora Marta and Maria Rosa were off to the bank, had opened the deposit box and promptly burnt the will. For which they themselves would burn in hell. Whereas we would never meet anybody more *gentile*, more *generoso*, than *il professore*.

Lucilla's bosom began to heave, it wasn't clear whether out of love or anger or some dangerous blood-dark cocktail of the two. Then Maria Rosa had herself fallen ill and become infirm. Lucilla had looked after her, as was her duty towards another 'Christian', taking her meals which she handed over at the door whose threshold she was never to pass. Because that woman put on airs, while *il professore*, who might have had good reason to be haughty, was *dolcezza* itself. And when things got worse, Maria Rosa had come and more or less lived in her own, Lucilla's flat; slept there for months, being nursed and helped to the toilet and so on. Until, finally, Lucilla could cope no more and the woman had had to go into a home. But towards the end of that period, in a fit of remorse, Maria Rosa had told Lucilla the story of the will and how it had been burnt and had agreed to write a further will herself.

Lucilla fiddles under the flap of a rather oversized new Regency writing desk, bringing out a furry-grey piece of notepaper which she then waves under our noses. '*Ecco, legga, legga, Signor Tino.*' Her fingers are stubby and impressively bejewelled. I take the *documento* with due respect. Uncertain handwriting announces the last will and testament of Maria Rosa Griminelli. The whole of Via Colombare number 10 belongs and always has belonged to Lucilla Zambon who built it with her own money. There is a single indecipherable signature, no lawyer, only the beneficiary as a witness.

But Lucilla's hopes are pinned on that scrap of paper. She raises her voice. She is furious, defiant. Her bony teeth are in evidence. 'The flat is mine, mine, mine.' But we are nice people, and when she finally gets hold of the property, on Maria Rosa's death, she will allow us to stay, although she will have to ask us to buy it rather than rent. But we can discuss all this at a later date.

Would we like a *cioccolatino*, a San Pellegrino Bitter? Would we like to watch television with her of an evening? She would be grateful if we could adjust her set. There is a programme on Tele Montecarlo with a man just like her beloved husband, here he is in this photograph. *Così bello*! Why did the men always die first? But she can never get a good picture on Tele Montecarlo. Signor Giampaolo has put up that new motorised aerial on the roof and it is sucking all the goodness from hers. Do I know anything about aerials? And could Rita perhaps phone her lawyer for her to have him explain something she can't understand, and tell him to hurry up with the case.

Lucilla talks on and on. There is simply no chink in her verbal armour, no hesitation into which one might thrust the dagger of a request to leave. Vittorina watches, silent, dark, with those sudden smiles when she catches your eye, smiles which say she understands your suffering, but this is Lucilla, this is how she is, *porti pazienza*.

In desperation, we begin our long retreat. First simply getting to our feet, then edging out of the lounge and across the dining-room with its dark, dying plants, its sad canary, heading toward the entrance. Along a low wall is an array of those tiny twisted-glass Venetian ornaments, reminding me of my infancy in Blackpool, when we visited a Great-Aunt Esther who had row upon row of the things on a dresser.

Do we think she should ask for the *condono edilizio*, the building pardon? You see, she had this wall knocked down, that's why it is different from our flat, didn't we notice, between the entrance and the kitchen . . . So much

more space. But without asking for planning permission
. . . and now with this pardon . . .

Does she have the right lawyer? What do we think?
Perhaps he isn't being tough enough. Surely the rent we
are paying should go to her. How much are we paying? *Il
professore* only left the flat to his wife for use while she
wanted to live there, but any rent should go to her, Lucilla.
And, of course, in that home Maria Rosa is in, Signora
Marta is putting pressure on her to sign another will
leaving everything to her. But it wouldn't be right, because
Rosa isn't capable of exercising free will now. She is senile.
Though the doctors are all *in complicità* clearly, with what's
being paid for her to be there. All *il professore*'s fortune. The
priest said . . .

Finally we make it to the hall. We are repeating *arrivederci*s, *buona notte*s, when I finally remember the purpose
behind our visit, the subject I had originally come to
broach. The nocturnal noises. We hope, I say, that we
never, er, bother them, when we play our stereo, when we
type late at night, when we have friends over. Noise carries
so much in these buildings. One can hear everything. We
wouldn't like . . . 'But no, Signor Tino, no, no, no, *troppo
gentile, troppo gentile*! We like to hear noise. We like to hear
footsteps, laughter, banging. The more the merrier. We're
two old ladies. It keeps us company. We feel less lonely.
Ma troppo gentile, ma che signore!'

And somehow Signor Tino just can't bring himself to say
what he wants to say. The way he can never quite make up
his mind to poison that dog.

14
Condono

The *condono edilizio* was first mooted in the early 1980s. The idea was to recognise that there are vast numbers of buildings in Italy which were put up without permission: villas and cottages in the north, whole blocks of flats down south. Since, officially, these buildings don't exist, they aren't paying the modest property tax (although they do of course receive electricity, water, post and so on, and residency certificates confidently assert that people do live in them and hence enjoy all the rights that go with officially living in a place). There are also, the new law would recognise, even greater numbers of buildings which have been altered in some way without permission: extended, restored, disfigured, rebuilt. Under the terms of the *condono*, the government would allow people to register these buildings or any changes made to them and thus get themselves *in regola* as they say, paying in return only a fraction of the fine they would otherwise have to pay if prosecuted. For the government this would mean a considerable *ad hoc* income and the prospect of larger regular revenues in the future.

No sooner had the splendid idea been put forward than building began in earnest all over the peninsula. Of course, the law would refer only to buildings completed some months before it was initially drawn up. But if a building isn't registered it is not always easy to say exactly when it was built. And perhaps the government didn't really care, since finances were such (are always such) that the larger the injection of cash, the better.

The law was passed by decree, quite normal practice, but a decree has to be ratified by parliament within sixty days. The *condono* was not ratified. Which was curious given the general enthusiasm. Some mischievous newspapers alleged that many of those MPs who voted against it were busy building their own illegal villas and eager to have them finished before the law was eventually passed, as they were sure it one day would be. But at the time, MPs had a secret vote in the Italian parliament, so it was impossible to tell who was involved.

Along Via Colombare somebody knocked down a handsome old barn and began feverish work on a luxury extension, which pretty well amounted to a second house. Passing of the law was again delayed. Almost opposite the luxury extension, the woman who swept the road regularly with her twig broom began to lay the foundations of a two-car garage with terrace roof leading through French windows to the first floor of her house. Wielding her broom, she bustled about the old workers in their dungarees with their bottles of wine and tupperware boxes full of cold pasta.

The law was now passed. But then the deadline for applications for the *condono* was waived on two or three occasions. To give a little respite. All over Italy the cement mixers rumbled; work went on apace. And I remember walking back along the more than usually dusty street one day, to find in number 10's postbox one of those magazines that somehow always find their way to ex-pats: *Investment International*, or some such title. They tell you how to send your children to English boarding schools, how to invest your money in offshore tax havens, how to prepare for the mental shock of return, how to let your Mayfair flat in your absence, etc. etc. On this particular occasion a review of European stockmarkets remarked, of la Borsa di Milano, that one could do no better than invest in Italcementi, the state-controlled cement company. Cement in Italy, the article said, had miraculously out-performed all other kinds of stock, thanks to the vigour, the creativity and the enterprising spirit of both manufacturers and building contractors. So much for the foreign perspective.

In Via Colombare we got a new fence to protect the really rather attractive beige-stuccoed, copper-drained three-bedroom extension which had replaced the old barn (beautiful, full of swallows nests, but no longer functional). The fence was made of tall, spiky, brown-painted iron railings sunk into a marble-topped cement wall, and it ended in a sheltered, terracotta-tiled entrance way complete with video-camera security. The tiny garden between the fence and the villa extension respected the cemetery style of dwarf cypresses and biblically inspired stucco statues. Opposite, the woman with the twig broom now swept her terrace of a morning, as well as the remaining half of the patio and a fair stretch of road outside.

But in the end this was a fairly innocuous form of anarchy. For around this time we took a week off to visit friends who live in the suburbs of Rome. Their house, a legal part of a new development, had simply been smothered by new building, much of it of the crudest variety, breeze blocks placed one on top of another with prefab roof, just enough to claim the *condono* and have the authorities accept the existence of a building which could then be developed in the future. Many houses were without utilities. Next door, the owner had converted the ground floor of his house into a bodywork repair outfit, blocking the narrow road outside with dented cars. Our friends had called the local *vigile* about the noise, the smell of spray paint, the inconvenience, reminding him that this was a residential area. The *vigile* went to talk with the culprit and apparently took a bribe.

Italian stories. One hears them more or less daily.

Back in number 10, there were various reasons for asking for the *condono*. The *palazzo* was a metre or so too near Negretti's house. Then the *solai*, for example, had tiled floors, whereas to remain in the tax bracket the house was in, they should have been left bare and 'non-inhabitable'. The same was true of the garage and the *taverna*. One has a building inspected, is the trick, its tax bracket declared, and then one changes it at will: peeling shutters in the city centre conceal luxury window fittings; pitted, flaking stucco is a front for polished parquet, granite and gold bathroom fittings. Everybody's at it. The humble façade, the lavish interior. Tall, glass-topped walls. Secretiveness.

Eventually, it was decided at condominium level (that is, by Lucilla) that number 10 would not ask for the *condono*. Because in the end it wasn't free, was it? However small, the fine would still have to be paid. And why bother? Lucilla was indignant. Nobody had really done anything wrong, had they? Nobody had hurt anybody. Anyway, the chances of the authorities ever catching you were infinitesimal; otherwise they would never have introduced the *condono* in the first place. And it was so dangerous to draw attention to yourself. Once they had your name in black and white, heaven knows what they might find out.

Lucilla was right. Some years later an income tax *condono* was passed by decree. People would 'reconstruct their tax careers', paying a modest fine. Thus the government would know how much tax to expect from such people in the future. But almost nobody applied for the pardon, since the very fact that the government had introduced it was an admission of their inability or unwillingness to catch anyone. Parliament then voted out the decree after the sixty days. This meant that while, over the previous two months, it had officially been the law, it was now considered never to have been the law at all. Upon which a few zealous magistrates attempted to prosecute those guilty few who had somewhat hastily confessed to their tax crimes in the hope of getting *in regola*. A lesson for the rest of us if ever there was one.

15
Discreto, valido, relativo

If Lucilla's most common expression was the flattering and subservient, *troppo gentile, troppo gentile*, a social tick she had presumably picked up in her deprived girlhood of floor-scrubbing and straightforward begging, Giampaolo Visentini's most characteristic utterances were always built around the three words: *discreto, valido, relativo*.

Imagine you are sitting in the Visentinis' tastefully and above all cautiously furnished sitting-room. You are drinking excellent *prosecco* which Giampaolo bottled himself, which he has put in the fridge three or four days before your planned evening get-together (in the back of the fridge, not the door, since that would involve its getting knocked around too much). Upon your arrival and acceptance of the offered treat, he has carried the bottle from kitchen through dining-room to sitting-room with the concentration of a bomb disposal expert shifting primed Semtex, has released the detonating cork ever so gently to prevent explosion, then tilted the bottle painstakingly slowly over an attractive pottery carafe bearing the name of some Sardinian seaside town – all this because it's so desperately important to avoid disturbing the sediment which is both the hallmark and curse of home-bottled wines. Giampaolo watches intently as he pours, brow knitted, long pale fingers strong and steady, his whole attitude conveying the slightly glazed worshipful concentration of the devotee. The contents froth out, the carafe fills, the sediment, which would have given the wine an unpleasant acidy taste, remains safely in the bottle and – *ecco fatto*, done it! Being bourgeois, it might be said, is never an easy way out in Italy.

Of course, if this is your first evening with the Visentini, if this is the first time you have drunk home-bottled *prosecco*, the whole elaborate rigmarole will seem nothing short of ridiculous. You can barely hold back a giggle. The caricatures are true, you're thinking. These Latins are obsessive about food and wine. What's going to change your mind is when you actually taste the *prosecco*.

And here at last it is. Lovingly as ever, but more relaxed now, Giampaolo pours from the carafe into tall slim glasses. '*Salute.*' You raise a crystal stem. The cold sharp taste stings the lips, demands attention. It's desperately dry, cutting like a knife through the sweetness of whatever goodies are being handed out. And as it fills your mouth, you become aware of wanting to hold it there. Bubbles froth on the palate. You are drinking something special.

So there you are, perched on geometrically arranged

chairs about a rug of soberly coloured squares and rectangles surrounded by polished tiles, chinking your tall glass with your host's. The Visentinis' daughter is there too: Lara, named after the heroine in *Dr Zhivago*. A strapping twelve-year-old, she giggles merrily when Rita cracks a joke. I'm offering compliments about the wine, asking if it is the same that we will be bottling together in the spring. There are the makings of a pleasant evening.

But Giampaolo is so solemn. And, perhaps not wishing to discuss wine with a layman, he launches into serious conversation. He's telling you about some new law. For he likes to talk about politics. Concerning drunk driving for example. Yes, the new law on drunk driving has been drawn up *discretamente* (quite well, with intelligence if not flair) and is in fact for the most part *valido* (sound, functional), but all of this is *relativo* (of only secondary importance) since the instruments for enforcing the law are not available, or if they are nobody has any intention of using them. He smiles, as if having performed a conjuring trick, takes a sparkling sip of *prosecco*, picks up another piece of *pastafrolla*.

And the formula, you discover as the evening progresses, can be applied to almost any area of life upon which Giampaolo cares to reflect. The Italian system of *autostrade*, he is telling you now, is definitely *discreto*, road surfaces and markings are always *valido*, but all this tends to be *relativo* since, with the exorbitant price of petrol and the very high tolls, one would need to be rich indeed before one could use it with any regularity.

Another long sip of this extraordinary wine.

Likewise efficiency in Italian companies, such as his own, is certainly *discreto*, the managerial class indubitably *valido*, but again these pluses are rendered *relativo* by a public sector which simply sucks blood from the rest of the economy.

And so, if you encourage him, he will go on all evening: the constitution, the electoral system, the TV networks; *discreto, valido, relativo*. It is a curious and, I believe, curiously Italian stalemate, in which ineradicable national pride (and why not?) exists side by side with a sense of cynicism (equally justifiable) and, at the end of the day, resignation. The judicial system has been 'conceived *discretamente bene*', and the constitution in this regard is undoubtedly *valido*, in that it establishes the total independence of the judiciary. But whatever the institutional make-up, it is inevitably only *relativo* given the endemic corruption that always allows the *mafiosi* to get off scot-free.

The mental pattern propagates itself like someone cutting pastry (or *pastafrolla*) with a die, or pouring wine into tall glasses. There is no question of simply showing anger or outrage for all the things that make the country a less attractive place to live than it might so easily be. The blunt analysis and sleeve-rolling gaucheness which forms the typical reaction of, for example, the English, inevitably carries the subtext that something could and should be done, and quickly: reform the poll tax, cut inflation, dump Thatcher, etc. etc. English people usually believe such things to be possible, or at least imaginable. But the Italian knows that nothing can or will be done in his country, and that if it is done it certainly will not be done quickly. This is his experience. After all, with all the shifting coalitions and merry-go-round of prime ministers, most people here haven't seen a real change of government in their lifetime. Thus an Italian's satisfaction, when he talks about politics, will lie in feeling that he has analysed the situation accurately, appreciated its ironies, seen the pros and the cons, absorbed the subtleties, and above all gone beyond the crude simplicity of foreigners who talk in ingenuous terms about changing things.

Discreto, valido, relativo – not one of them is a particularly complimentary or pejorative term. They are the cool words of the astute analyst, the man who looks at the whole show from a distance, then goes about his business as he would have done anyway, regardless, but happy to have had the chance to illustrate his powers of observation. In the final analysis: *'La legge non mi tange.'*

Fortunately there is Orietta's gossip to brighten up the evening. Lucilla has apparently called on the priest, Don Guido, to be a witness in the case she is bringing against Signora Marta. He has agreed. Which is interesting. And did we know that Lucilla has a fancy man? Simone, an ex-*carabiniere*. Yes, he comes three or four evenings a week. The daughter giggles and begins to explain about the vacuum cleaner. Lucilla has what must be a pre-war vacuum cleaner, but recently she has been borrowing Orietta's (Vittorina doesn't have one), claiming that her own is broken. Whereas, in fact, Lara, the daughter, saw Simone, the *carabiniere* fancy man, bumping down the stairs with the thing only a week ago.

To mend it? To use it? Can't he afford one?

Anyway, this is becoming a problem, Orietta says, since there's so much dust about these days with all the building going on in the street. She needs to use the thing herself two or three times a day.

Everybody nods gravely.

Orietta is small, doll-like, and clearly perfectly attuned to sedentary domestic life. She doesn't have a job, but every corner of the room shows evidence of her tireless cleaning. Only the other morning I watched her diligently polishing inch after inch of the long marble balustrade of the terrace balcony. There was concentration on her face, satisfaction, the devotion of the accolyte cleaning the altar. Not unlike her husband's expression while pouring his *prosecco*. Later we will discover that, when Giampaolo wanted to accept a more dynamic job in a much smaller company, Orietta forbade him. It wasn't safe.

She is also scared of earthquakes.

And of every possible disease. Thus, as so often with Italian acquaintances, we are not far into our first evening with the Visentini before Orietta is discussing her blood pressure. Which is a mite high. She shouldn't have more than two coffees a day. Also she occasionally gets attacks of tachycardia. She is appalled to discover that I don't even know my own blood pressure. As far as I know it has never been taken. Her face shows genuine concern. Apparently, we are touching on a real cultural difference here.

Orietta explains that after feeling somewhat faint a few days ago the doctor arranged for her to have an exhaustive series of blood and urine tests, together with an electro-cardiogram and a heart scan. She has thus been getting up early every morning to get to the hospital, wait in all the queues, fill in all the forms and fix all the appointments. She remembers last time she had a blood test her bilirubin was way outside the norms indicated on the test sheet, whereas cholesterol A was thankfully low.

I remark that I have never, to my knowledge, had a blood test. I don't even know my group.

Lara had a rash a few weeks ago on face and chest.

Although this cleared up almost immediately, she too was sent off for complete blood and urine tests, including tests for such things as syphilis. It appeared that her *trigliceridi* were rather high.

I can't decide if this is surprisingly intimate or rather frightening, or both. And I remember our landlady, Signora Marta, fiddling with her keys at the gate that first day, talking about her gynaecological problems.

With the gravity of a Houyhnhnm, Giampaolo takes this opportunity to reflect that, on the whole, public hospitals in Verona function *discretamente bene*, when compared with hospitals in other areas of Italy, and of course the idea behind the health system as it was initially conceived is indubitably *valido*. However, it has to be admitted that the apparent success of the local system is *del tutto relativo* since, if all the people who presently go private were to turn to the public system, it would break down in a matter of days.

Lucilla for example, and Vittorina.

'Really? They go private? But they're not particularly well off, are they?'

Giampaolo explains that the old women go to a local health-service doctor whom they tip generously. When they have any tests to do, he always tells them to go to a private clinic, of which he, as it so happens, is a director. And they pay a lot of money. And say, *troppo gentile, Dottore, troppo gentile.*

We thus discover that it is not so much, or by no means only the upper middle class and the important executive who go private in Italy. Above all it is the ignorant, the workers and peasant class who have tucked something away in their deposit box or in a few government bonds.

They can't believe the public system can work and then, of course, it's a status symbol to say, I am going to my private gynaecologist, my private cardiologist, my private paediatrician. From whom, more often than not, they will get no receipt.

Rita tells a joke her mother made up when her father Adelmo kept going to the hospital for tests upon tests upon tests. It goes like this. What does a German do in the morning? He jumps out of bed, grabs a cup of coffee and rushes off to work. What does an American do in the morning? He climbs out of bed, sips a cup of coffee, reads the paper for ten minutes and strolls off to work. What does an Italian do?

Long pause. Puzzlement of the Visentini in their spic-and-span sitting-room.

Urinates in a bottle and sets off to the hospital!

Only Lara truly thinks this is funny. The others have a sort of pained smile. Health is so important. Not for nothing did we say 'Salute' when we raised those glasses.

And Orietta touches her face. Do we think she should have her mole removed? This little one in the dimple on her cheek. She's afraid it may be growing. No it's not very visible because she powders it. Her doctor said to leave well alone, but she went for a second opinion and that doctor said to have a biopsy done. At a private clinic, Giampaolo adds.

Idly, Lara picks up the remote control and the television flicks on. With its usual brutality, the news is showing yet another Mafia killing. Corruption on a more impressive scale. The scene is always the same: the car caught at the traffic lights, riddled with bullets, the corpses in a heap on the front seats, perhaps an arm thrown out of the shattered window, blood trickling down on to the asphalt, spotlights all round for the TV cameras. They have shot General Dalla Chiesa, chief of police in Sicily.

Giampaolo plays with the controls to his motorised aerial on the roof to enable us to get a better view. Weeping relatives are being asked how they feel.

We finish our *prosecco* and go upstairs. Leaning out over the balcony to get some fresh air we are lucky enough to witness the departure of Simone, the ex-*carabiniere*. He's solid, sixtyish, thick head of bristling grey hair, and he has a package under his arm. Too small to be a vacuum cleaner though. He fiddles for the keys to his Fiat 128 parked a hair's breadth from our iron fence. Lucilla appears on her balcony, barely ten feet away across the façade of the building, although she hasn't noticed us. In the swinging light of the overhead streetlamp we can see she is heavily made up, dressed to the nines, wearing higher than usual heels, decidedly Felliniesque. She leans over the parapet and begins to whisper enticingly: 'Simone, Simone *caro*, when will you phone? Simone, when are you coming to dinner again?' One imagines him glimpsing her long teeth as he slides down into his car with the heavy sigh of one who has overeaten. *Ciao, bella,* he calls. She stands watching after him, pensive, huge breasts uplifted. It's sad to think of this woman being taken for a ride by her doctor. But then, as Rita remarks, she probably paid no tax in the good old days of the cleaning company, so it all works out in the end.

For the next few weeks I practise *discreto*, *valido* and *relativo* on any and every subject that comes up.

16
Una bustarella

They had shot General Dalla Chiesa, the man who had defeated terrorism, the man the government had appointed to defeat the Mafia. About the same time, a very close friend of mine paid his first bribe to a state official. These two facts are not perhaps entirely unrelated.

It's a complicated story, perhaps a little bit of a digression, but I'd like to tell it all the same because it shows how even the ingenuous foreigner who arrives here, as one arrives most places, more or less by chance, can so easily run up against the dark side of Italy.

This was an extremely close friend of mine. Like me he had arrived in Italy some time before, like me he lived in a little village not far from a sizeable town, like me he had grafted for a while with private lessons and commercial translations until good fortune had landed him one of the much sought-after jobs teaching English at the university, a position offering a decent, steady income for work that is pleasant and not overly taxing. He was delighted. Now he could relax a little. No more the breathless hurry to get from one lesson to the next, only to find the student has cancelled. No more the embarrassment of having to insist that patently rich people deign to pay one with a certain regularity. No more the smell of white-out in the early hours labouring over translations on the recycling of waste sludge in marble saw-mills, the unsurpassable tourist attractions of the nearby town. He was home and dry.

But the contract they made him sign at the university was a strange one. Although to all intents and purposes an employee, in the sense that he had a timetable and certain well-established duties, he was in fact officially free lance, the university retaining 18 per cent of his income as tax (had he not had *residenza* they would have retained 20 per cent), but paying no health contributions and requiring him to declare the money on a free-lance basis.

Now, since this friend of mine had a VAT number which he used for his translations, he went to the university accounts office to ask them what exactly his tax situation might be. Complicated, they said, and went into great detail. Which he didn't entirely understand. For Italian tax law might well be written in hieroglyphics for all the average citizen can understand of it. Never mind a foreigner. Rather than on actual income, everything seems to depend on the category of worker you are (artisan, lawyer, doctor, plumber, farmer, shopkeeper . . .) and the nature of the work you do (regular, casual, occasional, for one client, for various, etc. etc.), with different rules applying for each different category, different tax brackets, different deductions, different percentages for national insurance and so on and so forth. So that at the end of the explanation, which might also have been described with the much used Italian substantive, *mistificazione*, my sensible friend demanded to know the bottom line: could he retain his VAT number, do a few translations, and do the job at the university without paying VAT on it.

They said yes. And made him sign something. The usual *documento*. They also said that even if he did want to charge VAT on the job, they wouldn't pay it, but would deduct it from his salary.

Had any of the other thirty or so *lettori* opted for this alternative? he asked.

And was told none. Because it wasn't necessary.

But being a cautious lad, my friend also had an accountant. And went to see him. To clear the matter up. The accountant, however, could do nothing more than offer a second equally mystifying 'explanation' which simply defied comprehension, perhaps because, as the accountant readily admitted, the law in many areas was not only unclear, but frankly contradictory. It also changed with great regularity, and often government decrees, which were officially law, were not ratified by parliament and thus not only ceased to be law but were deemed never to have been law in the first place. Basically, my friend could do what he wanted. Since everybody else at the university was doing precisely that, my friend took this wise advice. He worked, he got paid and, at least in this regard, was happy.

Four years later he received a small white card in his mailbox. From the VAT office. He was required to present himself with great urgency, indeed within a date already past, for the printed card had taken more than a week to travel the six kilometres from the centre of town to his modest flat in the outlying village.

He got on his moped and rushed into town, found the VAT office, showed his card at reception, and was directed along a maze of corridors to a huge office whose walls were lined from floor to ceiling, door to door, with box files bulging with tax declarations. It quickly became apparent that the four moustached men behind four gun-metal desks were sorting through the VAT declarations of four years before.

My friend was breathing heavily because he had made it just in time. Like most offices in Italy, this one was open only in the morning since, unlike employees in the private sector, civil servants enjoy a 36-hour week, six mornings, six hours a day. It was now ten to one.

He handed his card to an older, weary, dusty, bespectacled man behind a huge, dusty heap of papers coloured the kind of garish pink and yellow that forms can be. In parenthesis, I find it is curious how colouring forms does nothing to make them more attractive. Rather the colours themselves, become, by association, somewhat frightening: those tissue blues, washed out mauves.

He apologised for the delay but the post had been slow. The man said the date was a formality and of no relevance. He then proceeded to look for the English teacher's VAT return out of the thousands, perhaps hundreds of thousands, which not only lined the wall, but were arrayed in great barriers of box files between the desks.

When the document was finally found, it emerged that while my friend had been wise perhaps to realise he needed an accountant, he had been unlucky in his choice. For the accountant had made a mistake. In the declaration of four years before, he had mentioned the university income and stated that it was exempt from VAT, but without indicating the code that would explain this exemption. The dusty old man now wanted my friend to tell him which code it was, so that he could write it in the space and the completed form be filed away and forgotten.

In passing, it's worth pointing out here that had the accountant filled in that space with any code, even a non-existent one, there would most likely have been no problem. For Italian tax inspection appears to be mainly involved in finding contradictory statements within any given declaration. Only very rarely do inspectors go out of their offices to see if the lifestyle of the taxpayer bears any resemblance to his declaration. Thus it is common and frequently repeated wisdom (in the bars in Montecchio for example) that it is far better to make no declaration at all than an incomplete or even minimally incorrect one. A line made all the more attractive by the fact that in this case one doesn't have to worry with an accountant. When Francesco Pazienza, a millionaire entrepreneur, was arrested in connection with the collapse of the Banco Ambrosiano and the death of director Roberto Calvi (hung under Blackfriars Bridge), it emerged that he had never made a tax declaration in his life, nor ever bothered with a tax code. He had thus never run up against the kind of problems experienced by my friend. And the same could probably be said of one or two people within striking distance of Via Colombare.

But the story that follows will offer a certain justification for that apparently antisocial kind of behaviour.

For my friend now made a terrible mistake. Lulled into a false sense of security by the bland innocuousness of this man with dust in his wrinkles and along the rims of his spectacles and peppering his anyway grey moustache, he said, truthfully, that he didn't know what code it might be. The man kindly suggested that he go away, consult his accountant, and return with this information inside a week or two. But here the young foreigner was quite criminally ingenuous, a born victim. He didn't want, he said, to have to return over such a small matter, nor to have to go and consult his accountant. It took him more than half an hour every time he came into town. Surely if he told the old man the nature of the work, he in turn could produce the code; they could then write it down and all would be over.

On the desk there was a little carousel of rubber stamps of all shapes and sizes, some adjustable, some not. The old man tapped the thing with his finger and it began to turn, squeaking slightly. Perhaps this was a warning.

Unheeded. My friend told him the nature of the work. Indeed of all his work. As a person who has nothing to fear from investigation and authority.

The older man became more interested, licked the dust off his lips, said he couldn't say offhand what code that would be; they would have to go and talk to a colleague.

The maze of passages again, grey carpets, fluorescent light. Indeed, apart from the occasional crucifix hanging under the heating pipes near the ceiling, this could perfectly well be an Inland Revenue office in Wapping or Huntingdon. But it isn't.

In another gloomy but more private office the colleague is of an entirely different variety. He is young, sanguine, peremptory and dust-free, despite the tomes and papers on his desk.

Such work, he pronounces, after hearing the story, should not have been exempt from VAT. There is no question of there being a code.

But my friend has a document provided for him by the university accountants whom he consulted precisely over this question.

Already he appreciates what a mistake he has made. But it is too late.

A document from the university? The younger man is scornful. No accountant worth his salt would be working at the university, getting only a million and a half a month. Would he? How could they advise him? In any event my friend, as a resident and contributor, is personally responsible for paying his taxes regardless of any advice received – even, the man adds triumphantly, if such incorrect advice were to come from this very office.

The dusty man has stayed to listen. Warming his hands over the radiator he looks out over the window at a building identical to the one the three of them are in, five, six stories, white concrete, regular square windows. In every room all the typewriters are supplied by Olivetti, as they should be.

'And you're still working at the university?' The sanguine inspector has assumed an interrogator's tone.

Yes.

So that this has been going on for four years?

Yes.

During which time your remuneration has been what?

My friend tells him. The other man's fingers are extra-ordinarily rapid on the keyboard of a calculator. 'You have evaded VAT for around nine million Lire,' he says.

But as the English teacher gasps, makes to protest, the inspector has suddenly become friendly. 'However, we should see this document you mentioned and your contract before we go into detail. Why don't you bring them in?'

He smiles, goes to pick up his coat. Is it because he's realised that it is time for him to go home for lunch? Or is there some other reason.

'When?'

'Oh, when you like. But don't forget.'

Leaving the building, my friend reflects that this kind of vagueness is more disconcerting than comforting. As was the unexpectedly pally smile on the young man's previously severe face. Extremely anxious as he is, he wants the matter settled at once, not left hanging over his head. And so he rushes things. When perhaps he might have been wiser to do what Orietta would no doubt have advised: had his blood pressure checked, waited till it had fallen.

In any event, he calls his accountant immediately, from a phone box outside the tax office, and tells him the story. At no point does the accountant apologise for his original mistake. If his client wishes, he says, he will go and talk to the tax office about it himself, but perhaps before he does so, it would be better if my friend got the document in question and the contract, took it to the inspectors, stressed his ingenuousness and insisted on his good faith. He has not, after all, pocketed any money in VAT and then avoided paying it to the state, as perhaps a shopkeeper might. He has merely omitted to charge the client VAT on top of the regular price, always assuming he was in fact supposed to do so. In this way he has not profited from the situation at all. Nor will the state have lost through the university's having detracted from their own VAT payments any monies supposedly paid to him.

My friend, however, is losing his nerve. He positively flaunts his anxiety by returning to the tax office with his documents the very next day. First there's the dusty man again, then the sanguine man, the one drily polite, apologetic, apparently innocuous, the other tougher, dismissive, immediately assuming the attitude of one who is fed up of hearing cock-and-bull stories.

Allora?

Here is the document.

The younger man looks at it; the older is window-gazing again. The document quotes three or four different laws, sections, paragraphs, amendments – convincing pomposity.

'*Incompetenti*' is the comment, and the VAT man opens a tome on his desk, finds a page, begins to read rapidly out loud from one of the laws cited. My friend, who is actually a dab hand at translating complex commercial insurance documents, can't quite follow it. Somehow it all depends on whether his non-university jobs are *continuativi* (regular) or *saltuari* (occasional). He earns, he says, about ten million a year from translations from a variety of clients, some new, some old, but he would be hard-pressed to say if this added up to *continuativo* or *saltuario*. The words surely require more precise definition.

The sanguine man undergoes one of his mistifying changes of behaviour. He smiles, he is relaxed. '*Sì, sì, sono d'accordo*,' he agrees. And adds: 'Five in ten people would probably feel you were in the right.'

'After all, given that I've made nothing out of it, no one can deny I'm in good faith.'

'*D'accordo, d'accordo.*'

The dusty man turns from the window to watch. My friend is smiling, seeing light at the end of the tunnel. The accountant seems to have advised him well.

Then the younger man lifts a hand to his face, touches his cheek, and says very politely: 'Though good faith is no defence under law, only a mitigating circumstance.'

'But . . .'

'And my interpretation remains, that you should have been paying VAT, that you have evaded VAT for a sum of approximately nine million Lire, and that you are thus subject to repayment of that sum, plus further payment of a fine.'

Flabbergasted, my friend can barely get out: 'How much?'

'Fines are usually equal to the amount evaded. A further nine million, with some reduction if you pay immediately, of course.'

A total of eighteen million Lire, or about eight thousand pounds. With his back to the window now the older man doesn't bat a dusty eyelid.

'But only a moment ago you said interpretation could go either way.'

'Naturally you could appeal against this and the judgement could indeed go either way. Which would clarify the law most usefully in situations of this kind. In the meantime you would be obliged to pay 33 per cent of monies due as a first instalment. You would also lose any possible reduction for immediate payment.'

My friend and the inspector are of about the same age and build. They stare at each other across the desk. One in disbelief, the other almost quizzical. And at last my friend plays his first smart move, even though his original idea is merely to gain time. He explains that some of his colleagues have recently fought and won a case to be recognised as employees of the university, not free-lance workers, this means that the job cannot be considered as subject to VAT. And recognition was retrospective. It would cover this period.

The sanguine man caresses his chin, narrows his eyes. He reminds my friend that in Italy the decision of a court does not establish precedence. It merely offers one interpretation of the existing law. The verdict in favour of his colleagues, if such a verdict exists, thus refers exclusively to those who fought the case, not to him. A second judge could perfectly well decide differently in his case. His status thus remains the same, and as far as he, the inspector, is concerned VAT has been evaded to the tune of 9 million. As an employee of the government he has a duty to collect evaded taxes and to punish those who evade them.

For the first time my friend lies, and this is another step forward. 'But I have begun my own case too,' he says. He is trembling.

'Ah?'

'So at present, in a way, everything is *sub iudice*.'

There is a long hard pause, much eye contact. The dusty man pouts, coughs drily. Finally the younger inspector politely invites my friend to come back once again, this time with a copy both of the sentence of the case won by his colleagues and of his lawyer's presentation of his own case to the *Tribunale del Lavoro*.

Which of course he hasn't got. Looking back at the building as he leaves, my friend remembers *The Castle*, the courtrooms of *The Trial*. Immediately, he phones his accountant. The avuncular man, in yet another cluttered office complete with crucifix, is kind and genuinely concerned. He hadn't initially wanted to go and speak to the tax people personally since, *'Finora io e te abbiamo sempre collaborato in modo amichevole'*: i.e., 'So far you have paid me under the table and I haven't given you a receipt for my services or in any way indicated in my books that you are a client of mine.' However, at this point he agrees it is time he went to talk to these people. Yes, he knows who it must be.

A nail-biting week. During which, to pass the time, and then, because, once there's an itch you have to scratch it, my friend goes to the university accounts office and again enquires, as if merely to reassure himself, about his tax position. Again he hears, as he did four years ago, that there is no need for him to pay VAT on his university income. He then tells the accountant, a forty-year-old man with the dress style of someone determined to stay young, an expensive mixture of Armani, Gianfranco Ferrè and Benetton, that the VAT office thinks otherwise and is at this very moment asking him to pay a heavy fine. To which the other man replies with great promptness that he can in no way be held responsible for the advice he gives. A brief slanging match follows, since this is one person, my friend feels, he can give a piece of his very worried mind to with impunity. As always, Christ looks on from his own particular cross. Plastic in this case.

Finally, the accountant phones. He has talked to the VAT people. Could my friend come into his office. They can't discuss it on the telephone.

And in the office he says: 'They want a Christmas present.'

'*Prego?*'

'*Una bustarella.*' A little envelope. A bribe.

'Did they say so?'

'God forbid.'

So how does he know?

He knows. And this burly accountant with thick bushy eyebrows now proceeds with nostalgic revelry to launch into the story of the very first time he offered a bribe. Oh, twenty years ago. He simply became so exasperated with the obtusity of the official he was dealing with that he said, 'OK, how much do you want?' and then fell silent, stunned by his own rashness. What if he had read the signals wrong? But he hadn't.

Later he learned the trick of dropping an envelope on the floor and asking the other if he had dropped it there. Another important indicator was if the official invited you out for a coffee.

It occurs to me, writing this down, that this sort of breathtaking breaking of cover – the dropping of the envelope, the invitation to coffee – is not unlike one's first declaration of attraction to a possible lover; there's sudden intimacy and self-exposure. It's exhilarating.

And, my friend tells me, his accountant was indeed exhilarated. In this case, the man began to explain, he had understood that they wanted a bribe, because otherwise they would have already proceeded to fill in the document requiring him to pay the fine. After which, there could be no turning back, the matter would be officially registered. And had my friend really evaded so much VAT, they would almost certainly have proceeded with the matter and nailed him. As it was, appreciating he was merely a victim of circumstance, they were inclined to let him off the hook in return for a small Christmas present . . .

'How much?'

Two days later the accountant phones to say the matter in question would cost 800,000 Lire. My friend should come to his office in a couple of days' time to say whether he intends to pay.

My friend is still very English. Though less than he was a month ago. In the past week he has joined a group of colleagues bringing a case against the university to be recognised as employees. So he now has a lawyer. An attractive young woman six months pregnant. And finding the idea of paying a bribe somehow offensive, the kind of awful initiation into a different way of life, a different state of mind, that theft or adultery might be, he phones this lawyer to discuss the problem. She is polite and patient, listening to the complex story. Until he gets to the bit about the little envelope, at which she suddenly becomes frantic. '*Per l'amore di Dio* we're talking on the phone.' Anyway, she will consult her accountant and ring back.

Which she duly does. Indeed, it's surprising how kind and helpful and civilised everybody is being. On the phone she's calm, matter of fact: 'The manner', she says – and my friend has written her circumlocutions down because he finds them so amusing – 'in which your accountant has chosen to resolve the particular difficulties in which, through no fault of your own, you find yourself, although perhaps not immediately attractive, and you do have my sympathy here, is nevertheless not so mistaken as you appear to think. If you follow his advice to the letter, I am sure you will be able to arrive at a *soluzione felice* without my help.'

But another anxious week has definitely italianised my friend that little bit more. For rather than simply shelling out the 800,000, as it now seems he will have to, he points out to his accountant that since the VAT office's complaint is based only on that one declaration of four years ago, they could perfectly well pull out the next declarations one by one, year by year, and have him over a barrel for the same amount again.

The accountant accepts this. It is agreed the 800,000 will be paid only if the VAT office can dig up the other declarations and allow the accountant to change them, otherwise the sum must be renegotiated. The VAT men, whom my friend never saw again, and whose names he does not know, are likewise reasonable. No they can't dig out the other declarations, yes they do appreciate the problem this represents, they will bring their request down to 400,000.

Pride satisfied, my friend pays.

'And 100,000 for me for negotiating the deal,' the accountant says, with still no apology for his initial mistake. And no receipt.

Before leaving the office, in the state of exhilaration that every initiation, every surrender of self, brings once one has decided to go through with it, my friend asks the accountant: 'But it's so little. Why would anyone corrupt themselves for so little?'

'No accountant worth his salt,' the burly man explains, 'would work in the VAT office. How much can they be getting, two million a month? They have to supplement it. A 100,000 from you, a half a million from me, it all adds up. And the rules are a lot simpler than the written ones.' Reflectively, as if this has occurred to him for the first time, he adds: 'There's only one person I know of in the VAT office who won't take something sometime. Lucky it wasn't him picked up your problem.'

My friend walks out into the bright street with the feeling of one waking up from a nightmare. In the end he's only lost two hundred and fifty odd quid. Not much to pay for a significant experience.

17
Una scampagnata

And when you do wake up from such occasional night-mares, when you turn off the TV with its bullet-ridden cars and improbable corpses (eight in a single village in Sicily the very morning I write this), when you close the newspapers with their intricate political scandals from top to toe of the peninsula, it will often seem that you are living in paradise.

There is no smell on the balcony this Montecchio morning. Perhaps because it is Sunday. The late October air has that look of water in a wineglass, so that one expects, on walking out of the front door, to step into a magic world. And magic it is. Old Marini's blackbird whistles brightly, perhaps remembering how fine the trees were on such sweet mornings, the sharp silhouettes of the hills, the nobly etched cypresses dark against the glowing gold of autumn cherry leaves.

We wait in the street for the old ladies to return from Mass, then set off with them, Orietta, Giampaolo and Lara on a *scampagnata*, a long walk up into the hills. We are going to see Lucilla's daughter, Marisa, who is not in fact her daughter, Lucilla now confides, but the child of a sister conceived and born adulterously while the husband was in prison and handed over to Lucilla at just a few weeks old to make the husband's release less turbulent. Lucilla's own and only child died at eighteen months, *poveretto*. From the long story she tells us about his illness it becomes clear that Lucilla quite probably provoked his death herself by applying scalding poultices to his entire body in an attempt to overcome some banal influenza. Shortly afterwards, a miscarriage led to her having *la totale* at only twenty. *La totale* is the grim Italian expression for a hysterectomy. Once again, I reflect that while people from the Veneto are generally reserved and formal, nevertheless when they get on to the subject of their health there is simply nothing, nothing they will not tell to the most casual acquaintance, from varicose veins to mastectomy, prostatitis to mere constipation. And, indeed, it's not long before Rita, Vittorina and Orietta are discussing various forms of tisane, or herb concoctions, which help to keep one regular. Vittorina has a plastic bag to put camomile plants in as she walks along. A new shop, it appears, is to open next to Bepi's and the girl is an excellent herbalist. She even has a mix for flatulence.

I remember how rigorously my own parents avoided discussion of such complaints. That was the English *omertà* perhaps, our own peculiar conspiracy of secrecy. Orietta is tackling an overabundant period now. Much confabulation.

To try Giampaolo on the subject, I remark that the other day the parent of a friend of ours informed us on very first meeting that her husband had only one testicle. Giampaolo neither laughs, nor winces, but with polite interest enquires: 'Tuberculosis, or war wound?'

We pass the Madonnina, at the end of the street, dead Christ on her lap, then a second tiny Madonna behind glass where the road leaving the village forks. *O Gesù salvaci!* – someone has attached a popular sticker to the wall just above. And how benign they are, these plaster guardians of dangerous junctions in their faded blue robes and dusty haloes, one hand inevitably raised in blessing. The glass has been polished. The Madonna is composed, wistful. A hundred metres further up the street, someone is still putting crysanthemums in a stone vase to mark the spot where a boy was killed on his *motorino* in the summer.

We climb steeply out of Montecchio to Olivè where so many parents send their children to the convent school because there are never any strikes and the Church is more efficient than the state. There is building work going on in what was recently an orchard, but the cement mixers are silent on Sunday. To the left, a fine old farmhouse has been restored with a warm beige stucco that has a honey look to it in the now yellow morning light. The white chairs and tables on the terrace outside, the patently movable dwarf trees and statues arranged in geometric design, offer, in what was once a farmyard, a last testimony to urban invasion. From here on *stile cimitero* gives way definitively to flourishing vegetable patches. Olivè is solidly indigenous.

A woman is attacking clothes with a soapstick at an outside sink. With every new fence a fierce dog barks. There's no pavement and, parked up against the walls, the cheaper Fiats predominate, with the occasional tractor. Weathered old men in trilbies and Sunday best descend to Montecchio for the second Mass, lighting cigarettes.

Then the asphalt gives way to dirt track. The road turns sharply left by a noble gate and goes into a steep cutting between high stone walls where a beautifully arched old bridge crosses above. With ivies hanging thick from the parapet, capers sprouting from the walls in vigorous tufts, the dust road almost white and the sky ever more deeply blue above, the scene seems made for one of those tiny paintings by Sisley or Pissarro that you find tucked away in the corners of rooms dedicated to grander canvases, paintings which convey such a sense of a single moment in a single place it is as if time has been made palpable. Even now, when I pass that turn in the road, I always remember it as it was that morning. It made such a picture.

Lucilla is volubly discussing *il professore* again. How often they used to come on walks like this! How cultured he was. How polite! Vittorina shakes her head, pouting silently, as if to tell us Lucilla is inventing. Clearly we are never going to get to the bottom of this. 'In my will,' the fat woman puffs, 'I've left everything to Marisa and Leone, but only on the understanding that they continue the case against Signora Marta.' She shakes her fist. Odd, I think, how despite her loathing she continues to refer to the woman so politely as Signora Marta. As if cowed by her urban credentials.

It's a long walk. We meet the main road climbing the side of the valley but, since it goes up in a series of tight bends, we merely cross it, following a little path that strikes up steeply from one hairpin to the next. The old ladies are surprisingly energetic, Lucilla amazingly managing perfectly well in high heels on the chalky white soil of the path. She has a posh coat on, although not her fur, plus a frilly blouse, a pearl necklace. Her bright make-up, I fear, will soon begin to melt.

Vittorina is plainer, but stalwart, peasant-solid with broad-brimmed straw hat, constantly bending down for her camomile. Orietta trails behind, already tired, limp. She hopes she won't have an attack of tachycardia. Giampaolo has that fine proud, upright, urban gait so admirable in Italian men. He wears a fashionable jacket, good walking shoes. Every Latin black hair is in place on his polished head. Lara is chattering about her homework. At twelve her Italian teacher has set her an essay entitled: '*La verità nella filosofia, nella matematica e nella fisica.*' It's mind-boggling. But not so tricky, perhaps, as *la verità* in the VAT office.

We are crossing another bend in the road when there is a sudden swishing sound, followed by grunts, heavy breathing. Turning round, it's to discover a pack of young and not-so-young men standing on the pedals of their sparkling racing bikes as they attack what seems an impossible slope. To a man they are fully kitted out with the cycling shoes, the elastic kneelength pants, the fluorescent sweat shirts, the caps . . . Not one without the perfect gear. A mobile love affair with sports equipment. One can do little but gasp with admiration at the energy with which they attack this slope.

'Not for someone with my blood pressure,' Orietta shakes her head.

'Or sloth,' says her daughter. Giampaolo maintains his reserve. Mentally I rehearse: as a sport, *valido*; the design of the bikes, *discreto*; but pleasure rendered *relativo* by the fact that by the time you get back you're fit for nothing but bath and bed.

Comes a sudden cry of '*Pista, pista!*' Make room! Out of the way! And from round the corner where the muscly backsides of the cyclists have just disappeared, flies a girl on wooden skis. The skis have small wheels at each end. The girl wobbles precariously, gives a heave on one of her ski-poles, and vanishes down the road – getting in vital practice for the season.

In sharp contrast to these healthy activities and all the talk of herbs and remedies, we now pass a cypress in a small clearing whose trunk is bristling with used syringes stabbed into the bark. Nobody has anything to say about this sad rejection of the usual social rituals. The old ladies shake their heads in incomprehension. Orietta worries that if the point of a discarded syringe should pierce the sole of her shoes, it could give her AIDS. But Giampaolo knows that the virus only lives for fifteen minutes outside the body. And we're back on safe ground discussing the reliability of the information they give us and whether the state should bow to Vatican pressure not to advise people to use condoms.

We trek on. The land, like that around Rivoli, is semi-abandoned. Elaborate stone terracing, now overgrown and ill-kept, reminds you that only fifteen, twenty years ago these hills were worked intensively. But not even the expensive blandishments of the Common Agricultural Policy have been able to keep the peasants at work up here. Now the only productive aspect of the landscape is the olive trees, their fantastically gnarled fairy-tale trunks and curious leaves, at once dull green and bright silver, adding a further touch of magic to the landscape, an autumnal play of stark, twisted, southern evergreen against paling breaks of deciduous copse. More prosaically, whenever the contours allow for it, there will be a long low prefab factory farm for chickens or churkeys. Approaching, you hear the sinister hum of electrics, then a busy clucking that explodes into excitement, or protest perhaps, as the birds sense your passing.

A couple of hours later, having reached the top of the ridge above the village, the whole fantastic landscape to the north opens up before us. Range after range of hills rise one after another to blue mountains. The panorama is vast, hugely open, intensely exhilarating. We stop and gaze. Two rapid reports from a shot-gun, then two more tell us hunters are about, although we have seen not a single wild animal along the walk, heard not a rustle. Bang bang, go the guns. Presumably aimed at some fluttering *uccellino*. *Poveretto*, says Vittorina, who enjoys cooking them so much. And, having absorbed the view, we press on toward the little village of Cancello.

When Lucilla retired she sold her cleaning company to a bigger one, but Marisa and husband Leone still work on in a management role. With the decent incomes these two no doubt deserve they have built themselves a house up on the hills. They would have liked to be nearer Montecchio but, unusually for Italians, they chose not to accept the offer of the flat immediately below Lucilla's. It is to this perversity that the Visentini owe their good fortune in occupying Flat 2.

At first sight, Marisa and Leone's *villetta* looks like an

English bungalow, for local zoning forbade them to build over a certain height. However the attic is *abitabile* – liveable – and opens on to a most attractive terrace cut in the roof. The ground floor is spacious and luxurious: tiles, parquet, rugs, two bathrooms, three bedrooms. But this wasn't enough for Marisa and Leone. Unable to build upwards, they decided to go down. The hills are limestone and easily cut. So there is a basement dug into the rock, comprising a garage for the Mercedes and then a huge *taverna* with absolutely all mod cons: TV, well-stocked bar, second dishwasher, fireplace of medieval castle proportions (including spit), etc. etc. And still it wasn't enough. For below that again, two floors beneath the rosemary, chives and minty grass of the hillside above, is the cellar. With bare rock walls, it is clammy, cool and abundantly stocked with wines labelled and labelless, alongside a variety of hams, salamis and sausages suspended from hooks in the ceiling.

Stiff Giampaolo is most impressed by it all. *Validissimo*, this idea of a second basement beneath the first. The temperature is just perfect. And the wine selection is certainly *discreto*. Whatever the inevitable 'relativity' of the situation may be, he chooses not to mention it in deference to our host.

We climb back up to the *taverna*. In bright and fashionable halogen lighting hidden in the false ceiling over the bar, I find myself surrounded by antlers, boars' heads, stuffed grouse and the like. And fleetingly I wonder what the same kind of people in England would aspire to. Perhaps the sort of showhouse I blundered into in South Wales on holiday last year: a simplified, wood-frame copy of some grand Victorian original, with twee furnishings, imitation Laura Ashley curtains, glass-covered book-shelves boasting leatherbound editions (surely fake) of Shakespeare and Dickens, and very sophisticated naughty underwear laid out on the pink silk lookalike counterpane in the masterbedroom.

But Leone and Marisa do nothing to hide their humble origins. They speak a broad dialect which I can't always follow. They have no cultural pretensions. If the floor is paved with a warm red *cotto*, it is because they like it. Likewise the designer tiles in the bathroom. They happen to like them. They have the money. And they are incorrigibly jolly as they serve us the usual abundant Sunday lunch of a pasta dish (*al pesto*), followed by various boiled meats and fatty red, quite delicious *cotechino* with *polenta* and salad. Then the inevitable *tiramisù*. And cheeses. A piece of Parmesan to sweeten the mouth? A piece of seasoned Piave? Or would you like some sheep's cheese? And now fruit of course: *uva moscata*, kiwis . . .

We are sitting around a table designed for thirty odd. There are photographs of big parties on the wall. But Leone's booming voice and merry stories make up for the lack of numbers. The wines come and go in the usual sequence, as they must: a Bardolino novello for the *aperitivo*, sharp and fresh from the vines, a smooth Barbera to bring out the flavour of the meat, a blood-red sickly Recioto for the sweet. And now a glass of grappa appears beside your coffee. There's giggling, backslapping. Even Vittorina is light-hearted, despite, at one point, some low-voiced conversation with Marisa about a Madonna who has been seen to cry recently in a church at Colognola Veneta. 'What about some chestnuts,' booms the incorrigible Leone. 'Chestnuts, chestnuts.' He's gathered them himself in some wood further north. Italians have always been off gathering or picking something for themselves. The chestnuts are placed over the grate on a sort of frying pan with holes, then wrapped in cloth in a basket and handed round. No salt. That would push the pressure up terribly. But another cork is pulled. It's all hugely pleasant and at the same time far far far too much.

'*Troppo, troppo gentile*,' Lucilla says at the door, appearing to forget that this is the girl she brought up as her daughter. *Troppo gentile*. Buxom Marisa in Sunday best winks at the others. Leone goes down to get the Mercedes.

But surprisingly, the seventy-year-old ladies are all for walking back. They don't want to be taken in the car. So we set out mid-afternoon in an atmosphere of dazed merriment and with a great deal of extra ballast to work off.

There is a lot more traffic about now as people return from their Sunday lunch in the surrounding trattorias. But not everybody is going straight back to Verona. Here and there, as we cross the road to follow the path, we find cars have pulled off the tarmac to park in the fields, and, while mother and children walk about looking for mushrooms, flowers and herbs, *papà* sits in the driving seat listening to the radio and nervously cracking his knuckles. Or alternatively, *papà* does go off walking with his wife and children, but all the while holding a tiny transistor to his ear, cracking his knuckles against his thighs. An elderly and very well-to-do couple stroll by: distinguished, snooty almost, arm in formal arm, mohair coats, traditional hats. But the man has his trannie at his ear. And he is biting the corner of his lips.

They are listening to the local football game. Across fields and slopes, it comes from behind, in front, above, below you – the sound of a nasal voice commentating play with the very same pomposity Lara is presumably supposed to bring to *La verità nella filosofia, nella matematica e nella fisica*. I overhear something like: 'The dynamic oscillation of mid-field deployment with interchangeable roles in zone configuration is indubitably sound when considered from an exclusively tactical perspective, but perhaps the precariously semi-advanced position of the two centre backs which this inevitably entails is not entirely suitable to the psychological tension in which players understandably though, it must be agreed, regrettably, approach a game that could prove the watershed of this intriguing championship.' It's bewildering and I for one certainly haven't the faintest idea what it means. But people are listening intently enough. After all, this is the place where the choice of referees for next week's games is announced together with political scandals and spiralling national debt on TV news headlines. The little radios hiss and crackle between the olives. Sunday afternoon. Verona are losing. Faces are long and severe.

We press on. Then, in the twilight of this beautiful day, hurrying down the hill paths, Lucilla begins to sing. She sings a sickly hymn tune: *Tu scendi dalle stelle, o re del cie-e-elo!* Then, more merrily, a grating old pop tune: *Ciao ciao bambina, un bacio ancora* . . . She is very loud, with a cracked, witch's voice, and completely tone deaf. The others join in, if only to drown out Lucilla. Then Rita and Giampaolo launch into some of the famous songs of the Alpini, the Italian mountain regiment. They are all First World War songs from when the regiment won a notable victory, turning back the Germans in the mountains with very great loss of life. There's a sort of spirited mournfulness to tune and words that reminds me of traditional Welsh singing. And the occasional refrain tells all: 'That long train that went to the frontier . . .'; 'On the bridge at Bassano, we'll hold hands'; 'Don't get yourself killed, soldier'; 'They are shelling Cortina'; 'Ta-pum, ta-pum, ta-pum'.

Italian friends tell me these old songs are corny, and yet I always find them desperately moving: the young men marching into the mountains, ill-equipped, to death and glory, for undoubtedly a certain sad glory there is to be had in such situations: 'But if I fall amongst flowers,' they sing, 'I don't care if I die.' 'Ta-pum, ta-pum,' go the guns. It always brings tears to my eyes. I must be hopelessly sentimental. And I can't listen any more. So I fall back a few paces to walk beside Orietta, who immediately asks me if I think it's wise of them to let Lara do so much volleyball. She's such a big girl already. Isn't there a danger she might get thick ankles, muscular legs . . .

We're still walking when night falls, although Montecchio isn't far below us now, the castle sharp against the glow of Verona behind. The radios have fallen silent. Ghostly among the hills, long thin lines of light flicker on. For the chickens its always fluorescent daytime. They produce more. I take Lucilla's arm as we negotiate our way along the last stretch of dirt track. She tucks my hand tight under her elbow. And so back home, after what must surely have been our most successful day as a condominium.

To hear, through the fence, from a hovering Lovato, the momentous news that *il professore's* wife, Maria Rosa died today. During our *scampagnata*. The battle for the inheritance of Via Colombare 10, Flat 4, opens in earnest.

18
Un panino due . . .

My first months at Via Colombare I bought my bread at Tosi's, a shop which is little more than a hole in the wall but still manages to sell every possible foodstuff in just ten square metres. There's a cash desk at the door, the wooden shelving is chock-a-block, the floor is made of old stone conglomerate, the cheapest, and, behind a cluttered deli at the back, old Tosi himself, bald head threatened by salamis above, cuts squares of pizza in the half dark and counts out bread rolls from bins. He always counts them out aloud. '*Otto mantovane, per favore*', you say, and he begins: '*Un panino, due panini, tre panini, quattro panini . . .*' Before we learn his name, we always refer to him as '*Un panino due*'.

When he's tucked your rolls into a brown paper bag, this

lean old man scribbles something with a practised shopkeeper's smile and you turn to the wife at the desk to pay.
They don't have a proper electronic till, which means
they're declaring a very low turnover, since above something fairly pathetic VAT-approved cash registers have
recently become obligatory. The *signora* doesn't have a
head for sums and invariably gives you less change than
she should. Meanwhile, Tosi is already counting out the
next customer's rolls: '*Un panino, due panini . . .*' He has
recently built a small estate of four *palazzine*, sixteen flats in
all, opposite the petrol pump. They go for more than a
million a square metre. A fortune. On the hill behind us he
is building two much larger villas surrounded by elaborate
iron fences for himself and his family. Rumour has it that in
the hungrier years of the war he would give people bread
in return for land. Certainly he now owns large areas of
hillside, and is eagerly courted by the local building
contractors. But for all his wealth, however gained, old
Tosi continues to count out panini: *un panino, due
panini . . .* And you say to his wife, '*Mi scusi*, Signora Tosi,
you haven't given me enough change.' '*O davvero?*' she
says. 'I am sorry.'

So when Bepi expands his greengrocery, adding a bread
and deli counter, I'm happy to switch there. Which means I
walk past Tosi's shop now, my plastic bag in my hand.
Perhaps the old man has come out of his cave for a moment
to stand on the steps beside the ancient enamelled blue
sign that says, '*OLIO D'OLIVA. OLIO DI SEMI, ZUC-
CHERO . . .*' He has a soiled white shopkeeper's coat, arms
folded. And to show that my betrayal is of no concern, he
makes a point of smiling his scrubbed shopkeeper's smile
from around a long hooked nose. For his old customers will

never betray him. Old Marini and his wife will never betray him, never go to a shop run by a parvenu like Bepi. Lucilla and Vittorina will never betray him. They're in there. Despite the fact that everything is more expensive. *Troppo gentile, troppo gentile*, Lucilla says to Signora Tosi, not counting her change at the door.

Bepi is sorting through piles of paper as he takes your money at the till. Scores and scores of loose scraps of paper: green paper, yellow paper, blue paper, printed, typed, scribbled. 'What are they?' I ask him. '*Scartoffie*,' he says: rubbish. And he laughs his barrel-chested laugh. In fact, they are all delivery notes and invoices from suppliers: a farmer who brings goat's cheeses in jars of oil, an importer who sends him Swedish salmon, a processor who prepares olives and red peppers, again in oil. It's a serious deli.

Bepi has a blunt pencil behind his ear in thick hair. I ask him if he does his accounts himself. He says yes. I ask him how he can possibly manage this with his gym, his karate, his dogs, his court cases, his occult studies, the house he is renovating. Of course he can't, he says. But then if *he* can't, *they* certainly never will, will they? We both know who 'they' are. 'And if they bother you?' 'I'll prosecute them', he says, 'for harassment.' And he means it.

Rather than giving you too little change, Bepi usually rounds your bill down. 'Five thousand two hundred and fifty? Oh, just give me five thousand.' He has an electronic till, but doesn't always open it. After all, I'm a friend. The government, one might mention, agreed to pay shop-keepers a percentage of the cost of introducing approved electronic tills. Mainly produced by Olivetti.

Mopeds whizz round the bend in the road as I leave the shop. One towing a bicycle. Outside Tosi's shop there are now four or five youngsters sitting on the steps behind their bikes eating oily squares of pizza out of sheets of paper. I walk to the other end of the village to pick up my *Arena*, and outside the newsagents there are other youths perched on more mopeds; these ones drinking Coca-Cola and eating crisps. Moreno, the tiny halfwit in deerstalker cap, is trying to talk to them and they are gently making fun. Going past the church there are yet more youths, yet more mopeds, hanging around in the gardens there. They hang around till late in the evening, summer or winter. Generally they are well behaved, I don't get the impression they booze at all, but occasionally a phone box, *the* phone box, will get damaged – or a road sign. And they catch colds, of course. Because it's mid-October now.

Giampaolo protests at the first local council meeting I go to. Kids are hanging around all over the place vandalising things and freezing their feet because there are no facilities in Montecchio, no green spaces and nothing for people to do. Actually, Giampaolo is not really very worried about this, since for the moment his daughter always returns at a reasonable hour; but word has got about that the cherry orchard behind the Madonnina at the end of Via Colombare is not to become a public park and recreation area, as originally promised in the plan for the village, but a cooperative housing estate. Which will mean tripling the traffic along our narrow street.

Giampaolo is well spoken, polite, but forthright. A modern, liberal man. There are cries of '*Sì giustissimo!*' But the Christian Democrat leader in Montecchio, who is also the weasely fellow in charge of the post office, calmly dismisses him. There is volleyball some evenings in the school gym, and the church lays on meetings for young people one or two nights a week. The reason kids are out on the street vandalising things is because they are not being brought up with traditional Christian values in good strong families (murmurings of approval from the older contingent). And it is calumny, he says, to suggest that the Party is in the pockets of the building contractors.

The Christian Democrats' local office is in an old church on one of the main corners in the village. They poll around 70 per cent of the Montecchio vote. The Veneto in general has a higher Christian Democrat vote than anywhere in Italy, including Sicily. The old church has a small tree growing on its unkept roof. Below, on the grey wall above the flood overflow ditch which runs alongside, someone has spray-painted: 'FOREIGNERS OUT OF THE VENETO.'

Only two hundred metres away, the Communist Party headquarters is a dark, poky place on the main street opposite Pasticceria Maggia. On a hand-painted wooden board above the door, the hammer and sickle are fading fast. Through the window, old men can be glimpsed at a bare wooden table on which stands a labelless two-litre bottle of wine.

The very same men are also to be seen some mornings sitting under straw hats on a bedraggled couch under a fig tree against the sagging wire fence that surrounds their allotments. The two-litre bottle, however, from behind which they look out over lines of enormous cabbages, is doubtless a fresh one. Youths roar by on their mopeds, confabulate in knots at street corners. After dark, when their parents could not see even if they drove right by, they kiss.

A modest crop of unmarried mothers patrols the streets

with their baby carriages, and in general have the sympathy of the population.

The very attractive *barista* in Pasticceria Maggia is such a case. Her child is eight years old, and perhaps aptly called Luna. The *barista* serves the people coming out of church. Out of church and into the bar in their Sunday best, which means furs for the women now the cooler air gives them an excuse. There's a parade feeling about it all. From one institution to another: the host, the *brioche*.

The church has the largest car park in the village, aside from the supermarket's, which nobody uses. A capacity of around a hundred cars. It is full Saturday evening for the Mass for those who want to dash off skiing first thing Sunday morning, or those who'll be so long in the discothèque tonight they don't expect to make it to-morrow. And it is full again Sunday morning for the Mass for those who want to show off clothes and well-dressed children and get a *cappuccino* afterwards in the bar and buy attractively wrapped trays of pastries for visits to relatives. Some of these people drive from three or four hundred metres away.

The church car park is also full for funerals and weddings. A bride and groom come out. They have married in their late twenties after being boyfriend and girlfriend since puberty. A photographer is waiting on the steps. But the groom is already lighting a cigarette. Anyway, the real photos will be taken later in an orna-mental park the other side of Verona where there is a lake and stone nymphs. The photographer will fade one face over the other against a pre-prepared full moon behind floating in the water. For the moment though, everyone is rushing out of church to try and get their cars out of the car-park before the crush. Since it's a wedding, they all honk.

Yes, it was certainly wise of the local government to provide such ample parking space, such a large area of asphalt in the middle of the village. But when there are first communions to be celebrated, even this space is unable to contain the flood of traffic and enthusiasm. The cars tuck in by the emergency overflow dike and down the embankment as far as the supermarket. The spiffily dressed relatives step out of black BMWs. Clean, *per bene*, as they say here: healthy, wealthy, right-thinking people. There is something almost Victorian about the overdressed children, the fussing mothers. Certainly they all know their catechism well enough, as one child after another is accepted into the community. And after the ceremony's over, it's off to a restaurant where a table has been reserved for twenty. The expensive festivities will go on all afternoon and the children will be given their golden chains and crucifixes and signet rings.

On his election poster, the local Christian Democrat uses a picture of himself and his wife standing with family and friends around a beautifully laid table with white embroidered tablecloth, tall glasses of bubbly, large slices of *panettone*. There is no message or slogan, just the candidate's name; but we can feel reasonably sure that this man supports all the best local aspirations, is the very avant-garde of the bourgeoisie perhaps.

The Christian Democrat's annual festival is called *La festa dell'amicizia*, The Festival of Friendship: good friends, good contacts, an aura of universal love and piety. With a subtle shift of emphasis, the Communists call theirs *La festa dell'unità*, The Festival of Unity. Conjuring up images of rump solidarity, a last stand. In the event, both festivals mean barbecue food and wine, dancing in front of a noisy band (the same one, quite probably) and lines of booths where trivial skills are rewarded with soft toys. If you go to the one you may as well go to the other too. As everybody does, in fact. Because both are a lot of fun.

My wife goes to see the priest who preaches to the faithful week in week out; Don Guido, the small, bespectacled, faintly squinting character who smelt something rotten in Bepi's shop. He sits behind his large desk in his modern *canonica* next to the new red-brick church which he himself had built.

What can he do to help?

Rita (for her sins perhaps?) is translating into Italian an American book about the papacy. The book quotes extensively in English from various encyclicals. Does Don Guido by any chance have copies of these encyclicals in Italian? She ought to use the originals, not translate them back herself. And she knows encyclicals are automatically sent out to all priests.

Don Guido has his black cassock on, loose about the shoulders, tight about the stomach. He makes a gesture, at once sly and resigned, of raising his hands, palms upwards. Yes, he gets all the encyclicals. And when they arrive he files them away – in the bin. He smiles. That's how it is. A modern priest doesn't have time for encyclicals, he has to deal with real life as it is.

While he is smiling, Rita notices something odd about the desk. Under that glass top he just raised his hands from to make his ironic gesture, are line upon line of tiny photographs. Photographs of faces. Passport size. And they are turned so as to look, not at the desk's usual occupant, but the other way, toward the supplicant, the interviewee. Rita recognises a face and draws a breath. They are Montecchio's recent dead staring up from the priest's glass-topped desk. *'Riflettete,'* says a little piece of card he has propped up: 'Think about it.'

Turning to leave she sees there is a photocopier in one corner. A notice says: 'Copies are free, but contributions are not refused.'

A popular private midwife in the village has the same line. Her prenatal examinations are free, but if people want to give her something . . . Women ask other women how much they should give. Not less than 50,000 a check-up.

Perhaps inevitably, the figure of the priest attracts all kind of stories, some probably apocryphal, some not. Famous for his careless driving, it is rumoured that late one night Don Guido had to call on a farmer to get a tractor to pull him out of a ditch. And in his car was an adolescent boy who had no cause to be there. Others maintain he has had more than one girl around the village. Recently, the *canonica* was robbed and poor Don Guido bound, beaten and gagged. All the same, he did not report the matter to the police. Why not? Because his son was involved, wasn't he . . .

Or so the rumour goes. But one quickly gets the impression that this is merely the kind of thing people like to say about village priests. The combination of celibate status and social prominence is too inviting for the fable-monger. And then it's important for the congregation that the priest be a wholesome sinner like themselves. Just as it is important for them that the men in the tax office take bribes . . . Certainly I have never met anyone who pretended to be shocked.

One evening in Via Colombare, Giampaolo adds a new

element to the Don Guido dossier by confirming that the priest has made something of a mission of going to preach to the prostitutes who hang around on the sheepskin seats of their white Mercedes near the station in Verona. Giampaolo admires him for this and feels he is *valido* as a priest and *discreto* as a preacher. The *relativo* aspect would appear to be that Giampaolo sees the Church as one of the conservative elements that keeps the local mentality so provincial. 'After all, prostitutes do have a social function,' he reminds us very seriously.

More prosaically, Don Guido keeps rabbits (also white and furry) behind the church, and hens and ducks too. When he meets children in the street he pulls boiled sweets from his pocket and tousles their hair. Then invites them to come and see his rabbits.

For Lucilla, Don Guido is a great religious intellectual, a kind, generous man, another person she can endlessly find *troppo gentile*. Especially now he has agreed to testify to how she nursed Maria Rosa those months after *il professore* died. A major point in her favour when it comes to authenticating the scribbled will.

Vittorina pays Don Guido to say Masses for her dead husband. She likes to light candles at twilight and mutter her rosary in the fat, waxy smoke. She buys any number of the religious publications displayed near the door. Miracles upon miracles of the saints.

Orietta is thankful to Don Guido because when, in confession, she told him she used contraceptives, he told her to act according to conscience. It was between her and God. There is concern and disbelief over another excellent bottle of Giampaolo's *prosecco*, when I point out that this is one of the main precepts of Protestantism.

But Don Guido is a little less Protestant when he goes to talk to Maria Grazia, the busty herbal specialist next to Bepi's who can advise such efficacious tisane. Her shop is officially a *sanitaria*, a sort of chemist's, but without the pharmaceutical side. It sells baby equipment, basic ortho-paedic aids, elastic stockings, corsets, maternity bras, bandages, Elastoplast . . . and condoms. Don Guido complains that being the fine churchwoman she is, she shouldn't be selling contraceptives. Maria Grazia thus has the unenviable problem of trying to reconcile genuine religious devotion with social conscience and commercial flair. She goes on selling her condoms. And, what's more, at less than the manufacturer's list price. When the representative comes round, he tells her the local chemist has complained. He knows she is undercutting him on the price. He sent a spy to buy some. The representative says she will have to comply with the list price, or he won't bring them. But Maria Grazia continues to sell at the lower price to people she knows. Because it is ridiculous that a condom should cost twice or three times as much in Italy as it does in other parts of Europe.

Does the Pope's strong stand on contraceptives have anything to do with Don Guido's complaints? Or is he a good friend of the chemist's? In any event we discover that Maria Grazia rushed into marriage as a result of an unwanted pregnancy. She had meant to be a doctor.

The Scholl sandals representative also tells Maria Grazia that the chemist has complained about her undercutting him. It is *concorrenza sleale*, unfair competition. She must comply.

A *Corriere della Sera* article shows that Italian shop-keepers have the highest margins in Europe.

Maria Grazia tells us that when she opened her shop, the first *sanitaria* in Montecchio, she couldn't understand why so many old women would come in asking for large, sterilised sponge gloves, right handed. Later she realised it was because they did not want to touch themselves 'in that place', when they took their bidets.

When a tax inspector comes to see if Maria Grazia uses her electronic till and gives receipts that correspond to the price paid, you can always tell, she says, because they hang around a few minutes, looking a bit lost, then choose the cheapest item in the shop, the herbal chewing gum she has on the counter, for example. She gives the man his receipt and promptly phones up a couple of other shopkeepers to pass on the message. If they haven't already called her. But not the chemist. Who is opening his own herb section now.

The inspector then goes on to *Un panino due*'s and asks him if he has the *pane comune* whose price is fixed by the government and used to determine the rate of inflation. A baker is obliged by law to have this bread. So the old man pulls out the one bag he bakes a day just in case the inspector comes. The government has fixed the price too low and anyway nobody asks for the stuff. Maria Grazia says it has no bran in it and makes you constipated.

Speaking about health, I ask Giampaolo jokingly if he doesn't suffer from tachycardia like his wife. He drinks so much coffee. Perfectly poker-faced, he says no, he suffers from *extra sistole*. He is having a series of tests done at the hospital. I have to consult my dictionary later to discover that this simply means he sometimes misses a beat.

Orietta, meanwhile, has been missing more than one beat recently, because they have changed the refuse-collection system. In the past, a man came down Via

Colombare on a bicycle affair behind a huge bin. He emptied the street's rubbish into it, then pedalled off to unload the lot into a truck. There was something very Dickensian about it. But now they have introduced the *cassonetto*, a very large fibreglass container on wheels with lids opening on top and fluorescent reflectors on the side. There's one every twenty or so houses. You take out your rubbish and next day the truck comes by, lifts the container with automatic arms and tips it up into its press. A jet of hot water washes the fibreglass inside, then it is lowered back into place again.

All of which seems marvellously efficient to me. The best refuse service I have ever seen. The truck passes regularly three times a week.

But the woman at number 8, wails Orietta, keeps moving the wheeled *cassonetto* so that it's always opposite our flat. And when it gets full, the lid won't close any more. The smell could bring germs and disease and death!

Emptying her own rubbish, Orietta heaves the heavy container with rubber-gloved hands back toward number 8. Emptying hers, the mongol-looking woman at number 8 rolls it back toward number 10. Back and forth. Back and forth.

Don Guido drives by in his battered car to bless a house restored without building permission. He will also do exorcisms and disinfestations. On San Biagio's day he blesses the village's children so that they won't get sore throats. Just this week, though, he has installed the first two black people to arrive in Montecchio in one of the flats the church keeps for the poor. A gesture of true charity in racist Veneto.

'WE SAY NO TO A MULTIRACIAL SOCIETY' appears

on a wall by Laghetto Squarà near the flat. Other graffiti complain about pollution from chicken factory farms. A truck from Germany has parked behind, come to pick up the things that stink so much in the chemical plant, whose owner is prominent in Don Guido's congregation . . .

And so one could go on and on. Rambling back and forth through Montecchio, dodging the fast cars and wobbling bicycles. For everything links to everything else: the priest, the *sanitaria*, Bepi, the political parties, the *cassonetto*, the mopeds and the huddles of youths in the night . . .

There is no one characteristic which makes Montecchio Montecchio, Italy Italy, or the Italians Italian. And yet, as in any place, the slow accumulation of details does gradually form a sort of mesh or matrix. There is this constant entangling, as though in the weaving of a tapestry or net. And the more entangled and connected it all is, the more inevitable it comes to seem. It takes on the weight, the impenetrability of a dense contingent world. Yes, you tell yourself, it had to be so, because this is what this place is like. The barber believes himself a faith healer, but never gives you a receipt. You open an account at the bank and ask what the interest rate is but, instead of telling you, they say, what interest rate do you want, what do you do, who is your employer? Health is desperately, desperately important, but the air is laden with industrial smells every morning. Everybody likes the Pope, and racism thrives. But of course. What did you expect? This is Montecchio. And perhaps the best test of initiation is whether, on being presented with some new element, you immediately have a sense of its belonging here, of its being a new manifestation of the same matrix, rather than just another alien fact, another surprise.

On a mild autumn morning you see a young woman in a seal fur climb out of a sky-blue Panda and start to fight with her remote control driveway gate which won't open. And you understand why she has a fur and why she has a Panda and why she paid more for her coat than her car. You also understand why she has a huge iron remote-control gate outside a modest house. You even have a fairly good idea why it's not working. She salutes you with a friendly smile. She's nice. You help her. She curses in dialect. Finally, the thing starts rolling and she drives off the few hundred metres to church.

Then toward the end of October, as *I morti*, the Day of the Dead, approaches, flowers appear in one of the village's back streets decorating a little stone plaque in a wall, behind which a chained dog laps water from an old bidet. You hadn't noticed the plaque until the flowers appeared. It says: *'Qui, sotto piombo nemico, caddero due patrioti.'* 'Here died two patriots, slain by enemy lead.' And you think of the old men in the Communists' office behind their two-litre bottles, of Lucilla begging on the streets of Vicenza, and Tosi counting out his bread rolls for acres of land: *'Un panino, due . . .'*

19

I morti

To put your car in the garage under Via Colombare 10, you inch along a crazy-paved drive the opposite side of the *palazzina* to the garden, then down a steep ramp behind the building and sharp sharp left into the garage. Among the many early morning sounds, as I sit at my desk translating sales forecasts for marble granulates, comes the roaring of a small motor, tackling the ramp from the garage. Suddenly, the roar dies; instead there's a sharp whine, then a puttering, almost immediately beneath my window. Then the whole noisy business repeats itself.

I don't normally go out on to the back balcony above the ramp. I don't go out because, directly opposite, across Negretti's garden where Vega tugs her chain, is a thin, tall crooked house like something from a children's book; the witch's house: flaking stucco, battered shutters, grubby lace curtains awry. And at the window exactly on a level with mine, an old old woman with long face, skin shrunken on to her cheekbones, and black shawl pulled tight about her hair, is constantly looking out, so that if I step on to the balcony my eye inevitably meets hers. Upon which, a ghost, very definitely a ghost of a smile will cross her face. My salute is hollow. The experience is not unlike seeing Don Guido's photographs of the recently dead. And, in fact, today is All Saints' Day, or as the Italians more commonly call it, *I morti*, the dead.

But the unusual sound of this car – roar, whine, putter, putter, putter, roar, whine, putter, putter, putter – is too intriguing, and I head for the balcony, studiously avoiding that ancient gaze.

It is the first time in the four months since we came to Via Colombare that Lucilla has got her car out. From above I can just see that the back seat of the tiny Fiat is full of flowers. She has a fair few cemeteries to visit today.

If she can get the car up the ramp.

On the flat patch at the bottom outside the garage she revs it furiously. With the choke full out, the air turns Fiat blue. The engine is racing. And off comes the clutch with a jerk. The car shoots up the ramp. But at the top she must turn sharply right to fit in between the railings and the wall of the house. Racing up so fast, she loses her nerve and hits the brake. The car stalls and comes whining back down the ramp, careering about dangerously close to the outer wall that shores up the garden, coming to rest askew on the patch at the bottom. Immediately, she turns on the engine again, putter, putter, putter, and is presumably getting up courage for the next attack.

After watching the show through two or three times, I go down to help. The car isn't warm enough, she explains. I nod in agreement. Would she like me to try? *Troppo gentile, Signor Tino, troppo gentile!* Although the car is not old, the white paintwork is dull and cracked. Giampaolo has explained to me that this is because she uses some old industrial cleaning fluids she has to wash it. Lucilla's approach to cleaning is nothing if not radical. Only a few days ago we saw her wash out the canary cage by simply holding it under the garden tap. With the canary inside. Flapping about terrified.

The Fiat 126 is a minuscule car. Lucilla has the problem of reconciling the physical needs resulting from short legs and great girth. If she moves the seat too far back she can't touch the pedals, if she moves it too far forward she is squashed against the steering wheel. I telescope myself to about half my normal height and climb in. There is a fresh smell of crysanthemums: flowers for her dead husband, flowers for her dead child, flowers for her dead brother, Vittorina's husband, flowers for *il professore*, flowers for Maria Rosa. I waggle the gear stick. In the centre of the driving wheel she has stuck a crucifix, in the well of the speedometer, completely obscuring it, a Madonna.

When I've got the thing out on the street, like a teacher giving a good boy a reward, she says she'd been meaning to tell me that if I want to, I can start using the *professore*'s place in the garage now; yes, I can tuck in between the heap of firewood for *taverna* evenings and the pillars with their memorials of the dead. I am duly grateful. Vittorina arrives in a very sombre black coat with velvetty tassles and the two elderly women set off on their lugubrious rounds.

How the Italians love their dead! *I cari morticelli*, the dear deadikins! Shortly after lunch, out of curiosity, we wander along to the cemetery, which lies just to one side of the industrial estate. As with a first communion at the church, the small cemetery car park is full and scores of vehicles have overflowed into the villas and factories of the industrial estate, and even out on to the main road to Mizzole. It's a public holiday. Some cars have out-of-town plates from as far away as Tuscany, Piedmont. For it is important to visit your dead, however far afield they may be. And it is important to do so today, on this Day of the Dead. For one must have a sense of occasion, of formality, of rhythm. November is the dead time of the year; the leaves are falling, the soil is cold and bare; one visits one's dead. Giampaolo, for example, has taken his twin car-burettor Giulietta to Venice to get a boat out to the island cemetery where his father is buried. Lucilla will even now be terrorising traffic on the road to Vicenza, Vittorina muttering her rosary beside her. One thus fulfils a duty, which is also a natural thing, not a burden, and then it is over. The fact that everybody else is doing the same duty at the same time certainly makes it more attractive.

The cemetery is rectangular and has tall walls, perhaps twenty feet high, like a little citadel. The crowd flows in from the car park, from the main road, from the pedestrian approach along an avenue of cypresses, and enters through the one big gate. Inside, there are white stone paths and more cypresses. The local authorities have cleaned everything up for the occasion. It's a job they've discovered the immigrants can do. The porticoes around the perimeter wall have been thoroughly swept. The marble is clean. Heading off directly to their loved ones' graves, people are dressed more or less as they would be for first communions, weddings and funerals: formally rather than sombrely. And they are all holding crysan-themums. Which have doubled in price this week.

The English, of course, bury or burn their dead and then largely forget them, at least after a few years. The main thing is to have them out of harm's way. But the Italians, like other Catholic nations I presume, behave differently. When I tell Orietta how my own father was cremated and his ashes scattered in the Thames from a plastic box whose colour and design seemed more suitable for the sale of ice cream, she is appalled, as if some awful sacrilege had been committed. But then he was a Protestant clergyman.

The fact is that Italians intend to remain on intimate terms with their dead for quite a while, and not merely by remembering loved ones as they were or placing framed photographs on mantelpiece or dresser. No, they want to sit by a grave and feel that there is a real whole body right there beneath them with whom they can somehow com-municate. Setting up this privileged state of affairs in a busy modern world where space, and likewise health, are at a premium naturally requires some careful organisation, as immediately becomes apparent on entering a cemetery.

It is interesting, in this regard, how devotion and bureaucracy go hand in hand. On walking through the sombre iron gates past hooded statues and beneath the confidently engraved *RESURRECTURIS*, you find yourself in a fairly small space with graves in the ground before you and graves, or burial niches, in the walls around you. The niches are six high, the coffins being slotted into the honeycomb wall like drawers in a dresser. And the graves in the ground don't look quite like English graves either. There are none of those leaning tombstones, that tufty look, that precariousness of stone and affections sinking lop-sided into the clay, so gothic and so romantic. Here on the contrary, everything is neat, rigidly perpendicular, brushed clean, the atmosphere of some quiet, tidy courtyard in a government building after hours.

Almost at once, you notice that the graves in the ground are of two kinds: one where the covering tombstone is full length and more, one where it is smaller. Where the stone is full length, what you have is not a single grave with a single coffin six feet below in the earth and stones, but a cement vault in which as many as four coffins are stacked on shelves right up to the surface which is then sealed over by cement. These are usually owned by families. After thirty years, a coffin can, if more space is required, be lifted up, the bones removed and a new coffin with a fresh corpse introduced in its place. Obviously this makes for some interesting family politics.

Where the tombstone is smaller, we have something closer to the Anglo-Saxon tradition: a coffin in the cold ground. But even here the organisation is rather different. The graves are not dug individually. A long trench is opened up with an excavator. Starting from one end, a coffin is placed on the bottom of the trench and covered with earth. The earth is then shored up with planks to prevent it falling into the trench, which awaits the next occupant. This gives the whole process a rather industrial feel. But this is not a problem, since the Italians are more ritualistic about death than romantic. And ritual is by no means alien to mechanics.

The trench fills up. When all the coffins have been down there ten years or more, they are then all dug up together, the bones removed and the space once again available for the freshly dead. This obviously has immense advantages over the Anglo-Saxon system of leaving people in the ground more or less for ever. It also suggests that a grave is there for as long as it suits the living to go and visit it, not out of some eternal respect to the individual's remains. Cemeteries are a social phenomenon.

However, the practical considerations are more complicated than they may seem, and the authorities must be careful. If the same earth is used over and over, it becomes too rich and greasy; as a result of which rainwater ceases to drain away properly and the third or fourth round of corpses will not get enough air to decompose on schedule. One imagines that this makes their eventual exhumation rather unpleasant, not to say unhealthy. In order to avoid this state of affairs, sand and gravel are thus constantly added to the recycled soil to allow air and worms to pass through. If you are interested, the *Arena* will always keep you up to date on developments.

The cement vaults cost money. They are family-owned and the recycling of spaces is under family control. The graves in the earth are free, and considered much inferior, if only because they suggest that the family did not have enough money or respect to purchase a cement version. On one such grave we find a headstone clearly designed to head off complaints from indignant in-laws. 'He wanted to be buried in the earth,' the wife has had engraved on white marble, 'and I did as he asked.'

Naturally, since these graves are not paid for, the families of the dead have no control over their recycling. The authorities merely inform relatives some months before they plan to exhume the plot. Relatives then have the choice of having the bones boxed and placed in a very small burial niche at a small expense, or they can opt for the cemetery's communal ossary. If the relatives have moved, died, or otherwise disappeared, it's the ossary by default.

Thus for some people the Day of the Dead will hold a sad surprise. They come to find their loved ones and discover the grave is gone. The letter never arrived. Perhaps it was lost in the post. Bureaucracy is bureaucracy in the end. Things can go wrong. They scuttle this way and that about the cemetery, wondering if perhaps they haven't forgotten where Father was: then tears, protests, the search for whoever can be held responsible.

An equivalent problem for the very rich might be to have the remains of their dear departed stolen from the expensive family vault. Then a few days later comes the request for a ransom. It happens occasionally. The rich are inevitably churchgoers here. Indeed, it's an interesting party game to ask people if they know of any rich, famous businessman or celebrity who is not a practising Catholic. When the head of the Ferruzzi family refused to pay a few billion Lire for the corpse of his dead father-in-law, the kidnappers sent a message to the newspapers, denouncing the industrialist for his shameful lack of respect.

But a more mundane unpleasantness that might occur in Montecchio's cemetery on the Day of the Dead has to do with the *loculi*, the niches in the wall into which coffins are slid. Colloquially, these are known as *fornetti*, little ovens. Since there is no earth to cover the coffins, they have to have a metal lining inside and are sealed so as to be airtight. The corpse thus burns itself up under its own steam as it were.

But the unpleasantness has to do with the flowers. Each *loculo* has its little metal ring for a vase. You remove the vase, chuck the old flowers, put in the fresh ones and put the vase back. But for the upper rows of *loculi* you'll need a small step-ladder to get up to the vase. Step-ladders are provided, although you may have to wait. Worse still, you may find, especially on the Day of the Dead, that holders of the bottom *loculi* (notoriously wealthier) have invaded the floor space with an extravagance of flowers. This means it will be difficult for you to site your ladder. You move the flowers. The person who placed them there returns and complains. Arguments are not unusual. Voices echo round the stone walls. The *Arena* prints a story about a group of old men who came to blows in Verona's *cimitero monumentale*.

'*Non fortuna, sed labor*', claims pompous gold lettering in black marble referring to the exploits of some local entrepreneur. As with the graves in the ground there is a hierarchy with the *loculi*. You can have the cheaper variety where you are pushed feet first into a long deep niche, or the more expensive version where you are introduced sideways and have a whole two metres of façade space. Which lends itself well to declarations of undying love or long lists of achievements, grandiose claims: *Industria ed onestà*, boasts another marble slab. The more preposterous dead. But for the most part the stones are simple: the name, the dates, a photograph, a tiny red light or *lumino*. These lights were once candles, but are electric now. All the *loculi* and indeed the graves are wired up. It's part of the package. The electricity board sends the bill and gives warning before cutting you off.

We walk about. There's a buzz of low voices, the clipping of heels along the porticoes where flowers abound, the scraping of step-ladders. A subdued murmuring echoes back and forth between the high walls, the graves. The word *'poveretto'* can occasionally be heard. It is very civilised. Sober, but not gloomy. There are smiles, exclamations, perhaps some tears where a knot of well-dressed folk are visiting the more recently deceased. The day is bright, the flowers attractive, likewise the sun on clean stones. People come, pay their respects, go. Old attachments are at once acknowledged, distanced, given structure. There's a sort of serenity about it, which is charming in its way.

We find *il professore*'s *loculo*: Umberto Patuzzi. The photograph is recognisable, although one had almost expected to see him standing beside one of his road signs – to where? Purgatory? Paradise? With his little backpack. Instead, he is wearing a collar and tie like the people walking along the gravel paths around him. And he, or perhaps Maria Rosa, resisted the temptation to put in a photo of a much younger man. He looks his sixty something years. Whereas Lucilla has already chosen her grave snap; and shown it to us. A flirty, well-built young woman of thirty years before. 'They feel sorrier for you,' she explains.

Beside *il professore*'s small slab is a square of blank cement: the freshly inserted Maria Rosa, as yet without her stone. It's disgusting, Lucilla tells us that evening, that Signora Marta, being the niece and closest relative, hasn't even ordered a stone yet. It simply makes it clearer than ever that she never cared for the woman, she just wanted her money. Well, she'll never get it. Nor her flat. Never, never, never! After her day dutifully carrying flowers around, Lucilla is burning with rage again. 'Because the flat is mine, mine, mine,' she shrieks, giving me a key to the garage at last.

And indeed our position in Via Colombare appears to be getting more precarious. Following Maria Rosa's death, Signora Marta produced a will apparently written in the last days of the old woman's life. It leaves all the property to her and she is eager to sell the flat as soon as she has the title deed in her name. Fortunately, Lucilla has produced her will too and is contesting Marta's, saying the signature must have been assisted and is thus invalid. Indeed, she is now accusing Marta of corruption and fraud and her lawyer has asked for the opinion of a handwriting expert. But Lucilla wants to sell too if she wins. Either way we lose.

And we begin to get telephone calls. The woman with the twig broom and the garage extension doesn't want to be nosy, but is the flat for sale? And who owns it exactly? Her nephew will soon be finishing university and . . . For a couple of weeks we get one or even two such calls a day. So and so has mentioned to so and so that Flat 4 Via Colombare 10 may be for sale and since their daughter is shortly to be married . . .

From over his wall, where he is digging the ground to let the frost in, Lovato watches. He hangs around, and when I'm out there doing some condominium duty, he motions to me to show he wants to speak. Is the flat for sale? His daughter and son-in-law are cramped living with them. There's only one garage for two families, and if . . .

Thus, it occurs to us at last that when all those people came out on to the street that first day we arrived, it wasn't just because they wanted to enjoy the spectacle of Lucilla's raving. No, they all have designs on our flat. Pretty well every family in the street. If it becomes available they want to be able to buy it. For the dream of so many of these people is not only to remain at home, but to have their children and grandchildren remain at home too. They would do anything to stay in the same village and as near as possible to all their relatives from birth until death; and afterwards too, the attraction of the vault as opposed to the grave in the earth being precisely that proximity: Papà at the bottom, then Mamma, the brothers, the sisters, the children and all the long slow recycling afterwards.

Most of them seem to manage it – to stay at home that is. The local paper tells us that some 70 per cent of residents in Montecchio were born and bred here (the figure is disturbingly close to the Christian Democrat vote). For myself, I can never decide whether this indicates a sad lack of any sense of adventure, or the true flowering of wisdom. The way I can never decide if the formal atmosphere of annual cemetery visits is the height of civilisation, or merely a suffocating cultural inertia. In any event, the effect on house prices in a place where the population long outstripped new building will be obvious enough.

Lucilla's lawyer is bullish. So Lucilla asks us if we would mind prospective buyers coming in to look at the flat. She can thus have a contract drawn up even before the place is actually hers. This is nerve-racking. We suggest she might do better to show them her own flat which after all is the mirror image of ours, and, frankly, rather better furnished. She responds well to flattery. *Troppo gentile, Signor Tino*. And people gaggle round the top of the stairs being shown into her flat. Lucilla's is always the loudest voice. The words *valido* and *discreto* are heard, perhaps in unconscious imitation of Giampaolo. Viewers study the fittings, practised hands swing the front door to and fro to feel the weight. Clearly, it will need reinforcing, another security lock perhaps, but over all . . .

176

I point out to Lucilla that we might want to buy the flat ourselves and that she did once say she would be happy for us to do so. Then, from a legal point of view, as sitting tenants we surely have the right of first refusal. She is polite but uneasy. For selling also means doing a selected person or a selected family a favour. But yes, she says, if we are really interested of course we can buy. She hesitates, then names the kind of price that chased us out of London in the first place.

On the phone, Marta quite bluntly asks us if Lucilla is showing any signs of falling ill. Her blood pressure must be so high with her being overweight and always shouting. Then this business of turning the thing into a criminal fraud case is crazy and very ugly. Just an opportunity for the lawyers to get rich. Our rent isn't even covering her legal costs now. Do we realise that? *Mi scusi*? And, yes, if she, Marta, wins she might sell it to us, but actually she's rather changing her mind and probably won't sell at all now. Her sister's daughter has a boyfriend and they are planning to marry in three or four years time and . . .

In three or four years time . . . I'm bewildered how far ahead these Italians can plan their love lives. And it occurs to me there must be some intimate link between being able to choose your death photo before you're even ill, or decide which relative your corpse will replace in the family vault, and this ability to plan your marriage for some date that sounds to me like science fiction. Life is so carefully controlled here in the Veneto, so attractively wrapped up: *cappuccino* till ten, then *espresso*; *aperitivo* after twelve; your pasta, your meat, your *dolce* in bright packaging; light white wine, strong red wine, *prosecco*; baptism, first communion, marriage, funeral; *loculo*, *lumino*, exhumation.

Driving up into the hills of an evening, to a trattoria, one looks back down into the valley and sees the cemetery: a neat rectangle of glimmering red pinpoints in the night, the electricity board keeping the sacred lights burning in perpetuity. Or at least till your ten years are up.

20
Statali, dipendenti, autonomi . . .

Another way of wrapping up your life in Italy is to become a *statale*, a government employee, a civil servant. Of course, every nation has its own way of dividing itself up. The English have their classes, the Irish their religious denominations, the Americans their racial origins: Wasps, Japs and the like. In Italy, apart from the drastic north–south divide, one of the most deeply felt group distinctions is that of the *statali* and the *non-statali*: the government workers and the rest. Basically, as the rest of the population sees it, the *statali* enjoy a network of privileges so fantastic and far reaching as to establish them as a class apart, something almost approaching 'party status' as it was until recently in the Eastern Bloc. To truly understand your neighbours, then, you must appreciate their position *vis-à-vis* this conflict.

The privileges of the *statali* (as perceived, of course, by *non-statali*) may be listed as follows: they are not obliged to work; they are not even obliged to turn up at work with anything more than token regularity; mid-morning and mid-afternoon they can take a long coffee break in the nearest bar and combine it with a spot of shopping, or with filling in their pools coupon in their favourite *tabaccheria*; they enjoy shorter hours than the private sector, which means they have more time for moonlighting; they can get cheap holidays in hotels and camps reserved exclusively for themselves; they can get very low-interest mortgages directly from their employers while they are given higher interest rates on savings at the bank; they have quite unbelievable maternity and paternity rights; they have a better health-insurance scheme; they have the right (so important for an Italian) to be transferred to their home area after a number of years' work elsewhere; they enjoy the most extraordinary pension arrangements which often allow them to retire well before they're forty on a decent index-linked income; but above all, and it's worth all the rest put together – they are absolutely and utterly unfireable whatever they do, wherever they do it, whenever and how often, it doesn't matter, they simply cannot be fired. They have arrived.

In the protected world they live in, some *statale* exploits have become quite legendary. Given that managers in government offices are for the most part unable or unwilling to discipline their staff, when things get out of hand the police or *Carabinieri* will, once in the bluest of moons, arrive in force to check up on who is there and who isn't, perhaps prosecute a few dozen absentees. Thus the *Arena* tells us how in one administrative office the *Carabinieri* came across an expensive fur coat on the back of a chair, but no person in that chair. The employee in question had clocked in and then disappeared, as she did every morning, returning briefly in the afternoon to clock out. The following morning the *Carabinieri* followed her, to discover that she was working as a call girl in a flat directly opposite her office.

Stories like this strike a very deep chord. Naturally, the immediate reaction is one of disdain, of self-righteousness. '*Maria Santissima*,' Lucilla claps her hands, 'when you think how hard I worked all my life, Signor Tino.' But there is also profound admiration. How smart of her to have fooled the state like that for so many years. And they haven't even put her in prison or anything. How *furba* (sly, shrewd) she's been. Then look at the fur coat she put over her chair. 'Pure sable, Signor Tino!' What a smack in the face that was. Good taste too. Perhaps I should have been a *statale*.

And, at a deeper level still, people think: if that is how the state wastes its money, mismanages its affairs, then why should I be paying my taxes? The truth is that the *non-statale* has a psychological need for the *statale*. They are two sides to a coin that is common currency here. For just as the chaos and corruption of the south justify the peccadilloes of the north, so the lazy, absentee *statale* (who notoriously *is* a southerner, or so northerners will tell you), justifies the tax evasion of the *non-statale*.

Always assuming he is in a position to evade tax. For though the *non-statali*, the private sector, will present a united front in their disdain for *statali*, they themselves split into quite distinct factions when it comes to taxes. Leaving aside all the many nuances, there are basically two groups of *non-statali*: the *dipendenti*, i.e., employees, and the *autonomi*, the self-employed; and there is as much, if not more animosity between these two groups as between both of them and the *statali*. Indeed, the *dipendenti* and the *statali*, with their taxes deducted at source, may often form a united front against the *autonomi*, since they are convinced, and not without good reason, that the *autonomo* pays next to nothing in taxes and, what's more, earns a great deal more than either of them do. Everywhere jealousy is the key.

Three classic conversations result. The *autonomo* (perhaps our shopkeeper Bepi) meets the *dipendente* (let's say office-worker Giampaolo) and they complain about the *statale* (somebody in the post office for example), his benefits, his proverbial laziness and rudeness, his constant presence in the *pasticceria*, his twenty-day sick leave over a sore thumb, Italy's hopeless inefficiency in the public sector which is preventing it from becoming a truly important player on the European scene, etc. etc. etc.

Or the *statale* (Lovato's son-in-law, for example, with his Prisma in the illegal prefab garage) meets the *dipendente* (Giampaolo again) and they complain about the quite shameless acquisitiveness of the *autonomo*: never a receipt when you pay for your *cappuccino*, when you have the plumber in, when you see your heart specialist about your *extra sistole*. These people are unscrupulous. They steal from the community. We all have to pay more because they pay so little. It has to stop.

And when the *statale* meets the *autonomo*? Well, there's caution, obviously, but a certain mutual respect, too, an air of self-congratulation even, as of two people who have made the right decisions in life. And why are these miserable *dipendenti* always complaining? If they're not happy they should change their jobs. Or if the name of a mutual friend comes up, perhaps the word *poveretto* will be used, as of one who is lost, beyond hope. For it is generally agreed that the *dipendente* of a private company has the roughest deal. With his rigid hours, his limited opportunities for moonlighting, his difficulty justifying sick leave, his slavery to the market, his taxes always deducted and his comparatively low salary, the *dipendente* is undoubtedly the loser.

Hence, there is nothing the likes of *dipendente* Giampaolo can do but assume the rather stony moral high ground and talk about the citizen of the future and a society where everybody will one day have a sense of civic responsibility. This Giampaolo does with great dog-in-the-manger frequency. And England, for example, is much admired because there the social contract between government and people is truly *valido* and the level of fiscal honesty (yes, Italians talk that way) is *discreto*, even if all this is rendered *relativo* by gloomy weather, bad food and a general lack of taste. Never does Giampaolo like to distinguish himself more from the provincial, narrowminded aspects of Italy, than when talking about *dipendenti*, *autonomi* and *evasione*, as if his own fully paid-up taxes were some sort of avant-garde, internationalist creed, a measure of moral stature, rather than mere misfortune. Although in the *taverna*, one evening toward Christmas, barbecuing trout from Montecchio's fish farm and drinking rather more than he usually would (because *novello* is no good after December), we do get him to reminisce with obvious nostalgia about the good old days before PAYE was introduced (in the mid-seventies), the days when you declared next to nothing and nobody could do anything about it. So from his high ground, in the time machine of the *taverna*, the condominium *dipendente* will turn a wistful wine-soaked eye back on the cities of the plain. Which were, and for others still are, so much more fun.

I am tempted at this point to proceed to the rather grand reflection that thus, while the English have their lower classes, their middle classes and their upper classes, the Italians in turn have their *dipendenti*, their *statali*, their *autonomi*; so very deeply are these distinctions felt here, so bitter are the resentments, so sweet the triumphs. But the analogy could be nothing more than superficial. For this is not a hereditary system (a railway-union request that jobs be made hereditary was recently turned down), nor a family affair. On the contrary, father and son can all too easily be turned against each other. Old farmer Lovato, for example, with his years of hard autonomous (though mainly tax free) work on the soil, obviously feels not a little contempt for his wimpy son-in-law from the same background who has bagged a prize *statale* job as cook in a nursery school: just five mornings a week, plus all school holidays and the endless benefits: a day off to give blood, a day off for a union meeting, a day off for a urine test . . . The young *statale* pulls the Prisma out of the garage and cleans it meticulously beside his father-in-law's hard-worked cabbage patch. Or sits in the window opposite our lounge, building an elaborate nativity scene to grace the church porch a month hence. While old Lovato digs and eyes our flat . . .

Then there is more mobility between these groups than one would expect to find in a class structure. A *dipendente*, given the chance, or an *autonomo*, should his business take a dive, might well decide to become a *statale*. And a *statale*, on retiring at some ludicrously early age (*'i pensionati baby'*, they call them) might well become an *autonomo*, although he is unlikely, it must be pointed out, to want to become a *dipendente*.

Orietta, for example, a woman who has turned worrying into a fine art, who quakes when the ground trembles in Calabria, shivers when it snows in the Val d'Aosta, would very much like Giampaolo to become a *statale*, because then his job would be safe beyond any market logic for ever and ever and she could look forward to middle and old age with serenity in the full knowledge that the family will be able to pay for a well placed *loculo* at the end of the day. And Orietta is by no means the only wife pushing her husband in this direction. The search for security is an obsession here far far beyond anything I ever came into contact with in England or the States. I imagine this is linked to post-war insecurity, to the rapidity of economic change, the survival of a peasant culture forever seeking protection from bad weather. And, presumably, it's not unconnected to those frequent visits to the hospital for blood and urine tests, and then in a different way to the entrenched conservatism that surrounds all local customs and traditions here. Which is rather attractive. In any event, the more people despise the state, the more, nevertheless, they appear to wish to depend upon it, to become *statali*. As one dear southerner, Pasquale, self-declared anarchist and evening-school teacher explained to me: 'During the year the state cradles us, and in the summer holiday they just rock us to sleep.'

21
Concorsi

But how can Giampaolo become a *statale*? By doing a *concorso*. One appreciates that the reader may be getting weary of so many Italian words, but this is one that quite definitely defies straightforward translation. My dictionary, for example, offers a whole range of meanings: 'a throng of people', 'a coincidence', 'a competitive exam', 'complicity in a crime' . . . All of these, I fear, are appropriate.

The idea is as follows. A *statale*'s job is a very easy number, a meal-ticket for life. This the state tacitly acknowledges. Indeed, they have deliberately allowed this situation to develop in order to ingratiate themselves with the population. But, given the unfairness inherent in the fact that these jobs cannot be available for quite everyone, it becomes absolutely crucial that their allocation be seen to be fair. No favouritism must operate. Only merit will be considered. Merest merit.

Thus, the local railway station cannot, for example, simply put an advertisement in a local job centre saying they need three cleaning women and give out the jobs on a first come first served basis. Because then the station master might take on friends, or friends of friends – as a favour. Worse still, in the south, the Mafia would get control of things. So no, the railway has to hold a *concorso*, a public exam, and this must be announced at national level. Because again it would be unfair to exclude people from the south, even though they may, of course, after a couple of years, request transfer back home, thus contributing to overmanning there while reopening the vacancy in the north . . .

Our 'competitive exam' is thus announced in the papers and on posters inside and outside public buildings. Our 'throng of people' applies. Perhaps a thousand. Sometimes twenty thousand. Everybody wants to be a caretaker, a receptionist. 'Fifty Staff taken on to Process Applications for Dustbin Men', might be the typical headline of some small article in *Corriere della Sera*. It is never clear how these selecting staff were themselves selected. Whether there has been a *pre-concorso*, or what. It is as well, one suspects, not to enquire too precisely into the matter.

But what qualifies a person to be a dustbin man? Well, a certain level of intelligence, a certain mental attitude; so a written exam. Then a certain level of reliability, a certain personality; so an interview. But above all, health of course, and so a medical . . .

Which is where we come to the *concorso* as 'coincidence', or 'complicity in a crime'; or both.

The story I have in mind is Giampaolo's, a splendid Italian tale which I think sums up more or less everything that need be said about *dipendenti*, *statali* and *concorsi*. In one of the departments of Giampaolo's company works a highly skilled young technician who is very clever at his job. So clever that, under the table, the company is paying him more than his fellow workers to keep him. This lad's father is a Christian Democrat, has always held his membership card, and the son too is a member of the Party and lends a technical hand with Party activities, setting up the dais at the *Festa dell'amicizia* and such like.

After a few years at the company, the young technician marries. Both his own family and his wife's feel that the couple would be much more secure if he had a job as a *statale*. There are threats of recession. The State is the only organisation which will never fire you. Even if it means taking a cut in salary, security and peace of mind are the overriding concerns. And there will be the months of paid paternity leave when they have a child.

So the talented young man decides to take part in a *concorso* to become a bus-driver. And he goes along with his father to talk to his local Christian Democrat councillor. It is time the councillor did something for a family which has always voted for the Party and always been ready to help out. Otherwise what reason is there for being members? *D'accordo*, agrees the councillor, *va bene*. Which is as much as to say: Will do.

But our young technician is a conscientious, honest boy, with a sense of loyalty. He goes and warns his foreman that he will be leaving the company in six months or so, thus giving them time to train up someone else. Because he has applied to be a bus-driver, he explains. And, yes, he knows hundreds of people have applied, but he is sure he will be selected because he has spoken to Christian Democrat councillor X who knows Y who is on the committee.

The foreman promptly buttonholes the managing director. This boy is the cleverest and most efficient we've ever had, it will be a major setback if we lose him. The managing director, who is a Christian Democrat and friend of the same local councillor (here's our *concorso* as 'coincidence', although not such a great one perhaps), phones the said councillor. 'What is this, stealing our workers? It takes years to train someone to that level. How can a private company even begin to compete with the state with all the ridiculous benefits you're offering? I'm sorry, but this isn't on. You've got to stop him being selected.'

This places the councillor in a delicate position. The written exam and the interview have already been done, he explains. The boy is already through. He apologises profusely. 'I can't change those now, I'm afraid. If only I'd known.' Until at the last moment he has a brainwave: 'There's still the medical though.'

And we arrive at 'complicity in a crime'.

The doctor is looking at an X-ray. 'Don't you get any pain just above the pelvis sometimes?' The confident young technician says no, he never does. 'Really? Try and remember. In the small of the back. A dull ache?' 'No, never.' The doctor frowns, hangs the X-ray up on the viewing screen. 'Come and look at this. Here, you see, too much space between these lower vertebrae. Quite a common malformation, nothing to worry about in the normal way of things.' He is shaking his head. 'But I'm afraid it would soon result in disc hernia if you started driving a bus six hours a day.'

And incredibly everybody is happy: the doctor is happy because having done the councillor a favour he is now owed a favour in return, he has a card to play for the future; the councillor is happy because he has ingratiated himself with both young technician and managing director, they will see him as the right man to vote for, their own personal access to power; the managing director is happy because he has kept his worker and demonstrated his ability to wield influence; the skilled young man is happy because he never really wanted to be a bus-driver anyway.

Only the families of the young couple are left with a lingering feeling of regret, of wistfulness for that safe haven. A *dipendente*'s life is not an enviable one – he depends, as the very word suggests, on the whims of the market, the whims of his employer – and they had wanted the best for their children.

Whenever this story is told, by myself, by Giampaolo, people burst out laughing. The kind of laughter which greets those jokes that confirm a caricature. Yes, how they enjoy this harmless breach in the general *omertà*. And where could you get a story like that if everything was done in an honest, open way? According to merit. Or even if everything was done on a straightforward and acknow-ledged basis of nepotism and favouritism. No, it is the superimposition of the bureaucratic and apparently fair over the private and determinedly unfair, the public umbrella, we might say, over the personal intrigue, which breeds so many such stories, and which creates such a delicious tension in so many areas of Italian life. The rules are only a veneer, and indifferently glued on at that; like the Pope's diktats, or the catechism – no more than the thinnest coat of paint. While in the soft old wood beneath, the jolly worms honeycomb past each other in the dark. Busy and alive.

Curiously enough, I got confirmation of Giampaolo's story one December evening travelling back from town on the bus. It was rush-hour time, the bus was packed, so I went ahead to stand at the front behind the driver and watch the black countryside flinging by, the starkly twisted shapes of the bare vines against the twilight, the pinpoints of light rising up the hills to the north. In Borgo Venezia, another driver got on and came to stand beside his colleague. Barely a foot away from me, they talked about the most recent *concorso* for maintenance jobs in the garage. The new arrival had heard from someone in the know that these jobs were to be divided up equally on the basis of the local strength of the political parties; three people chosen by the Christian Democrats, one by the Socialists, one by the Communists . . . This made it unlikely that a friend of his would get in.

The speaker made no attempt to lower his voice to prevent me hearing. Nor did he show any sign of outrage or even unease that in this case a *concorso* was more a question of complicity than an exam. He might have been talking about a patch of dull weather, or the difficulty of finding fresh *tortellini* in the late afternoon, some irritating contingency. His colleague at the wheel drove on at great speed between the cement walls beside the flood ditches, stabbing at brake and accelerator as we hurtled through the narrow stretch where, if a bus or truck comes the other way, there is no room.

I moved back down the bus to the door. Two old women were knowledgeably comparing their blood sedimentation speeds as exhibited on the familiar health-service printouts. A group of fourteen-year-olds discussed whether horsemeat was nicer than beef, whether *polenta* was better with melted cheese or without. Then they argued about what kind of car Ruud Gullit drives. I climbed off. A bulldozer had been having a go at the old factory at one end of Via Colombare. A notice announced the construction of a complex of flats and shops. Reassuringly, the Madonnina was still in her place at the other end of the street, promising to protect us. Electric light gleamed on the more tangible security of iron railings. Simone's car was outside the gate at number 10, come for an abundant dinner: *baccalà*, *polenta*, Valpolicella. An electricity bill addressed to Patuzzi was in the postbox. The *cassonetto* had been pushed down toward number 8. Vega was barking, the TVs were on, and all was apparently well with the world.

22

Mussulmani

One of the sharpest images winter conjures up here is that of dry sticks. It will be hard, perhaps, to sing the beauties of dry sticks, but I shall try.

Maybe the fact that these sticks are seen against a blue sky is the first thing that need be said. For, after the autumn rains, much of winter in the Veneto is dry, bright and very blue: a crusty, colourless, cold ground under brilliant sunshine.

The leaves finally fall in late November. They fall from the vines, leaving strong, gnarled shapes behind. They fall from the fruit trees, the peach and cherry orchards. There is no wind and the thin dark branches are perfectly still against the heavens with an almost shiny blackness of polished bark. Often, tin cans and strips of plastic have been tied among the twigs – to scare the birds when there was fruit. Now they look like decorations for a ragman's ball. Along the edges of the fields, or winding along by ditches and streams, the fiercely cropped plane trees take on the despondent monumentality of surviving columns from some ruined portico.

In the smaller farms on the hill slopes above, the rows of vines are often supported by the cherry trees. A horizontal wooden slat is strapped to the tree; four or five wires are stretched from one slat to the next, one tree to the next, and the vines, twisting and splintery, cling on between. When winter comes and the luxuriant summer foliage of pergola and cherry leaf is gone, the rude peasant mechanics of these slats and wires is left stark in the bright light, like the tangled rigging of some beached clipper. There are the complex twists and turns of natural growth, branches and twigs curving back on each other, then the sharp manmade angles of sawn wood, and the graceful physics of sagging wire swooping from slat to slat, to end in small unused coils round the last cherry bough. All of which is seen against the terraced climb of the hill, the silver green of olives higher up and the sombre vertical dark of the cypresses.

Everywhere the *contadini* are cutting sticks. They prune the vines, moving slowly along the rows, arms constantly raised with knife and secateur. It must be tiring work. They bring out the year's now reddish brown tendrils, hardening into sticks, and burn them in low bonfires in the fields. At the bottom of the hill, along the ditches, they cut the young branches from the nobbly heads of the plane trees and tie them into bundles such as old women carry in fairytales, then leave them to soak in streams or big water tanks sunk in the ground. Kept pliable, they will do for tying up next year's vine shoots.

And they prune the fruit trees and the olives, sawing off whole branches, dragging away huge tangles of wood in their tractor trailors to be cut up for firewood on the powersaw in the farmyard. As we walk, the hills echo monotonously with the squeal of steel discs slicing through wood. There is something mournful about it, a lament for the lost summer, for last year's growth.

They cut longer sticks from poplar and birch trees, poles three metres long perhaps, and these they strip and leave standing in clumps in their farmyard, to serve as fence posts and railings, vine supports, shafts for pitchfork or shovel. Tall, leaning at an angle against a barn whose two main beams are themselves resting on the cleft branches of two ancient cherry trees, the birch wood is a smooth blue grey in winter sunlight. The walls of the barn are old packing cases, boards, strips of corrugated iron, an assortment of planks which once served other purposes, a sheet of pink plastic, an iron bar. On the other side of the building, a cable is taut between the tarpaulin roof and a concrete post driven into the hill. Unlike the thriving cemetery, there has been only token observance of such notions as perpendicularity here. Why doesn't the thing fall down, you wonder? Why doesn't it blow away? I stand and stare: the winter branches, the canes and cut sticks poking at the sky, the beams resting on the cherry tree, the tracery of crisscrossing wires; such a tangle of man and nature, the antique and the provisional, the old seasonal rhythms and the shamelessly makeshift. When the leaves are gone it's so clear.

We are in the farm, not far from Via Colombare, where

we pick up our eggs. A big German shepherd strains at the end of a chain which slides along a wire strung from barn to cowshed. Sixty plus, the farmer's wife is in her slippers and dark woollen stockings. She speaks good Italian and is bright and witty. Her husband is in the office, she laughs, and her thumb indicates the cowshed, which forms one side of the 'L' of the house. We go in to chat for a moment. In fact, there are two farmers here, brothers, pushing seventy. Their lease runs out in a few years and then the land will most probably cease to be a farm and the builders will move in. A builder bought the place some years ago and is pulling all the strings he can to get permission to put houses here. Sooner or later some contact he has, some favour he has done for priest or politician, will prove the winning card. For, although the regional plan designates the land as agricultural 'in perpetuity', no one has any illusions. After all, the surveyors are already marking out the orchard at the bottom of Via Colombare.

The cowshed is ancient, dark, with swallows' nests in the beams and soiled ropes knotted to iron rings in the stone wall, polythene over the windows. The smell of the eight cows standing in their straw and shit is overpowering. Here they stand and sit all year. They are never let out. The terraced land with its fruit trees, vines, and strips of wheat or maize is not suitable for grazing. The men go out to mow grass for feed in summer, and in winter there is the hay in the ramshackle barn. They have one milking machine and the two urns they fill stand in a little stream behind the shed to await collection. Perhaps this sort of arrangement explains why in summer the milk here sometimes goes off almost as soon as one has bought it.

Giuliano and Girolamo, they're called. They wear dirty

blue dungarees and brown felt hats. They speak in such fierce and garbled dialect that it is difficult to latch on to single words. One is merely left with a general impression of what has been said. Which may or may not be correct. Girolamo, the younger, but obviously the boss, is gritty and sarcastic. He likes to mock our city clothes and easy life. He scratches behind his ears, slaps a cow's thigh, smiles the smile of the old fox. Ailing and very bent, Giuliano is sweeter, although virtually toothless. He has just had his prostate removed – his *'prospera'* he amusingly calls it – and there are the usual detailed enquiries after health, all the more so because, before the operation, Rita recommended him to her brother who is a urologist at the hospital. Although this recommendation didn't improve Giuliano's lot in any significant way, a human contact is considered very important. It is a favour we have done them. Perhaps this is why they have agreed to sell us their eggs despite having an arrangement under which they're supposed to deliver them all to a local shop. Or maybe they say that to everyone.

Giuliano frequently carries a spade or hoe or just a pole around with him so he can lean on it. He is pleased I am English because it gives him an opportunity to reminisce about his prisoner-of-war years in Scotland and Wales, which seem to have been very happy ones. He lived with local farming people and they sent him out in the fields every day to do more or less what he does here: weed vegetables, cut grass. He settled in well. But when the war was over they gave him only twenty-four hours to decide whether to stay or return. And he would have stayed but for the thought of pasta. The thought of a plate of pasta put him on the boat back to Italy. I wonder if his toothless grin is meant to indicate that he appreciates what a caricature he is offering. Girolamo, on the other hand, returned from forced labour in a German factory, near dead with starvation. Even a plate of Scottish potatoes would have been good enough for him. He scorns his brother's sentimentality.

Because now Giuliano is complaining that the Ministry of Defence has stopped sending him his Christmas card. Every year after the war he used to get a Christmas card from the British government. Until that 'Tachair' came to power. She stopped it. Margaret's cuts, we discover, struck deep all over the Continent. But it would be unkind, one reflects, to speculate out loud on what would have happened to a farm like this had she ever got her way over the Common Agricultural Policy.

It's funny. These old farming people seem both suspicious of us and at the same time eager to take a break and have a chat. Occasionally, they invite us in for a glass of something. The big, nameless bottle with a strong dry wine stands in the middle of a long, scrubbed wooden table. The floor is bare stone, the walls powdery whitewash. There are straight-backed chairs and no armchair or sofa, but a huge colour television stands in one corner and two grandchildren are watching. It's curious how impervious everybody is to the Rome accent of all the announcers.

Since it's Sunday, the conversation – not at my prompting I can assure you – gets on to religion. Rita explains we don't go to church. The farmer's wife says brightly that their son-in-law doesn't go either, but that he is not a Jew. This is a little disconcerting, until we appreciate that all she means is that he is a believer, but that he doesn't go regularly, just at Christmas and Easter: i.e., the only imaginable non-believer in her universe is a Jew, and her son-in-law is not one of those. Nor, she clearly assumes, are we. Her warm smile suggests an indulgent subtext: you young people are understandably a bit lazy and selfish, but later you will go to Mass every week just as we do.

Rita, however, has an infuriating habit of being honest in conversations like this. 'That's not exactly the situation,' she says.

'You must be Protestants,' says the well-travelled Giuliano, perhaps remembering bare Presbyterian pews in war-torn Galloway, comrades carving images of the Madonna.

'Not exactly,' Rita says again.

'What then?' Girolamo is scratching vigorously behind his ear, smiling his mocking, foxy smile. Every Sunday morning, as we make for the *pasticceria*, we see him and Giuliano heading off to Mass, awkward in their old smokeblue suits and dark ties.

'Nothing,' I finally join in. 'We are nothing. We don't go and that's that.'

'But you must be something. Everybody has some religion.'

Girolamo turns out to have a conversational manner not unlike his German shepherd's way of straining threateningly back and forth on its chain. He begins to mock us. Everybody has some master, even if it's only money. What am I living for? I must be living for something, and that is my religion. So what is it? He sounds disconcertingly like sermons I used to listen to twenty-five years ago. But one feels it would be churlish and above all pointless to launch into an argument. For of course we both know what we know: his world of sticks and pruning, mine of town and translations.

'You must have some religion,' he insists, as if having cornered his prey. And he drains his wine belligerently.

I can't think what to say.

'We're *mussulmani*, Muslims,' Rita solves the momentary embarrassment and raises a laugh from everybody. Although Girolamo continues to eye us darkly. Going back out into the farmyard, trying to change the subject, I ask him if he ever lets the dog loose from its chain. To which the old man casually replies with the common expression: '*Non è mica un cristiano*. He's not a Christian, is he?' Similarly when you rebuke a naughty child you might say: 'So, are you a Christian, or a beast?' For these are the only two categories of living creatures the old idiom allows: Christians and beasts. Apart from the Jews that is. I almost forgot.

And when the world is going from bad to worse you can say: '*Non c'è più religione*.' There's no religion left any more. As if that were the problem. And you repeat it, shaking your head: '*Non c'è più religione*.' It's something Lucilla, with all her Madonnas and crucifixes and sacred hearts, has been saying a lot of late. Because Marta's lawyer has managed to have the hearing over the presumed forgery of her will postponed for another three months. For the moment, things appear to be going swimmingly for us parvenu *mussulmani*.

23
La tredicesima

Winter in Verona means chestnuts toasting over coal braziers in Piazza Erbe; it means the crowded market for Santa Lucia where suspicious-looking gypsy folk sell every kind of candy, nougat and dried fruit from brash mobile caravans. It means shops and supermarkets full of huge, colourfully packaged *panettoni* with special offers on Johnnie Walker and local brandies.

In Montecchio, winter means steam on the windows of the *pasticceria*, swollen watercourses, mist rising thick from Laghetto Squarà on frosty mornings, polythene bags over oleander bushes and lemon trees and Christmas decorations on the big cedar in the main square.

In Via Colombare, winter means the stout woman with the twig broom sweeping away the leaves almost before they have fallen. It means old Lovato digging his square handkerchief of vegetable garden down almost a metre to let the frost right in. It means the genuine mink of the woman whose husband drives the Alfa 75 and the fake mink of the mongol-looking woman opposite who cleans offices in town.

At number 10, winter means sweeping and mopping the stairs with the same monotonous regularity we watered the garden in summer. It means freezing to death because the roguish builder who put up this place installed tiny, inefficient radiators. It means a plastic Christmas tree appearing on the first landing and schlocky red and gold decorations pinned to the satin-finish wooden front doors. At night it means Vega wailing to the cold stars as he paces the frostbound soil outside, and the constant constant whine of Lucilla's central-heating pump.

Although each household has its own separate heating system, the boilers are not located in the flats but all together down in a tiny cellar; and Lucilla's is mounted against the outer wall in correspondence to one of those reinforced concrete pillars. Thus, every time her system starts up, the building hums. And she keeps it on all night.

Giampaolo goes upstairs to complain. As for everything else in Italy, there is a law about when you can and can't turn on your central heating. It was brought in after one of the oil crises. You can't turn on before 1 November and you must turn off after the end of March. During the day you can't turn on before six in the morning and you must turn off after eleven in the evening. And between six and eleven you can't have it on more than a total of twelve hours.

Naturally, like the emergency provision about watering gardens, this law is generally ignored, except perhaps by the stingy owners of large blocks of flats where the rent collected is supposed to cover the cost of heating. Giampaolo, however, hopes to use the rules to play on Lucilla's fears of authority and convince her to stop bothering us with the sound of her pump every night.

It is typical perhaps of a *dipendente*, an encyclopaedia reader and a modern man to appeal to the law. And Giampaolo does seem to know them all, how far they are *valido* and how far their value is *relativo*. I can hear him talking politely and persuasively to her at her door, right outside our own. But on this occasion Lucilla isn't impressed. Because her health is at stake. She has been coughing a lot. Then she is dieting, which makes her cold and constipated despite all the herb teas she is trying. When Giampaolo, polite as ever, backs down, she tells him he is *troppo gentile* and asks if he would like to come in and drink a glass of something with her. She is having trouble getting Telepace, the Vatican channel, on her TV . . .

Winter. I sit at Patuzzi's great desk where he must have leafed through many a sunny brochure on similarly bleak days, fantasising about the ever more exotic road signs he could pose beside. The temperature is well below zero, but the breath of the cadaverous woman opposite barely steams her window pane as she stares out with infinite patience. To one side, between her house and ours, a tangle of branches reaches up into the sky. It's the one tree in Negretti's garden. And on those branches are what I at first, in my ignorance, imagine to be oranges: beautiful big round abundant fruit hanging by invisible threads from a tracery of leafless black twigs above. In the staring twilight, they start to glow, reminding me of Marvell's lines: 'He hangs in shades the orange bright, Like golden lamps in a green night.'

But we're not in the Bermudas, despite Patuzzi's ghost. And the evening isn't green, but grey, a blue smoky grey. And of course these aren't oranges at all, but *cachi*, a very soft fruit with a peel like a plum's, only thicker, and inside a lush pulp with a tremendously sensual texture and sticky sweet taste. They are the only fruit I know of I've never seen in a London greengrocery. They are too delicate to travel. Even Bepi doesn't like stocking them because they ruin so easily. Negretti lets most of his fall to the ground in a blackening orange mush over dead leaves before telling his sons to go out and pick the last few. Then, one-handed as he is, he does a little pruning with a chainsaw. Twigs and branches fly. The old woman with her shawl watches impassive till evening deepens. Then she leans out and draws her decrepit shutters to, turning to give me a last wan smile before they close. It seems unlikely that her house has any central heating at all.

Vittorina comes out of her Christmas-decorated door to find me mopping the stairs. For it is our turn. She is obviously disturbed to find me doing this menial work rather than my wife. Is Rita ill? If I had told her, she would have taken our turn. 'No, she's fine, but she has a rush translation job on,' I explain. Clearly it is not sufficient explanation. Vittorina looks troubled; cleaning the stairs just isn't a man's job. Her husband Giosuè, for example, whose grave she is off to visit, never cleaned the stairs. I tell her how often I wish I'd been born into the world and values of fifty years before. She takes this perfectly seriously. And maybe it does have a little sniff of seriousness about it. For if there's one thing I hate it's cleaning these marble stairs, and reflecting how carefully Orietta and Giampaolo will look at them afterwards, how they notice if you don't get your mop into the corners or if you sweep dust under doormats. I have heard them criticising Vittorina's performance. There's something that spells death for me in obsessive cleaning. The cemetery is a clean place. Could it be the English let their cemeteries get untidy so that they won't remind us of death so much?

Giampaolo walks in with a carpenter holding a huge polished shelf about eight feet long and almost three inches thick. They apologise for muddying my stairs, but Giampaolo is paying for the carpenter's time. Then Lucilla comes out on to the stairs above. 'Rina! Rina!' she calls. I tell her Vittorina is out taking flowers to Giosuè. Lucilla asks if I would come up to her flat and help her with the Yellow Pages. She can't remember the name of her dressmaker and would I read out all the ones in the phone book. I lay down my mop.

For some reason, everybody is having something made for them. Perhaps it's because, with the world outside being so icy and damp, winter naturally becomes a time for home improvements. Giampaolo is changing the focus of his sitting-room, the position of the TV. Instead of having it on a raised platform in the far corner he has invited the same carpenter who previously did that job to relocate his impressive set alongside a row of equally impressive encyclopaedic volumes on one of two huge, specially made shelves which pin directly into the walls with no visible brackets. The whole plan is undertaken with the utmost seriousness. A plug socket will be moved to directly behind the TV so that no wires need be visible.

At the same time Vittorina, in the flat opposite, is getting another carpenter in the village to replace her kitchen furniture. There are long consultations as to the height and depth of cupboards, the position of the lights, the need to change the fridge so as to have one the right width for the new cupboards, etc. etc. People here seem to enjoy this so much more than just going to a store and buying the readymade thing. Over the years they establish a relationship with their carpenter and then during dinner-table or *taverna* conversation they will boast that he is the best in the *provincia* and they would give you his name and number if only he wasn't so busy he'd never have time to fit somebody new in. They talk about *il mio falegname di fiducia* (my trusted carpenter); and quite probably they have an electrician *di fiducia* too, and a bricklayer *di fiducia*, and a tailor or dressmaker *di fiducia*, and undoubtedly a butcher. Indeed, the Veronese rarely seem happier than when talking about their somebody *di fiducia*. A social status is implied, the status of the person who doesn't just buy what the market offers, nor stoops, as the Englishman might, to DIY, but discusses and creates together with his craftsman. It's the status, almost, of the patron.

But as in any relationship, there are drawbacks. The most common being that the somebody *di fiducia* is too busy. And the reason he is too busy is not just the enormous demand there is here to have everything done and made privately, but the fact that the somebody *di fiducia* is actually a *statale* working on the side in his spare time. Our postman, for example, is frequently to be seen about the village busily engaged in illegal masonry work or installing radio-controlled gates and garage doors. A man from the health clinic is trowelling on stucco. And this sort of situation can lead to a quite schizophrenic attitude on the part of the client, one moment praising the skill of his carpenter, or mason, or gardener *di fiducia*, and the next berating these *statali* and all their privileges and craftiness. Still, at least when the man gets his early retirement he will have more time for your domestic projects.

Inspired by the general enthusiasm, we have found a carpenter ourselves and are getting him to make a bed for us to replace the uncomfortable medieval thing which always makes me feel like I'm sleeping in the central panel of a triptych of tortures. Recommended by a student, our *falegname di fiducia* is young and enthusiastic, talks green politics more intelligently than most, rapidly produces an attractive design for a simple bed with bay oak surround, quotes us a price that is a good 30 per cent below anything in the shops and then disappears. He is so busy that we won't see the bed for another six months and more. It's the price you pay, Orietta says sagely, for using a good carpenter. But it's worth waiting.

I go up the stairs I have just mopped to help Lucilla rediscover her dressmaker. She had her kitchen furniture recarpented only a year or so ago. On a nut tabletop she has a pink *gingerino* waiting for me. 'Now, Signor Tino' – and with simpering and obviously relished embarrassment, shifting her tubby bulk from one slippered foot to another, she explains. She has to have her bras made for her specially. Yes. Otherwise they are not comfortable. You know? Normally she would ask her dressmaker '*di fiducia*' but the woman was too busy (this sad admission indicates that the client's importance is only *relativo*); so she went and asked somebody else, but has now forgotten the name. Seeing that the bras were due to be ready this week, perhaps I can find the name for her in the Yellow Pages, assuming it's there, since of course she didn't use the Yellow Pages herself to find this person, but got a friend to give her the name of her *sarta di fiducia*. And the friend is off on holiday.

I look up *'Sartorie per donna'*. It turns out there are about twenty in Verona. I ask Lucilla if she remembers the name of the street. Only that it was in the centre. But they all seem to be in the centre, more or less. We arrive at a name she thinks she recognises: Riccadonna. I dial the number for her and hand her the phone. She has her synthetic pink dressing-gown on, fluffy little-girl's slippers, a glimpse of varicose ankles. Her hair is in a sort of plastic cap, covering curlers, I assume. Perhaps Simone is coming tonight. When she gets through, she puts on the most extra-ordinarily servile, obsequious voice: *'Buon giorno, buon giorno,* I am Zambon, the signora of the seven bras, are you the dressmaker I ordered from?'

It is the number seven that somehow renders it so magically incongruous – seven seas, seven seals, seven bras.

The second place we try asks for specifications, which Lucilla duly gives, but I am not familiar with cup sizes. On the third, remarkably, we hit the jackpot. The seven bras are ready and waiting. I write down the name and address on the notepad in her kitchen. As I do so I notice out of the corner of my eye a covered birdcage next to the waste bin on the balcony. Lucilla has cleaned out her canary, *poveretto*, once too often.

'Troppo bravo,' she tells me at the door, as if I had been responsible for finding the right name. She is clearly pleased that Vittorina is out. She likes to have men do things for her. And she says, if only I could afford to buy the flat when she becomes our landlady she would be very happy indeed to have us stay.

Giampaolo, meanwhile, is not at all happy with his *falegname di fiducia*. Incredibly, this trusted man tried to install one of the big new shelves the wrong way round, couldn't understand why it didn't fit inside a piece of wall that juts out, and smashed off a very large piece of plaster. What's more he refuses to accept that the damage was his fault, claiming that he should have been told the alcove was not perpendicular to the main wall. They argue by the Visentini's door for ten minutes until the carpenter hurries off, lamely pleading another engagement. My mop in hand again (for I still have the last flight of stairs down to the garage to do), Giampaolo insists on taking me in to show me the damage. His long slender fingers probe the smashed plaster. What do I think? It doesn't look that bad, I tell him. But he shakes his head. Obviously, he will have to call in his mason *di fiducia*. Yes, there's a man who's done a variety of jobs for them in the past. Because one could never plaster a corner perfectly right oneself. People would always notice. Worse still, he's going to have to decide whether to fire his *falegname di fiducia* half-way through the job, or have him back. Again he shakes his head. The attachment to a person *di fiducia* is such a deep one, Giampaolo clearly sees the man's behaviour as a kind of betrayal. Not to mention the added cost of the mason. Which on a *dipendente*'s salary is a tough proposition. Orietta brings in the vacuum cleaner to take up all the dust and plaster. '*Grazie al cielo*,' she sighs, 'that we're getting near Christmas and there's the *tredicesima*.'

The *tredicesima*! Here's another little peephole into the heart of modern Italy. For what other country in the world has a *tredicesima*? None I'm sure, unless at the end of some very slippery pole the Land of Cockaigne truly does exist.

Or perhaps Italy is the Land of Cockaigne. It's something the Italians like to say sometimes. Or they say: 'Go to America? But Italy is America!'

The word *tredicesimo* means nothing more nor less than 'thirteenth'. But *la tredicesima*, the adjective turned feminine noun, means your thirteenth salary of the year. Thirteen, it's worth noting, is considered a lucky number in Italy.

What happens is that in the first weeks of December, the *statali* and *dipendenti* in general receive an extra month's salary. This is a legally required part of any employer–employee relationship. In the negotiations which originally brought the development about, I am told, back in the 1960s, the *tredicesima* was perceived as a productivity bonus to be paid only if the employee had behaved well, not been absent more than a certain amount, and so on. But given that almost nobody takes it upon themselves to judge the performance of anybody else, at least in the state system, payment soon became automatic. And some companies, notably banks, even introduced *la quattordicesima* and I believe in some cases a *quindicesima*.

Such extravagant arrangements give the hard-working *autonomo* perhaps his only real chance to gripe about the cushy lives of the *dipendenti* although since he is aware that most of the extra money will be spent on his goods and services in the general Christmas binge, he doesn't complain too much. Indeed, the imminent arrival of the *tredicesima* perhaps explains why Giampaolo and the ladies have all decided to get their carpenting done and bras made now. For, as pensioners, the ladies have their *tredicesima* too. They are briefly rich. Lucilla sets off into town for high heels and diamond-patterned black tights. Two men struggle up the stairs with Vittorina's new fridge. One can only wonder what they might do if they ever got the money they want for our flat. Give Giosuè a new headstone? Muffs and minks? A new sitting-room suite? Extra Masses said?

Going back down to replace the doormats after the stairs have dried, I hear the postman's Vespa arriving, as it usually does, toward lunchtime. I wait for him. Apart from some junk mail for Patuzzi, there is a magazine for Vittorina, *I fioretti di San Gaspare*. My dictionary translates *fioretto* as, 'an act of mortification'. The magazine is published by *L'ordine dei frati del preziosissimo sangue*, which the saint founded. Most of it involves stories of miracles following hard upon praying to the saint. One reader writes to say that, after years of painful prostatitis, his problem was resolved by a single supplication to San Gaspare. Perhaps old Giuliano should have been informed. And it occurs to me that Italians have a long and uninterrupted tradition of miracles. Of which maybe *la tredicesima* is just a recent and very civilised manifestation.

24
Viva, viva, Natale arriva!

It will seem odd perhaps that, having spent all my teens in London, I had to come to Italy to discover real fog. It is a peculiarity of the *bassa padana*, the Po valley. Protected by the Appennini from the prevailing west wind, the sun shines brightly on the vast triangular area of flat, damp soil between Milan, Venice and Bologna. The snow-covered mountains to the north keep a constant stream of icy air rolling down to meet the warmth steaming up from fields and ditches. And the result is the thickest fog imaginable stretching for mile after mile after mile. Sometimes lasting for weeks. The winter version of summer's *afa*.

Stepping out on to our balcony this December morning, the world is milky white and quite silent. The terraced hill has gone, the castle has gone, likewise the abandoned mill.

Along Via Colombare, the Madonnina has vanished and with her the woman with the twig broom, whose patient sweeping can nevertheless still be heard, pushing dirt she can barely see away into the fog. The dry sticks of Marini's vegetable patch opposite are sombre pointed shadows, spear tips of an army of wraiths. A few poplar poles lean against a spectral fig tree, eaves and balconies drip, and all the street's railings are hung with dew-soaked spiders' webs.

Leaning on the marble parapet we never polish, it's such a pleasure to breathe in this soft spongy air. It's as if the whole Veneto had been very gently, very efficiently anaesthetised. Even the smells have gone, smothered where they rise. Everything is whitely quiet, waiting.

Then into this beautiful, hushed world comes a sudden fierce jangling, turning the corner from the Madonnina end. A grating jingle blares through a megaphone, followed by a voice speaking in dialect: '*Mamme, bambini, ragazzi, ragazze*, come and see, come and see, three *panettoni* for the price of one, three *panettoni* for the price of one!' The voice stops with unnatural abruptness. The jingle plays again, harsh, idiotic, strident. When it stops there is the unmistakeable rumble of a diesel ticking over. The still, damp air begins to smell. And now I can just catch the ghostly shadow of a white Fiat Fiorino delivery van. Out blares the voice again, incredibly loud, the kind of volume one expects at the Last Judgement, booming through fog: '*Mamme, bambini, ragazzi, ragazze!!!*' Odd, I think, how he excludes fathers, unmarried adults and the like. The van stops three times along the two hundred metres of Via Colombare, sells a dozen or so *panettoni* and is gone.

As many as four or five of these *ambulanti* may pass down our semi-suburban, semi-rural street in a single day, summer or winter, rain or shine. There's the man who sells brooms, dustpans, brushes, kitchen mats, pan-scourers. He's a regular. He passes around ten o'clock, his wares piled on the top of his tiny Fiat 650 van. A broomstick lunges forward through the fog like a lance.

Another fellow sells mattresses. He has a dozen or so piled on the back of a small lorry. Like the *panettoni* man he has a recording crackling through an overloaded speaker system: *'Un' occasione d'oro per sogni d'oro.'* A golden opportunity for golden dreams. Every Tuesday without fail. He is burly, brisk, darkly moustached. But how many mattresses can he sell to thirty or so houses?

One suspects the knifesharpener of being wilfully picturesque. He has a grinding stone geared up to the drive of his moped and a little shelter affair arranged over the handlebars. He squints, hunched. In normal conditions you can see the sparks fly. Through the fog there's just the sinister shriek of metal on stone. You're reminded of the Green Knight, sharpening his axe; another sound heard in dead of winter.

Or there are the one-off *ambulanti* offering the most amazing deals. A huge lorry noses along the street, squeezing between parked cars, watching out for shutters left carelessly swinging. Four best-quality wooden kitchen chairs for 60,000 Lire. Just thirty pounds. Is that possible? Or on another lucky day you may get the chance to buy a whole terrace set of tables and fold-up chairs for 100,000 Lire. Sometimes I wonder if, rather than being behind the lorry when the stuff fell off, they didn't just take the whole lorry and start driving around the streets.

Of the regulars, the cheese duo are the most impressive. These two fat, jolly men have a super-long, purpose-built van which folds open at the side to reveal a cheese counter that wouldn't look out of place in Fortnum and Masons. Turning the corner by the Madonnina, they have to reverse and manoeuvre. The relaxed megaphoned announcement of '*Formaggi, formaggi, eccoci qua*' suggests far more confidence in their clientele. The vehicle ticks over in the fog. Orietta slips out in coat and scarf to buy some seasoned Asiago and Parmesan. It's cheaper, she says, than in the shops. I wonder why.

'Thieves,' is Bepi's only comment when I mention the *ambulanti* to him.

Coming back, Orietta makes her usual detour to the *cassonetto*, heaving it so far the other way it's almost lost in the grey damp.

The *marocchino* is even more discreet than the *formaggi* fellows. Officially, *marocchino* just means Moroccan. In reality, the word refers to a stock figure in Italian life, the Moroccan carpet pedlar. Male, anywhere between fifteen and fifty, he patrols the streets with a heap of carpets over his shoulder and colourful tablecloths on his arm. In summer one almost melts at the sight; if you bought anything it would surely be drenched in sweat. On winter days you suspect the carpets are worth their weight in gold. You're surprised he wants to sell them at all. In any event, the *marocchino* is admirably stoical. His face is a cipher. Apparently, he expects nothing, fears nothing.

The bell rings. Rather than buzzing somebody in immediately, or even quizzing them through the intercom, I have learnt to go out on the balcony for eye-to-eye contact. The Arabic man stands there in the damp cold, his rugs over his shoulders. Would I like to buy something? I say no, thank you. He doesn't insist. And this is another admirable side to the *marocchini*, they will never bother you, never shout anything or use a megaphone, never try hard to persuade. Perhaps this one might have done better if he had tried. For the truth is we could use a few rugs on our freezing tiles. It's just that I'm not used to buying this way.

He presses Lucilla's bell. We can hear. Inevitably, she lets him in. How many times have we been obliged to listen (for conversations on the stairs are audible everywhere), to Lucilla talking to Mormons, Jehovah's Witnesses, water-purifier salesmen, survey interviewers and the like. But this morning she actually lets the *marocchino* into her flat. He leaves about half an hour later, I fear without having sold anything. For a *marocchino* could never be *di fiducia*, the way the cheeseman is for Orietta. I hope at least Lucilla offered him a *gingerino* and told him he was *troppo gentile*.

From my balcony I watch the man walk stoically off into the fog. Even from this distance I can see that his carpets are not Moroccan at all. Most probably they are produced by some small sweatshop in Reggio Calabria operating from an illegally built prefab. He keeps a steady pace, stopping only at the house of the man with the Alfa 75 where the postman is mounting new railings on a low cement wall. Then the fog swallows him up. A short distance away there will be an old Fiat 128 serving as a base for himself and three others. They keep the carpets in the boot, move from village to village. Perhaps they sleep in the car too. The *marocchini* are rumoured to be homosexuals without exception. Certainly, they bring no women with them. And, curiously, they rarely aspire to a place in regular Italian life the way other immigrants do. I have never seen a *marocchino* here who did anything but sell carpets.

Since it's Christmas Eve, we drive into town for some last-minute shopping. On leaving the village, the fog is desperately thick along the narrow road, though no one is going particularly slowly. Each car hangs on to the tail lights of the one in front and hammers through, even though this means being far too close to avoid an accident if one had to brake. And since we are one of the only vehicles on the road without fog lights, the car behind has to hang on even closer to us than we to the car in front. What this means in terms of the dynamics of an eventual pile-up, I've no idea.

Suddenly a *carabiniere* looms right in front of our bonnet, waving a red stop sign. And we realise we haven't even seen the big traffic lights. Comes the sound of sharp braking all along the line. Four officers in fluorescent plastic jackets are risking their necks to keep the junction operating. I wonder, will we see a parking spot even if we pass one?

In town, the medieval and Renaissance buildings are splendidly mysterious. The illuminated clockface comes and goes in the fog at the top of the fourteenth-century Tower of the Lamberti. The Roman arena is sombre despite housing an exhibition of East European nativity scenes. Christmas carols, all English, are being efficiently cranked across the fog-draped trees of the main piazza, interrupted by the crackle of fireworks, illegal but abundant. Diving into the shopping streets the stuccoed façades have been bled of all colour by stabbing neon beneath. And anyway, nobody is looking up at them. They have things to buy.

But despite the *tredicesima*, Christmas is not quite the spree it is in England. This is partly because, at least in the Veneto, the children have already had their presents. Santa Lucia, 13 December, was the day. So the pavements are no longer choked with grandmothers determined to gratify excited infants. Decorations are everywhere evident, but fairly modest in the end: lights strung across the streets, red carpets on the cobbles outside shop windows, paper festoons in the three department stores. An unconvinced Father Christmas with the name of a shop on his armband is handing out sweets. And, of course, there is the everyday streetlife, which takes on a special poignancy at Christmas: a gypsy woman sits begging in a doorway, the baby in her arms swaddled against the fierce cold; young blacks proffer trays of cigarette lighters and pirated cassettes; despite numbed fingers, a tramp is playing a popular tune on some kind of bagpipes: *Viva, viva, Natale arriva* . . .

In Standa, the cheaper of the department stores, people are picking up a few last-minute details to add to their home-made nativity scenes: an extra sheep or two, fake hay they forgot to pick up for the plastic manger, a star with a little bulb in it. There's an array of polythene packages. The magi are available separately or as a group.

But most interest is concentrated on food. Serious food. The delicatessens are packed, despite prices that would raise eyebrows anywhere. There is no one traditional Christmas lunch in the Veneto, but it would be a mistake to imagine this indicates lack of interest in the occasion. On the contrary, it avoids any danger of getting into a rut. Parma hams and salamis are coming off their hooks at an extraordinary rate. All kinds of goodies – Russian salads, black olives, green olives, a sticky crystallising orange mixture which calls itself *mostarda vicentina* – are being spatula-ed into plastic tubs. A bristling old fellow picks up a whole form of Parmesan. For how much? A hundred pounds? Two butchers (*di fiducia* of course) are unloading duck, turkey, geese and chickens from the surrounding farms and factory farms, plus all the best beef cuts. The die-hard *contadini* are looking for *cotechini* and the where-withal to make *polenta*. A curious shop window offers fresh pasta of every colour: green spinach pasta, swampy artichoke pasta, red pepper pasta, brown chocolate pasta . . .

We pick up the turkey we have promised our American friends and a few bottles of this and that from a display offering a remarkable range of cheap Scottish whiskies, many quite unheard of, I suspect, in Glasgow and Edinburgh. Glenlivet, however, is thankfully cheaper than it ever was back in London, although slightly watered down to meet local proof regulations. Driving back to Via Colombare just as twilight stiffens the fog, we find our astonishing postman still messing with stones, bricks and railings beside the Alfa 75, and we take the opportunity to give him his Christmas bottle of grappa.

He doesn't understand. He looks at us nonplussed in the foggy dark, his breath steaming warmly, white droplets on a black moustache. I explain that it's a tradition in England to give your postman something. The tracery of blood vessels on pink cheeks suggest that he is not unused to a glass or two. A token of our appreciation, I say, somewhat foolishly, for perhaps such words have never been addressed to a *statale* before. He takes the bottle, sets it down by the railings, thanks us, but remains somewhat wary, as if we must be expecting a favour in return. Perhaps in the end he will put it down to a fog mirage.

Giampaolo is unloading a Christmas tree from his car. In Italy they are not sold cut as in England, but with their roots in a pot. However, to get a cheap price, as every *dipendente* must, Giampaolo has driven some twenty kilometres to a hypermarket where they sell trees that, yes, have their roots, but tied in a plastic bag. Very *valido* as an idea and the price was *discreto*. He will plant it in a pot for Christmas, put it out on the balcony through January, then move it into the garden before the spring to join Lucilla's sad madrigal of ornamental evergreens. Orietta seems dubious as to its chances of making it that far. Probably it will have her hoovering pine needles every ten minutes right through the holiday. There must, after all, be something *relativo* about the deal.

Preparing tomorrow's food in the evening we turn on the radio. Rita has recently taken a liking to Radio Santa Teresa, our local religious channel. Or one of them. Two priests are discussing the Madonna's house believed to have been brought by angels to a convent in Loreto near the Adriatic coast. With sobre enlightenment, the priests explain that, in fact, this is a tenth-century Palestinian dwelling brought over from Bethlehem by the Crusaders. Having chatted for a while, they open the telephone lines for questions. Immediately, a woman's voice crackles through. She is very excited: 'Don Marcello, Don Marcello, do you remember me, Maria, from Nogarole Rocca?' Don Marcello doesn't remember her. 'You baptised my children.' From the cracked sound of her voice this must have been some considerable number of years before. 'Praise the blessed Virgin', Don Marcello says warmly.

Another woman phones, from Caprino this time, up in the mountains. She is so depressed, oh but so depressed. 'Actually,' Don Guglielmo reminds her gently, 'we were asking for questions about the blessed Madonna's house in Loreto and the value of devotional relics in general.' She bursts into tears. She is so depressed she doesn't think she can go on living. She would never have imagined life could be so awful. 'Unburden your sorrows on the Holy Virgin,' Don Marcello tells her. She has tried, she has tried, but she can't. It makes no difference. She honestly can't. She sobs loudly on our old valve radio. And it takes these two embarrassed men literally ten whole minutes to get her to agree to unburden her sorrows on the Virgin and get off the line. 'The Madonna be praised,' she finally sniffles. There's an audible sigh of relief from Don Guglielmo.

After which about a dozen more women call, at least half of whom seem to know one or other of the priests personally. Not one of them has anything to say about the tenth-century Palestinian remains in Loreto, or indeed about Christmas. Their menfolk, one suspects, are elsewhere.

Shortly after eleven we hear the clunk clunk clunk of the Visentini turning their security locks about two hundred times as they prepare to go out for midnight Mass. A few minutes later, Giampaolo comes up to our flat to inform us that our cat has got trapped in the garage and has walked all over his white Giulietta, which he had just cleaned. There are black paw marks all over it. The Italian distaste, on Orietta's face rather than Giampaolo's, for animals which are allowed to penetrate the four walls of the domestic bunker, is only too plain. I solemnly promise it won't happen again and mollify them both with Christmas gifts which they weren't expecting: a scarf for Giampaolo, simple brooch for Orietta, perfume for Lara. We have, as Italians say, made a *bella figura*, a good impression.

Best of friends, they offer to give us a lift to midnight Mass to save us getting our own car out. Although we hadn't been planning to go, we accept. Walking out into the street, we catch the familiar sound of a small engine revving wildly, shooting off as the clutch is released, then whining, dying and finally puttering into life again. Giampaolo goes down to help Lucilla get her car out.

The fog is impossibly dense, the traffic very brisk. The church car park, needless to say, is packed to overflowing. Inside, despite the fact that we're ten minutes early, the church is already a solid mass of fur coats. People obviously came some while ago to stake out their places and now there are no seats left. I am surprised at this lack of forward planning on the meticulous Giampaolo's part. Although perhaps the fault is our cat's.

We stand at the back near the nativity scene Lovato's son-in-law has been working on for so long. Stars wink in three phases, water runs in a little stream, ox and ass nod their heads. It's an elaborate affair. Although, as in all nativity scenes, there is no sign that the animals perform their natural functions. On the hill, the shepherds have a little carafe at their feet, which is a nice touch. They may not, after all, be so unused to UFOs.

More people crowd in. There's a buzz of chatter, greetings, handshaking, kisses. Everybody knows everybody. People you usually see smoking on street corners or double parking outside the bar are queuing up to light candles. Some of the youngsters are obviously dressed, under their coats, for the discothèques they will be heading off to as soon as the service is over.

Things get under way a few minutes late. Don Guido intones the liturgy in a style my father, an evangelical Anglican, would no doubt have scorned. But there are advantages. The quickly read, toneless words impose a sense of order and ritual without one having to pay attention to whatever they might mean. The congregation are prompt with their responses and know very well when to stand and sit. They move as one well-trained animal. And they enjoy this oneness. Since we are anyway obliged to stand, my ignorance passes unobserved.

Looking about, as the others mouth prayers they learnt in childhood, I can see Maria Grazia from the *sanitaria* who supplies contraceptives at below list price. To her left is Montecchio's most famous politician, presently Verona's councillor responsible for traffic. His wife has a nice full-length fur, although, surprisingly, the family are on the list for the co-operative housing to go up behind the Madonnina. Beyond them stands the builder who is putting up the luxury villas on the hill above Via Colombare. Giuliano and Girolamo are there too, and Un panino due, and the woman with the twig broom, again in a fur . . .

But these fur coats seem to be causing problems. For, although it's cold outside, it is desperately warm inside. Big modern radiators are pumping out heat. Before the altars, down the side of the nave, a thousand candles are burning. Orietta wriggles uncomfortably, frowns. But she hasn't put on anything sufficiently attractive underneath to be able to take her coat off.

Up in the chancel, a small choir of young people sing a very upbeat Christmas carol to the accompaniment of guitars and drums. Nobody seems to know the song.

There is very little tradition of Christmas carols here. And, anyway, nobody is invited to join in.

Don Guido preaches a sermon from the chancel steps with the aid of a microphone on a stand. He also has a microphone on the altar. This means he never has to raise his calm dull voice and assume a rousing evangelical tone. He is not a leader, but a medium, a go-between. Predictably, he preaches generosity. We must remember the poor at Christmas. Christ was born in a stable. There is absolutely no criticism, veiled or otherwise, toward his overwhelmingly bourgeois congregation. He is rehearsing the values on which their respectability rests. As so often with things traditional in Italy, I am unable to decide whether this is attractive or sinister, an expression of civilisation, or decadence. My Protestant truculence no doubt.

And after the sermon, we move into the Eucharist proper with the modern guitar band playing and a girl singing, very pleasantly and professionally. Indeed, it's a treat. People walk to the front, the host is popped into their mouths or placed in their hands. Moreno, the halfwit, goes up three times but is not turned away. To deal with such a huge congregation, Don Guido has four helpers, a younger priest, three nuns. Other young people, many of whom shoot by me every day on *motorini*, are walking up and down the aisles with baskets, collecting money.

Then Orietta faints. The heat was too much. She should have taken her coat off. Fortunately, there is such a crowd of people round her, she couldn't possibly fall. Giampaolo rushes her out to the car and off home. No doubt this will mean a fair number of tests at the hospital. We stay behind for the hot chocolate Don Guido advertised at the end of his sermon and discover that below the church there is a very large *taverna* complete with bar, and drinks. Now this is civilised! In the crush, we come across Vittorina and Lucilla, determined to show off their furs to the last, although Lucilla's thick make-up is running a little in the oppressive atmosphere. '*Auguri, auguri, Signor Tino!*' she calls, '*buon natale, buon natale*', then returns to her cemetery chat with other older widows. 'The stingy niece', I can hear her telling them, 'still hasn't ordered a stone for the *poveretta*. So I ordered one myself. To shame her. I told my lawyer to tell her lawyer I'd ordered it, and I didn't want to be paid, and do you know . . .'

Walking home in a freezing fog filled with car exhaust now as the worshippers disperse, I wonder where this morning's *marocchino* might be. Has he found a stable to sleep in perhaps? With ox and ass. Not unfeasible in these parts. And I remember an article I read in the *Arena* only a few days ago: in the recent cold weather many *marocchini* have been sleeping in the empty *loculi* in the walls of the city's main cemetery, wrapped in their carpets. Well, at least they won't have to hear Vega barking.

25
Buona fine, buon principio

The fog persists, thick and extraordinarily white – not the gritty, yellowish variety you occasionally encountered in London. Penetrating even the narrowest streets, it deadens the anyway dead days between Christmas and New Year, muffling the sound of fireworks children are letting off between slices of pizza outside Un panino due's. And when there is a deep frost the night of Santo Stefano, you wake the following morning to find every tree crystallised from roots to topmost twig: the clinging fog on their branches has turned to white ice. So that walking out in the country, breath tasting of blood in the throat, it's to find icing-sugar cypresses standing on a great cake of frost-bitten landscape. The leafless vines have become disturbingly spectral, fields of crucifix-like contortions, bled white by frost and fog. The tall stone walls beside the road ring with the cold sound of voices. Figures approaching through the murk intone the end-of-year greeting: '*Buona fine, buon principio.*' Happy end, happy beginning. It's been a week and more perhaps since you saw the sky.

And yet, if you walk and walk, you can have that pleasure. For Montécchio is at the very northernmost extreme of the *bassa padana* and its fogs. The hills begin here, and you need only climb. Following more or less the same route we took with our neighbours in the mellow autumn, we head for Cancello, at the top of the ridge far above Via Colombare. And, after a mile or two, there's a sudden thinning of the atmosphere. The fog becomes merely mist and haze. A pale disc of sun comes and goes. The landscape takes on pastel shades, a faded tapestry of beiges and dull greens woven up and down the steep slopes where farmland is retreating before heath and thicket. Another few hundred metres and, almost before you realise it, here comes the explosion of colour and light: a sky more eiectrically blue than it ever is in summer, a low but whitely dazzling sun that immediately narrows the eyes, and, to the north, the vast, sharp panorama of the pre-Alps sparkling with snow.

There are cars parked by the side of the road. Well-dressed people are stretching their legs. '*Buona fine, buon principio.*' It's nice how these greetings are extended to every stranger one passes. Other cars race by with skis on their roofs. Immediately, the light encourages a mood of fun and sensual pleasure. And with the light comes heat. The air is full of the smells of damp earth and vegetation warming in the sun.

Turning back to look at the plain, you appreciate how the

fog stretches, like cloud cover seen from an aeroplane, as far as the eye can see: white, flat, monotonous, with just occasionally a church spire, or radio tower poking spookily through. And having made it up here and rediscovered such brilliant light and scented air, it makes you furious to think you'll soon have to walk back down to that under-world and live heaven knows how many more days in the half-light and cold. Indeed, if you were in the habit of dividing people into groups (and writers inevitably are), you could do worse than to distinguish between those Montecchiesi who are happy with their foggy lot, who sit it out stoically, like the Visentinis, seeking comfort in hearth, home improvement and fifteen TV channels; and those, on the other hand, who are obsessed by that bright paradise only a few kilometres away and who pass the entire winter with their ski-racks or bike-racks on the tops of their cars, counting the days to the next long weekend. In between the two extremes are the hunters, country folk, like old Marini, quite at home in the fog except that, if they're going to see anything to shoot at, they have to make the effort to get up here. Every few minutes the hills echo with gunfire. Little children gather the orange, yellow and blue cartridges along the path.

This silent winter fog, that suffocating summer *afa*, they must play their part in forming the local character. The seasons here don't offer the exhilarating heroism of battling through strong winds, horizontal sleet, deep floods and snow-drifts, the glorious centuries of stormy weather the British can boast. Instead, the inhabitant of the North Italian Plain faces these long long periods of relentless attrition, a loss of sunshine, of visual clarity, coupled with oppressive heat in summer and damp, penetrating cold in winter. Never the kaleidoscopic movement and brusque surprises of an English cloud formation. For day after day, heaven and earth remain inert, motionless, in an anaemic torpor. The taciturn Veneto, a research student at the hospital tells me, consumes twice as many pharmaceuticals per head as other more fortunate areas of the peninsula.

Orietta is popping pills for her tachycardia as we prepare for the New Year's Eve celebration in the *taverna*. Lucilla knocks on our door and asks Rita to come and read the instructions in tiny print inside the box of some medicine or other. For her blood pressure. Could it combine nastily with the other drugs she is taking for her constipation? Vittorina won't take the pills she has been prescribed for her low pressure, counting rather on San Gaspare. Giampaolo, meanwhile, is congratulating himself on having decided to go for the flu vaccination this year. Everybody at the office has been down but him. Taking sick leave most likely, Orietta thinks wrily, the *dipendente*'s only revenge. Sitting together in their flat, Giampaolo constantly fiddling with the remote control of the aerial on the roof, we watch the President's New Year message, in which, referring to the recent devastating bomb on a train in a tunnel between Florence and Bologna, he makes the famous remark: 'They tell me that the secret services are honest, they tell me they are working non-stop to find the culprits . . . ' Later there is to be something live from the Moulin Rouge which Giampaolo shows a lingering interest in. There's so much enticing soft porn on Italian TV. But now it's time to go down to the *taverna* for a big barbecue and plenty of wine and *prosecco*.

Towards midnight the fireworks begin to crackle in

earnest. It sounds like a gun battle. Nearer to home, the Negretti's adolescent boys have bought a full-scale disco-thèque outfit and installed it in their two-car garage where they are making other young Montecchiesi pay a couple of thousand Lire for the pleasure of sixteen-year-old Mario's disc-jockeying. Every time we stop talking in the *taverna* we are assailed by the line: 'Up, down, like a yo-yo, life is just a giddy up and go go.' Lara asks me what it means but I refuse to translate. It's too stupid. The reinforced cement columns throb. Heaven knows how Vittorina and Lucilla are managing to watch their variety shows upstairs. Giampaolo tells me that legally he could phone the *carabinieri* and get them over, since doubtless the noise is above legally established decibel thresholds and the Negretti certainly don't have a licence for holding public gatherings. However, he feels this would be unkind at New Year. I ask him how he decides whether to call the *carabinieri* rather than the *polizia*. Do they have different duties? He tells me that their duties are exactly the same, indeed they frequently compete, and refuse to share information in the hope of arriving at their criminal first. He calls the *carabinieri* merely from personal choice and because their station is a kilometre or two nearer. Isn't our Margaret Thatcher always talking about personal choice?

Towards one o'clock we go upstairs. The fog has lifted, as it sometimes will at night. The air is quite clear at four or five degrees below zero. From our balcony we can see rockets rising into the sky from surrounding villages. The restaurants offering their New Year's *cenone* at 200,000 Lire a head will still be packed. Tomorrow's news will tell us exactly how many people the fireworks and celebratory gunfire killed in Naples, how many people who paid for their *cenone* in advance turned up to find the restaurant closed, the proprietor gone forever, how many people driving back at dawn in thickening fog went into walls and ditches. Obliged to put up with Mario Negretti's disc-jockeying into the early hours, we while away the time with the 1,000 piece jigsaw the Visentini have given us, showing the snowy peaks north of this fog.

The following morning, the Visentini are off early to see their relatives in Venice, but Giampaolo has left precise instructions that I must go and see Lucilla before ten o'clock. I will be the only man in the house and it is bad luck for a woman to see another woman first on New Year's day. Thus, before Lucilla can go downstairs to chat with Vittorina, I will have to go and greet her. Interestingly, the more religious, mysterious Vittorina doesn't insist on observing this superstition, while for Lucilla it's a matter of life or death. When I mentioned this paradox to Vittorina a couple of weeks later, I actually got a squeaky giggle out of her. Cilla just wants to see a man, she said.

And, indeed, when I knocked and announced myself, Lucilla was in a state of suggestive *déshabillé* which twenty years ago might still have turned an *ambulante*'s head. *Buona fine, buon principio, troppo gentile, Signor Tino*. I bend down to kiss her on both made-up cheeks and she tells me she hasn't even been answering the phone in case it is a woman. Actually, she's not sure if the phone counts, but she thought she'd be safe. As always, she insists I come in. Do I know how best to look after the plants she has been given? Four *stelle di Natale* (poinsettias), a traditional Christmas gift, are lined up on the tiled floor, still in their transparent plastic wraps. They are so beautiful, but somehow she can never keep them for more than a month or so. *Sì, sì grazie*, she did get her seven bras, *troppo gentile* of me to ask, although she wasn't entirely satisfied. *Il professore*, on the other hand, knew everything about plants. He used to advise her as to how . . .

Two weeks after these New Year celebrations, we receive a letter from Lucilla's lawyer advising us in the most grandiloquent terms that from now on we are to pay our rent to her. We show our ignorance of such matters by not appreciating that we could perfectly well ignore this. I immediately telephone Signora Marta, who says she will get her lawyer to send us a further letter ordering us to continue to pay to her and quoting the various articles of the law which justify this approach. 'And how is the old lady?' she enquires as always. 'She must be seventy something after all, why doesn't she just enjoy her old age?' I tell her that while Vittorina has been quite ill of late, Lucilla is doing just fine. Marta says that she herself is so upset by having these criminal proceedings brought against her, she is now being forced to take an assortment of tranquillisers. When she wins the case she will sue Lucilla for damages.

After which, the legal war goes on with letter following letter. The first court hearing is finally held, then promptly adjourned – because Marta's lawyer doesn't turn up. A date some three months away is fixed. It is impossible for us not to reflect how all this is playing into our hands. Not only will nobody be able to sell the place until the case is settled, but it would take a very courageous Marta indeed to raise our rent in these circumstances. The affair seems to be without either *fine* or *principio* which can only be *buono* for us.

26
Strada delle zitelle

I date our final acceptance as first-class citizens of Via Colombare to the moment when it became generally known that Rita was to have a baby. It would have been Carnival time, February, the shops full of monster masks and d'Artagnan outfits for five-year-olds. It was also around then that we discovered the Centro Primo Maggio, a place which has always made me feel that little bit happier about living in Montecchio.

Rita wanted tests done at the hospital and asked Orietta how to go about it. No one could have been better informed. Nor more delighted about the news. A baby in number 10, *Meraviglioso!* Giampaolo, too, was genuinely delighted. His serious man's face broke up into excited boyishness. The vibrations in this spic-and-span, austerely stylish apartment were suddenly very cosy indeed. Lara almost jumped for joy. The little brother or sister she hadn't had, she cried!

Of course, the Visentini were discretion itself. They respected your privacy, spoke to no one. It was a point of honour. With them any remark, however banal was considered highly confidential. But about ten minutes after Rita had mentioned the development to Lucilla (since every secretive society must have its source of gossip), the whole of Via Colombare was informed. And our social status rose vertiginously. We were no longer two fly-by-nights who did strange jobs and brought queer visitors in scruffy cars with foreign plates. We were responsible people putting down roots. We were creating a family and thus probably Christian even if we didn't go to Mass. Walking along the street now, there was no question of people not responding to my *'buon giorno'* and *'buona sera'*. On the contrary, everybody smiled their complicity. Rita was buttonholed by women who had barely spoken to her before. When was it due? Was she suffering from morning sickness? Did we want a boy or a girl? Which hospital were we thinking of going to . . . Heads nodded sagely in the cold air. For there was no fog now, just a long dull wait for spring. After which, the baby.

Anyway, it would probably be a girl. Yes it would certainly be a girl. Why? Because every child born in Via Colombare in the last few years had been a girl. And oddly enough all their names started with 'M': Marta, Monica, Milena . . . Perhaps we could call ours Mariangela, or Miranda. Although not that many children had been born in the last ten years, of course, because not only was this the street of the little girls (at this very moment playing

volleyball over railings in winter sunshine), but it was also
la strada delle zitelle, the street of the old maids.

It hadn't occurred to us before, but now one came to
think of it there was a marked preponderance of unmarried, middle-aged women in the street: the woman
with the twig broom, for example, and her slimmer sister;
then the dark-haired sprightly sister of the insurance
pedlar; and the woman at the corner by the Madonnina
who sat at her window behind a loom and had a dog on a
chain outside which barked ferociously behind tall iron
gates and appeared to answer to the name of Book.

'Perhaps it's because of the Virgin,' the woman with the
twig broom laughed, all of a sudden on very easy terms.
She had wiry permed blond hair and a fierce mole at the
base of her nose. We didn't understand. 'The Madonnina,'
she said, pointing to the statue with its patient sad face.
And she added with a note of disappointment, 'I don't
suppose you'll be leaving number 10 now, my nephew will
have to buy in the co-operative.'

Walking back home, I objected to Rita that the Virgin had
surely only been a virgin prior to the birth of Christ. After
that she had had other children whom Jesus referred to as
his brothers. It was thus unlikely that she would want to
influence the women of Via Colombare to become old
maids. Rita told me I was wrong. The Virgin had never had
other children. But I have a whole youth of church
attendance and Bible studies behind me. I was sure. 'And
Joseph?' I asked. 'What became of him then?' We were
walking by the low pink wall of old Marini's garden. He
was pruning his fruit trees.

'Celibate.'

'But if . . . '

'Well, he could hardly go to bed with the mother of Christ, could he?'

I'd never thought about it quite in this crude way. I suggested we go and talk to Don Guido about it. Even if he chucked away his encyclicals he could surely clear up this one for us.

But in the end it was enough to enquire of an authority like Vittorina. Yes of course the Virgin had remained a virgin for the rest of her life. Anything else was unthinkable. Otherwise how could she be the model of virtue? She would come down to our level. The old woman, herself childless, seemed genuinely puzzled that anyone should have imagined otherwise.

I quote this banal misunderstanding merely to show how even a supposedly well-educated Protestant like myself can for so long be unaware of some key piece of dogma underpinning the Catholic culture he is living in. Joseph had thus been forgotten. Jesus hadn't had any brothers, as I had been taught. Mary was the model of celibacy, which was a blessed virtue. She had somehow managed to combine this self-denial with pious motherhood, thus making herself the perfect woman. Indeed, a statue of hers was still reputed to be crying in Cologna Veneta after more than three months, although the priests were refusing to allow the tears to be analysed. Radio Santa Teresa had discussed the matter, but without ever taking on the question as to why the virgin might be crying. Because she was still unhappy about her son's crucifixion despite his resurrection? Because the local congregation was sinful? Or to demonstrate that devotional images were more than mere blocks of wood or stone? Sometimes Radio Santa Teresa would broadcast a whole rosary repeating

Santa Maria, Madre di Dio, time after time. It was quite relaxing. And now the virgin was also being held responsible for the preponderance of female births in Via Colombare. And likewise for the fact that so many of the women in Via Colombare remained unmarried . . .

Naturally, I began to hope that our baby would be a boy (as the Virgin's had been, come to think of it).

But such a hope was precisely what was expected of me anyway. 'I imagine you'll be wanting a *maschio*, Signor Tino?' Lucilla said. 'It's only natural for a man to want a *maschio*.' And she laughed, as if to say, 'Too bad for you the creature was conceived in Via Colombare of all places.'

I thus decided to say to other inhabitants of the street that I would rather like to have a girl, while secretly hoping we would have a boy, and at the same time feeling irritated with myself for getting drawn into this superstitious mare's nest, which in the end nobody on Via Colombare particularly cared about, just as none of them particularly cared whether the Pope insisted that contraception was murder, or whether a visiting priest had once dared to tell them not to come forward for the host if they hadn't paid their taxes. There is this magical duplicity about Italians. I'll never get used to it. You think they're superstitious bigots, but then they're more open-minded than you are. None of them would ever have criticised Christ for plucking his ears of corn on the Sabbath. It's as if they were a nation of Protestants, or even free-thinkers, who just happened to be deeply attached, for reasons of style and aesthetics, to the Catholic way of worship. Because they appreciate its richness. It fills their lives.

But a more pressing question than the sex of the child was whether we should use public or private health care for this pregnancy. Giampaolo Visentini, being the new man, favoured use of a public health system which was, he claimed, extremely *valido*, although he appreciated that some people might doubt that. Indeed, he himself had paid privately when Lara had had to see a dermatologist over a rash she'd had, because the waiting list at the state hospital was so long. And he'd been furious, he added, when the consultant's secretary had not given him a receipt after he'd paid his 70,000 Lire.

The problem, Orietta explained, was that if you went to the hospital for your visits, you couldn't guarantee seeing the same gynaecologist every time, nor could you know whether he'd be there when the child was born. The doctors had plainly decided on this system in order to further their private practices outside the hospital.

We were thus persuaded to go private. A gynaecologist *di fiducia* was recommended by a friend and we went. Disconcertingly, despite having an appointment, we had to wait just as long as one usually waits in the doctor's surgery. Then at the end of his examination, the little man who went by the apt name of Dolcetta prescribed a list of tests so long we wondered if there would be time in the remaining six months to perform them all. And since a scan was urgent, he said, we should do that privately too, not waste time at the hospital; and he gave us the name of a clinic, where, we very quickly discovered, he himself worked, and presumably took a cut of the 100,000 or more they wanted for a scan. At which Rita decided to drop the man and go for the lowest of the low, a health service gynaecologist who came to the small public clinic in Montecchio once a week. Not being a hospital consultant or even a hospital doctor, his assistance was generally spurned and making an appointment was refreshingly easy. The man turned out to be a southerner with a light, jolly patter, and a determination, he surprisingly boasted, to make the public system work. We couldn't have been better served.

27
Centro Primo Maggio

It was accordion music which first drew us to Centro Primo Maggio. We were walking along a little footpath that leads off the main road behind the new church where Don Guido keeps his rabbits and hens. Running between two deep ditches, the path is ill-kept: to the left is a patchwork of vegetable allotments behind crumbling houses, plastic bags over warm-weather plants, plane trees pruned to knobbly trunks, dogs on chains, skulking cats, and a complex crisscrossing of lively streams. I am conscious, as I describe this, that it does not sound especially attractive, whereas in fact the rich haphazardness of it all and the general rejection of any recognisable geometry is constantly picturesque. Someone has built a little raft to push from one side of a ditch to the other: a chair strapped to a

240

wooden door over petrol-can floats. There's an old man in his allotment asleep in a decaying armchair with a hat and a bottle of wine. A woman is dropping sprigs of rosemary into her apron. On precarious scaffolding, an older workman and young apprentice chip at the ruined stucco of a house. And there is bric-à-brac from the past: a complicated pattern of stone walls guides one of the streams into an old sheep dip; here and there steps lead from a house down to the water and a large, flat scouring stone. A sturdy middle-aged woman will appear, and descend the steps with a red plastic basket full of dirty laundry. Where the houses back right on to the water, you see pipes gushing out suspicious effluents into the stream. All these people have colour TVs and decent cars.

We had just begun to hear the strains of jolly accordion music when we came across the ascetic Lorenzo, standing thigh-deep in the larger of the two ditches, almost a river at this point, patiently hacking away under water with a sickle tied to a long metal pole.

He is cutting the choking underwater weeds, he explains, which are a result of excess oxygen in the water due to extravagant use of fertilisers up on the hills, plus the dumping of waste by pig breeders.

Off his own bat?

He laughs: he and some friends have formed a co-operative, a non-profitmaking company, which is paid by the council to keep the village's streams and ditches in good order. It's a victory won after a decade of protest about public lack of concern for the local ecology.

But isn't it cold in the ditch? A great clump of weeds detaches itself from the bottom and floats clear with the current. Lorenzo has a big bag tied to his belt into which he drops a muddy Coca-Cola bottle.

Not at all. The water is warmer than the air, and he has his waders on. He likes the job. But has decided to leave Montecchio.

Lorenzo has ginger hair, tightly curled, and a thin nose. Despite having left the Jesuits, his sharp features betray the stubbornness of the man with a cause.

Because the people here are so traditional, he says, so timid, so cynical, so set in their ways. They're never willing to get out there and fight the environmental battle. Lorenzo turns out to be another of those Italians who aspire to escape provincial claustrophobia.

'I'm thinking of going abroad,' he says, just as Bepi does, although the two people couldn't be more different.

First he tried the Church, he said, where they wouldn't allow you to have a single thought of your own. And now it's not much different in the end trying to improve the situation here in Montecchio. Every new idea is greeted with suspicion.

He begins to press us to come to the next meeting about the flyover the council are planning to build right by the hill with the castle. Feeling guilty, we agree to come – the cause is certainly a good one – but to change the subject we ask him what the accordion music is. Lorenzo gives us directions to the Centro Primo Maggio.

The path ends in a flight of steps climbing to a road where cars chase down a desperately narrow, crooked strip of tarmac with no space for a pavement below the tall walls of three- and four-storey houses. Opposite the path, however, the houses end and the road opens up into the village's second lake, which is much like the Laghetto Squarà, although without the Roman blocks. A battered crash barrier stops the hurrying cars from falling in. To the left of the lake are the gates to a large old factory covering acres of land. This was once a tannery. Now Mondadori, Italy's largest printers, are using it as a paper-storage warehouse. You thus step out from the path to find a huge German truck with two trailers rumbling back and forward to try and get out of the gate, around the crash barrier by the lake, and then on into the forbiddingly narrow canyon of the street beyond.

The other side of the lake there's a grassy pasture, and to the right, a group of *case popolari*, council flats. We walk down towards them and towards the sound of music. Other people are converging there too, in carnival outfit. Or, rather, the adults are for the most part in plain clothes while their little children are fairy queens and assault robots. Carnival is fairly tame in Montecchio. So tame we didn't even know the procession was today. In any event, no inhibitions are being dropped behind demonic masks. For a more extravagant celebration people will go to Verona, where bizarre floats wind through the streets for hours and youths cover shop windows in shaving foam.

The *case popolari* look really OK. True, the stucco is cracking here and there and the balconies are smaller than they might be, but by London standards they look fine. And the people living in them seem to be doing all right too. There are plenty of expensive cars about. Like the *statale* (and very often he is a *statale*), your *casa popolare* occupant is on to a good deal. He pays a rent way below the market rate and, after twenty-five years, the flat will automatically become his. Meanwhile, he polishes his Alfetta. The only drawback being that, ten years after the place was built, the council still hasn't found the money to put in pavements or asphalt the parking spaces. The

ground is grit and stones. One thus has to wash one's
Alfetta rather more often than even an Italian might want.

And the little princesses are getting their silver slippers
dirty. The accordion speeds up. We follow a small
d'Artagnan through the estate to find, on the other side,
just where the country begins, a rusty green gate in a
sagging fence and the legend, 'Centro Primo Maggio'.
Inside, under a bare pergola, a small group of middle-aged
men in Sunday best are playing accordion, guitar and
drums. Despite changing tune every couple of minutes,
the sound and rhythm is always the same: Der-der-der-
der, di dum, diddy dum, diddy dum, der der der der, di
dum, diddy dum, diddy dum . . . A table is stacked with
paper cups; there are big plastic bottles of lemonade at one
end and even bigger bottles of wine at the other. In the
middle are plates of *galani*, fried dough cakes dunked in
icing sugar. The children hurl handfuls of confetti, some of
which gets in my wine. And a little boy bursts into tears
because he has got his Zorro outfit dirty.

Then the Re Magnaron, the carnival leader, arrives. The
magnaron is a tiny fish that swims about in the dikes and
ditches here and once formed the traditional carnival dish.
With his scaly head and sequinned cloak, the man playing
the role looks like something from a Ben Jonson masque.
Guffawing loudly, tossing clouds of confetti, he leads off
the fifty or so cowboys, penguins, batmen and fairy queens
on their infant procession through the village. But we have
already fallen in love with the Centro Primo Maggio and
decide to stay behind. There will be time for the parades
when we have our own children.

It began as a Communist Party social club. Immediately
to the left of the gate is a large low prefab with bar, cluttered

tables, a pair of space-invader machines, a copy of *Unità*, the Communist paper, a poster of Berlinguer, a hammer and sickle, and an assortment of those ubiquitous old Montecchio men with their hats and wine bottles. Playing cards. Opposite the hut is the pergola, perhaps twenty yards long, vine tendrils stretching over a curving iron frame to offer a shady space on summer days and a small dance floor for festive evenings. There is a strip of cement for bowls, which is fenced in to prevent the heavy balls from flying out at passers by. A notice exhorts customers not to argue. Beyond, a very large scrubby lawn is scattered with rickety chairs and tables as far as the flood embankment and emergency ditch fifty yards away. To one side of this lawn a big barbecuing stand prepares hot sausage meat, *bruschetta* and aubergine slices on toast for lunch. Then there are a couple of tennis courts, a children's playground, a cement table for ping-pong and, at the very end of the complex, an ambitious dirt track for BMX bikes. For the Communists must appeal to the younger generation, too.

But it is not the facilities which make Centro Primo Maggio what it is. I haven't spent a hundred lazy Saturday afternoons here for that. It's the extremely attractive atmosphere of *laissez-faire*, the civilised and gentle nature of the people who use the place. There's nothing aggressive in the culture of Montecchio's working and peasant classes. At least, not that I have observed. And if they drink too much, they do it slowly, sitting on the veranda of the prefab, watching the crimson wink of Bardolino in the sunshine. They are at ease, relaxed, there is never the slightest threat of hurry or unpleasantness. Nor does one experience that sense of claustrophobia you get in downtown middle-class Verona, and even in Pasticceria Maggia sometimes, that obsession with fashion and elegance, fur and leather, the scrubbed faces of the men, the heavy make-up of the women, the crinkly dyed blond of respectable girls fanning out on to sheepskin shoulders, the hubbub of posh Veneto la-di-da.

None of this at Centro Primo Maggio. It's the sort of place, I have sometimes thought, that Orwell must have dreamed of. You salute your faith-healing barber who clearly appreciates you more now you have admitted to sensing a tingling feeling when his fingers touch your head. You salute the shoemender, who runs a little Elvis Presley fan club and has pictures of the King all over his tiny shop. You wave to the supermarket boys as they play tennis, the girls who serve in Bepi's shop. And Ercole, tall, lantern-jawed, who fills up your car at the local pump and ran as an *indipendente di Sinistra* at the last elections, nods to you as he helps the younger boys with their bikes. Prices are comparatively low, although it would be a mistake to buy a *cappuccino* here. Wine or *espresso* or both are the thing. Just inside the door of the prefab, a small space is made available for a couple of *marocchini* to show their wares without going about and bothering people. And there's a black man selling cheap leather goods and Russian watches. You pick up your wine, take it out into the garden and wonder how long you can resist the smell of sizzling pork and aubergines.

Not that there aren't encroachments from the modern yuppie Italy and its well-healed pieties: the anxious mothers, for example, who are watching their children do as tennis teacher tells them on the new, carefully groomed, clay courts; and then the bright young men who have just finished playing and are ordering, instead of beer or wine, the fashionable, healthy, super-vitaminised mineral drinks heavily advertised on television. They are so conscious of their virtue, these young men, as they discuss the technicalities of their game with TV-expert solemnity, I feel almost sorry for them. Outside, hordes of eight-year-olds in the uniform of the Montecchio biking club are strapping on their helmets before tackling the BMX course. Every single girl and boy has his or her special biking shoes, biking pants, biking gloves . . .

But it all coexists so happily at Centro Primo Maggio: as if the contemporary fads were nothing more than pink froth on the same old blood-red wine. And it's fun watching the bowls, or on summer evenings the people dancing to the squelchy tunes of the accordion beneath the now fragrant pergola: der der der der, di dum, diddy dum, diddy dum . . .

Whenever I go, I always feel this is Montecchio at its best.

28

Il frate indovino

Another thing that raised my status in Via Colombare, and at number 10 in particular, was the fact that I was the only man around one morning when disaster struck. We were sitting in the kitchen. The news was reminding us it was time to make our VAT declaration. It is touching the way the public service seeks to prod the citizens' memory in this way. Such and such a category, the newscaster tells you – artisans, shopkeepers, solicitors – has just three days to make such and such a declaration. Or: people with cars registered in January have just a week to pay their car tax, although there may be a reprieve since not enough forms are presently available.

The apologetic Roman voice was suddenly interrupted by a pounding on the front door. Lucilla, in her pink, brushed nylon dressing-gown, face harrowed by melo-drama, was hopping from one foot to the other on the landing by the remains of her Christmas poinsettia. She had been unable to get Vittorina to come to her door.

This then was what all the shouting had been about earlier on.

Had she tried the phone? Vittorina has a phone by her bed. Lucilla rushed back into her flat and was so upset she couldn't dial the number. '*Che agitassión, che agitassión, Signor Tino!*' she cried. We helped her. A tubby hand grabbed the receiver. There was no answer.

Could Vittorina be out?

No. Lucilla claimed she had heard her moaning behind the door. At which Rita phoned for an ambulance while I rushed downstairs. Orietta came out, and whereas I would have imagined this was just the kind of thing that would have brought on her palpitations, she was in fact very cool and sensible. We must try and get into the flat. Lucilla's spare keys perhaps? But Vittorina had left her own in the door inside. So, a window, Orietta suggested.

I went outside and pulled myself up on to Vittorina's terrace balcony beneath which I had watered grass all the long summer before. Forcing apart the slats of her shutter just a crack, I was able to see that the french window behind was open to let some air in. I asked Orietta if she had such a thing as a breadknife and she hurried off to find one. It was late February. Rain was falling in the street behind me, and, unusually for these parts, there was wind with it. I remember the cheese van turned the corner with a coolly megaphoned '*Formaggi!*' Then Orietta brought out a selection of useful-looking knives and only a very few moments later I had sawed two small squares out of the plastic slats so as to be able to reach in and release the catches inside. I heaved the shutter up a little, crawled underneath, and found Vittorina stretched limply on her cold dining-room tiles in nineteenth-century underwear.

On being let in, Lucilla had a fit of hysteria. It was plain she could already see herself beating her fists on the coffin. She howled out loud and tugged at her short hennaed grey hair to feel the pain. Neighbours rushed in from the street. Together we got Vittorina into a sitting position on an armchair. The women rubbed her hands and feet. Others comforted Lucilla and helped her loosen off her girdle.

Somewhat embarrassed, I decided I had better retire to the kitchen until the ambulance came. It was thus that I found myself reading a rather odd calendar pinned to the door of one of Vittorina's freshly carpented cupboards. *Il calendario del frate indovino*, it said. And this immediately struck me as curious, for a *frate* is a priest, a friar (the calendar was published by a religious order), while an *indovino* is a decidedly secular fortune-teller. Another peculiar thing was the way the colours and graphics of the poster-size pages seemed to come straight out of the early sixties (old cornflakes-box illustrations spring to mind), whereas the dates referred unequivocally to today. In the middle of the page were the days of the month, each with its saint's name in bold type followed by runner-up saints in small print: i.e., 1 March, *SAN SILVIO*, Sant'Albino, Sant'Ercolano. Then, around the calendar proper, a series of different coloured boxes offered oodles of advice, predictions, maxims and mottoes, information for farmers, satirical jokes, cartoons and ominous sayings. Plenty for me to while away five minutes with:

'*Seeding*: given a waning moon, now is the time to plant peas, beets and spinach in a sheltered area.'

'*Women*: Die-hard reactionaries refuse to recognise that in a Christian society women have responsibilities as great as those of men, and sometimes greater. Like motherhood.'

I wondered quite who the reactionary here might be. And if the piece on seeding had been written by the *indovino* persona, was the comment on women the work of the *frate*? Vittorina of course had had no children, no motherhood to justify her femininity. Nor even virginity. Although she subscribed to this same potent mix of the religious and secular: the quote from the Bible and the day's horoscope beside. And then my eye caught this disquieting reflection:

'*Thought for the Day*. Every morning in Africa the gazelle wakes up and knows he will have to run faster than the lion if he is not to be killed. Every morning in Africa the lion wakes up and knows he will have to run faster than the gazelle if he is not to die of hunger. When the sun rises, it doesn't matter if you're a gazelle or a lion, you'd better start running.'

Clearly this boded ill indeed for poor Vittorina.

The Croce Verde ambulance arrived, an orderly offered a possible diagnosis of stroke, Vittorina was swathed in blankets and carried off. The stretcher-bearers refused to let the sobbing Lucilla into the vehicle so a neighbour, the insurance salesman's sister, one of Via Colombare's *zitelle*, travelled with her. At the last moment, Orietta hurried out with a plastic bag containing nightdress, cutlery, soap, towel and toilet paper, all of which Vittorina would need if she was to stay in hospital for any length of time. Lucilla retired to her bed with its pink canopies and called the doctor to come and measure her blood pressure, slipping the man 20,000 Lire for doing what the state already paid him to do. Imaginatively, he prescribed tranquillisers. '*Troppo gentile*,' Lucilla told him and called us in to ask if we would go and get her prescription.

The chemist is still a figure of some authority in provincial Italian society. A long queue of people with no time to go to the doctor were thus waiting for his advice. And, unfortunately, there is only one chemist in Montecchio since the local council has not given permission for another to open. This gives our chemist a powerful monopoly, especially since such simple products as aspirins, milk of magnesia and the like can only be sold by chemists. The prescription charge is around two pounds, then you pay a percentage of the cost of the product, this depending on the nature of the medicine required and your own particular status.

The process is complicated. The chemist has what looks like a plasticised log table on the counter and taps on a calculator, doing percentages, adding and subtracting. I wait, but then the woman in front of me doesn't have a prescription for the valium she wants. Which must only be sold under prescription of course. *Sotto voce*, a long argument begins. *Per favore, dottore*, she pleads. After furtive glances to check who is in the shop, he finally gives her what he shouldn't. At the full price. Then he asks me to sign two petitions, one to have the flood ditch outside paved over for more convenient parking, another to complain that the government is being very late in making its payments to chemists for medicines sold under prescription. Politely, I refuse. Down south, in Calabria, I think, there is an area where pretty well every chemist has been kidnapped at some time over the last few years. Ransom payments have not presented an insuperable problem. Walking home, I observe that I am already feeling that peculiarly Italian envy of the more fortunate employment categories.

We go and visit Vittorina in hospital. The building compares well with the National Health ones I knew, although there are a few beds in the corridors. The nurses are mainly small, slim, southern men and wear green pyjama affairs and slip-on clogs. At night Marisa has been sitting on a straight-backed chair by Vittorina's side. Almost everybody who is seriously ill has a relative spending the night with them.

But Vittorina is recovering fast. She's sitting up and smiling. It's just that she can't move her left arm or leg. In a slurred voice she is embarrassingly profuse in her thanks. She does hope Lucilla will let us keep the flat. And driving home, it occurs to us that, yes, we do have a strong card to play here. I will point out to Lucilla that since I mostly work at home I am generally on hand to deal with the kind of emergencies that might befall old and ailing women. Whereas a new tenant, even one as capable and *gentile* as Signor Giampaolo, would probably not be.

Always assuming Lucilla wins, or that the case is ever settled at all.

Arriving back in Montecchio, we noticed a small knot of people outside the church, elderly women and children, one or two of the latter furiously rubbing their foreheads. How odd. Until we recalled it was Ash Wednesday. 'From dust you came and to dust you shall return.' Don Guido had been signing the cross in ash on their foreheads. This was one religious festival that it was as well perhaps Vittorina had missed.

Although death, as they like to say, is not always unwelcome. And if the saga of Marta vs. Lucilla was to be interminable, it was not long after Vittorina's return home that the final curtain did at last fall on another long-running drama. The weather had turned rough: spring storms, March winds. And, at night, when the wind blew, you couldn't keep the shutters down because the plastic slats would rattle irksomely. This meant that if Vega chose to bark, five, six metres from our window, the noise was even louder. It seemed to ring in your skull.

One night we were kept awake for ages as the dog yelped, howled and bayed; railing at the stormy wind we imagined, participating in her doggy way in the change of the seasons, the approaching equinox. Right through the small hours it went on, urgent and tortured, as if the creature were barking inside your brain, tugging you back from the threshold of sleep with its teeth. How we moaned and swore and wondered at our own impotence. Until the following morning, wearily cleaning my own teeth before some lesson, I pushed open the frosted glass of the bathroom window, for no other reason really than to feel the air on my face and see the world I knew was there. Except that today it wasn't, quite. For under the budding *cachi* tree was stretched, as if in sacrificial offering, the horribly distorted corpse of our canine tormentor. Poisoned.

Rita! Rita! A moment's delighted celebration, an enthusiastic embrace. At last, at last! Someone had done for the mutt! How splendid life was going to be!

And then came the first doubts. Everybody must

imagine it was us. Oh no! The Negretti family were only too aware how much Vega disturbed us. We had talked quite openly about poisoning the creature. And there had been those phone calls we'd made. In the early hours. If nothing else they must make us the prime suspects. Not that we feared Rocco Negretti would go to the police. It wasn't his style. But what if some stupid vendetta were to begin? After all we had the cat now. Would it be safe for her to go out?

That evening we talked to Giampaolo and Orietta. Vega, they had heard through the grapevine, had definitely been poisoned, but nobody knew whom by. They looked at us intently. We denied any knowledge. There was a rumour, they said, that the animal had eaten some rat poison Negretti had used in his cellar. But this seemed extremely unlikely, given that the dog was never allowed into the house. Vittorina, grim faced, mouth twisted as she spoke, was mysterious: 'That animal got on one too many people's nerves,' she said darkly. Across from my study window, the old skull-face between lace curtains was sibylline as death itself.

Other inhabitants of Via Colombare seemed not so much reticent as genuinely uninterested. Who cared who had killed old Negretti's dog, as long as the next one he got didn't bark so much?

We mulled over this strange case of wish fulfilment for some time. And watched our cat carefully. Nothing happened. In the end our conclusion was that Negretti must have poisoned the animal himself to be rid of it. For only forty-eight hours after Vega's death he came home with a huge black Doberman and launched into a breeding experiment that is still going on to this day. The sight of the great black creature terrified us at first; how loud would this monster bark? Until we realised that a Montecchiese breeding a dog is quite a different proposition from a Montecchiese merely keeping a dog. For a breeding dog is worth money and hence deserves respect. With the result that first Ursa and later Sirio, Musca and Canope (this obsession with the night sky was one of the more attractive sides to Negretti's character) were well fed, regularly brushed, and barked very little at night.

29
Primavera

I don't know why, but I picked up a copy of the *frate indovino* calendar myself. I had noticed it hanging in three or four houses now. It seemed popular in a sort of Reader's Digest, ready-source-of-wisdom way. And who would be without a ready source of wisdom? Thus, come spring-time, an entry entitled *Per Tutti* tells me: 'Remember that love exists regardless of age, and that the love that lasts longest is also the strongest. However, we should also remember that young people are a constant prey to sexual impulses, especially at certain times of the year. Fortu-nately, these can be quietened and actually disappear in individuals who manage to establish loyal relationships with their parents, their true friends, and their spiritual guides.'

A world where adolescents are not troubled by sexual impulses! One's first reaction is to burst out laughing, to assume that our *frate* is way out on a celibate limb here. Who could ever want such a thing? Yet when I begin to pay attention, it does seem that a very large proportion of my students at the university not only do seem to want, but actually appear to have achieved the God-fearing serenity he describes. And a fair number of youths in Montecchio too. There is a decorousness and calm about them at once admirable and disturbing. 'No, I don't want to leave home,' they tell you. 'I like living with *mamma e papà*. There's nothing I'd like to do that I can't do at home.' Or 'Francesca and I will get married and live together in about five years' time when I pass the state exam to become an accountant in my home village of Buttapietra.' They seem quite untroubled by matters sexual.

I ask how many of my students go to Mass (one can pretend this is a linguistic exercise when teaching English). More than half regularly and most of the rest occasionally. Yes, they go with their parents. Even their grandparents. (Of course, in a way, this is wonderful, even enviable.) I ask what they did last weekend, and hear from three or four students that they went on a spiritual retreat. To be together and pray for peace. The girls dress with Latin elegance and seem very self-composed. But Friday night they went to a discothèque. Oh yes, Federica, and what did you wear? (revision of chapter 4). Black skirt, black tights. And you Cristina? Black skirt, black tights. And you, Monica? Black skirt, black tights. Do the boys wear ties when they go to discothèques? Some do, some don't. And what did you have to drink? Fanta, Coca-Cola. No wine? No wine.

One constantly suspects that some cover-up job is going on. Something you can't understand is happening. Surely they can't all be like this, so very sure of themselves, untroubled by life's passing. And I ask questions at random. How did you get to the discothèque? In *papà*'s car. What kind of car does he have? A Mercedes estate. Oh, and how long did you stay? Till two in the morning. And does anything actually happen at these discothèques? What do you mean, happen?

Is this truly serenity, the wise calm of the youth who has a good relationship with loyal friends, sensible parents and spiritual guide? Or reticence and obtusity? And how does it square up with those unmarried mothers of Montecchio, disconsolately pushing their prams around the broken fountain of Piazza Buccari?

'By far the most widely practised method of contraception in Italy', explains Maria Grazia in her *sanitaria* (she loves these conversations), 'is *coitus interruptus*. You know? Not something young men are notoriously good at.' A rueful expression crosses her face. 'And then spring comes so suddenly here.'

It certainly does. Late March, early April's the time: San Francesco, San Sisto, Sant'Isidoro . . . The lingering mists, the cold colourless days, the heavy rains are suddenly gone. The sun powers through, so hot you find you're desperately overdressed. And the women would have loved to wear their furs just one last time. But it's too late. You wake one morning – San Celestino my calendar tells me – and the sky is awhirl with swifts and swallows. How they liven up the hills and farms and river bridges with their voracious, darting search for food, and sex presumably. Cherry and peach blossom simply explode. All the trees at once. Line after line of them up the hills between the still gaunt vines. Already the bees are crawling in and out of sugary petals. The polythene comes off the lemon trees. The earth releases all its pent-up smells. And in the evening dusk, white cherry flowers glow like beacons, to the croaking of a thousand frogs converging on Montecchio's ditches – to lay their spawn.

How loud those frogs will croak! It's obscene! And no wonder that one or two of the less-well-spiritually-guided tend to fall by the wayside: in the soft grass, the primroses and periwinkles. After all, the *frate indovino* did warn that there were vulnerable times of the year.

At number 10, a condominium garden committee agrees to have a man come in and prune all our flowering shrubs just before they can bloom. He cuts and clips, returning a year's growth to austere geometric shapes. And the buds had looked so promising. Rita is furious and sticks the cuttings in jars about the flat. If she had had more time, Lucilla says, she would have moved the hibiscus the other side of the little cypress. But what with Vittorina being ill . . .

On Palm Sunday everybody comes out of Mass with olive branches in their hands. Specially blessed by Don Guido. The children make a pretty picture. Their well-dressed parents look rather sheepish. *Il frate indovino* says:

> *La domenica dell'olivo, ogni ucello fa il suo nido,*
> *e se gocciola la frasca, sarà bello il dì di Pasqua.*
> (On Palm Sunday, all the birds their nests do lay
> And if the branch drips rain, Easter will be fine again.)

In the event, *la domenica dell'olivo* is fine this year, and likewise *Pasqua*. So much for our *indovino*.

On Easter Monday, *Pasquetta*, as it's called, the tradition is to set off into the hills for a mammoth picnic with barbecue equipment and bottles of wine. As always, the formula of religious festival plus heavy eating appears to be invincible. Everybody is on the move with hampers and ice-boxes. Marisa and Leone take the two old ladies up to Cancello. Bepi is throwing a party on his grounds at Rivoli. More modestly, we walk along the valley to Mizzole with Giampaolo, Orietta and a well-prepared picnic basket. As we cross the main road, a stream of cars drives by with sacks of charcoal strapped to luggage racks.

Outside the village, the valley is luridly green today and the spring light, you notice as you saunter along, is different from in England, somehow. At first you think it's clearer; perhaps because, after weeks of mist and rain, you can see the mountains again now, far far away. And it gives you a tremendous sense of space to see them there, still in their majestic winter white. But it's not really a question of clarity. Nothing could be clearer than the light in England when a gusting wind is blowing every scrap of haze and exhaust away so that you feel you could see the whole length of the Edgware Road, if only you wanted to. Anyway, by ten o'clock, as seen from Montecchio, the Alps have already disappeared in a gathering heat haze. Visibility soon loses that sharp edge it will keep all day in windier climes.

No, it's the suffusedness of the light which gives the spring its power here, its distinctly erotic feel. Quite simply, the light seems to have got in everywhere, to be on all sides of everything. Perhaps because it bounces off the pastel stuccoes so, and the white limestone of the window surrounds, simmers dazzling on terracotta roofs, shoots off dusty grey asphalt – a light that is glare, haze and heat all together. So that clothes simply fall off the women. In the space of a couple of weeks we've gone from furs to thin blouses and fashion T-shirts. People move bathed in fragrant brilliance, which somehow gives you a feeling that things are happening in slow motion. For the light has that effect too. Especially if you are in the habit of taking three bottles of wine on a picnic, stretching out under the first cherry blossom and simply watching as the more adventurous hikers push on.

And lying there, you hear your first cuckoo raise its cheeky call, and the larks twittering high in the sky, and the urgent hum of a thousand bees (for many orchards have their own hives), and the frogs and toads croaking shamelessly as they flop through the long grass to the water.

What chance for spiritual guides at moments like this? Surely even the best of biblical armour can offer no real immunity to such a strident call to be living and doing. What hope for Montecchio's Catholic youth? The *frate indovino* must be tearing his tonsure.

Then across the heavily scented grass comes an insistent modulated drone. Nearer and nearer, louder and louder. Until all at once a leatherclad figure bursts out of a nearby ditch, roars through the vineyard where we are picnicking, and attacks the first slope of the hill in a spray of dirt and stones. Followed by another, and another, and another . . .

For ironically, it's science that comes to the old Church's aid. There is the internal-combustion engine. With the same ritual inevitability that lifts the sun higher every day and draws the sap up in the trees, the local adolescents answer migrant birds and reawakened bees with a great shriek of unsilenced mopeds and motorbikes. Throttles are opened and closed, opened and closed, revving rhythmically in the spring air. Cannily, Don Guido, a man who knows the lesser of two evils when he sees it, permits the lads to go round and round the church car park in frenzied circles. Then they race to Un panino due's for a slice of pizza, then to Giulia's at the other side of the village for Coca-Cola fresh from the fridge. While, back in Via Colombare, the Negretti boys gun their mother's Cinquecento jerking back and forth, back and forth across the big terrace among the broken flowerpots and clothes pegs: three yards in reverse, a great screeching of brakes, three yards in first, three yards in reverse, three yards in first. The blue smell blots out all the stirring scents of the air. The noise drowns the seductive cries of the *ambulanti* with their seasonal offers of deckchairs and skimpy beachwear.

Walking the winding pavementless village streets to the bar of an evening becomes hazardous. Hoards of *motorini* scream by, rearing up on their back wheels, skidding and swerving. Could this be, one wonders, some pact between Fiat and the Holy See, a conspiracy to displace the libido of Latin adolescence and restrict casualties in the spring offensive to a minimum? Orietta confides that she and Giampaolo are now worried about Lara who has taken to hanging around with the moped brigade outside the church and is reported to have been seen holding the hand of a tall blond boy. I suggest she should consider herself reassured.

Mid-April. We cycle through a cherry-blossom countryside. Walking in the hills the hedgerows are so full of primroses, narcissi, violets, hyacinths, it's almost unbear-

able. The strips of winter corn are shooting up. Everybody's busy with their vegetable patches. The farmers are
spraying their trees with the usual assortment of noxious
chemicals.

And then it turns cold and rains again. Not only rains,
but sleets, for an hour or two actually snows. The snow lies
ice-white on the white cherry blossom. Old Marini shakes
his head. Not a year for fruit, he says.

Giampaolo is shaking his head too. It is almost time for
us to bottle the *prosecco* he has been keeping in three huge
wicker-covered demijohns down in his cellar. The problem
being that *prosecco* should always be bottled when the
atmospheric pressure is high or rising. This sudden return
to winter is a disaster.

But the weather is going to be good next week, I tell him.
I have heard the long-range forecast. All we have to do is
hang on and we'll have sun and blue skies again. The
pressure will rise.

He frowns, twists his mouth.

What's the problem?

Prosecco should really be bottled with a waxing moon too,
he says. And the full moon is Sunday. He knows the
weather is supposed to be fine next week, but by then the
moon will be waning.

I protest that I thought he was a man of science. Surely
his encyclopaedia doesn't come any of this lunar stuff. This
is the realm of the *frate indovino*.

Giampaolo is such a nice man because he knows when
he is being ribbed and rather enjoys it, yet at the same time
persists perfectly seriously with his line of argument. His
encyclopaedia, he says, doesn't actually say anything
about bottling *prosecco*. But the fact is that he has a certain

amount of respect for popular wisdom. He believes that some day the scientists will find some reason behind the farmer's attention to the moon. More pertinently, we have spent quite a lot of money on our sixty litres of *prosecco* and he doesn't want to risk its coming out wrong.

But what could happen?

It might turn out flat, he tells me glumly. It's the waxing moon that makes it bubbly.

Well, I'm as anxious to avoid that as he is. For the next few days, every time I meet him, on the stairs, in the garage, or out on the lawn trying to remember where he put his bulbs so we won't mow over them (for we'll have to start mowing the lawn again now) – every time I meet him, our conversation is about rising and falling pressures, waxing and waning moons.

Couldn't we just wait for the next waxing moon?

We could. But that will take us to mid-May. It will be absolutely our last chance. Otherwise the fermentation process will have gone on for too long.

Giampaolo hangs a barometer on his balcony and wears a worried look. We discuss the expediency of bottling willy-nilly on the last day of this waxing moon, regardless of pressure. My own instinct is to bank on the atmospherics, rather than the moon. He looks at me, wondering if I know something. I hasten to assure him I don't. He must decide. Or perhaps he should ask old Marini. No, these Montecchiesi, Giampaolo tells me, only deal with local wines. They would have no idea what to do with a *prosecco*. Thus, while worrying about the moon, he nevertheless manages to express his Venetian, modern man's superiority to the provincial locals.

The days pass. The moon is now a perfect round silver

coin in the sky. How can it possibly affect our *prosecco*? I stand on the balcony, watching it rise full as full between rainclouds over the derelict factory. To wax no more. Mid-May it will have to be.

30
Il 25 Aprile

On 25 April flags hang from windows and balconies along the main street through Montecchio. It's Liberation Day. People whose homes face on to major thoroughfares are obliged to fly the flag. Most of them do. Somebody has forgetfully left a pink towel over the railings of their balcony. In a beam of sunshine it clashes gorgeously with the red, white and green.

Walking towards Centro Primo Maggio, for it's a public holiday, we hear the strains of a brass band. In dark uniform an endearing mix of adolescents and middle-aged stalwarts are playing a military march. They arrive at the monument to the fallen more or less as we do. Not the monument in the main square dedicated to the soldiers who died – they have already been there – but a more modest, modern affair located at the corner below the ex-tanning factory where another small estate of *case popolari* begins. Here a copper plate records the names of eleven civilian Montecchiesi killed in the bombing. A recycled wreath lies at its foot.

The band lower their instruments and a couple of youths in jeans are busy setting up an amplifier. A small crowd gathers, families in their Sunday best, shifting weight from one foot to the other, children tugging at coats. Every few minutes they have to part to let a car, or a team of racing cyclists through. On the opposite corner is one of the noisier bars for village youths, its window daubed with a cartoon view of the New York skyline, symbol of un-imagined decadence.

An old, portly man in uniform, complete with medals, starts to speak into a microphone, although there are only thirty or so people. He begins with the normal introductory formalities employing the pompous Italian of public dis-course, so that for a moment I imagine this will be one of those politician's speeches one grows accustomed to here where any possible message is obscured by an intermin-able clutter of qualifications and relative clauses. ('It depends' – I quote more or less at random from a newspaper by my side – 'if this development is to be seen in the light of a possible *rapprochement* between forces by their nature intrinsically unsympathetic to what I think one would have to call the future interests and indeed hopes of the nation, conceived as that group of people who, for reasons of history, race and culture, consider themselves to form an identity distinct from, though not opposed to, other national identities, or whether . . .')

But no. Having got over his carefully pre-prepared

introduction, his list of names to be thanked and organisations mentioned, the old man has given up on his notes and is talking in a very simple way about the war and the dead now. He remembers how Italy fought on the wrong side, how soldiers went to freezing Russia in light summer uniforms, how these civilians were killed by the bombs of their ex-allies. He pauses, clears a hoarse throat. 'If their death is to have any meaning at all,' he says, gesturing to the monument, 'it must lie in the kind of Italy that we have managed to build after the war, that we are able to build now. And at the moment, this Italy of Mafia, tax evasion and public corruption does not do honour to their names, we cannot feel we have built on their sacrifice.'

He continues in this remarkably strong vein, although speaking calmly and intelligently. His old man's sincerity is impressive, the more so because of his scrubbed red nose and the deep wrinkles, weather-, age- and drink-induced. He has none of the professional speaker's polish; he ers and ahs, feeling for what to say next. Turning round to the monument, having problems with his microphone, he begins to read out the names, one by one, as if they were people he knew. And maybe he did. 'Albertini Mario, Pizzini Giuseppe, Stefanelli Emanuele . . .' The little gathering listens gravely; and it's a moment of unusual candidness, this old man in the spring light, speaking hoarsely into a microphone, reading out the names of the dead, surname first, then Christian name, as if at some impossible roll-call. Then the band strikes up the national anthem and everybody disperses for their *cappuccinos*. On our way to the bar, we find a bunch of fresh daffodils has appeared by the plaque to the three who fell under enemy fire as the Germans retreated. It would be intriguing to know who put them there. The Dalmatian imprisoned behind jumps on and off the old bidet that serves as its waterbowl.

In the bar the price of our *cappuccino* has gone up another hundred Lire, but since this price is fixed by a government body, we can hardly complain at Pasticceria Maggia. The price of an *espresso* is fixed, the price of a *cappuccino* is fixed, the price of a newspaper is fixed, the price of petrol, diesel and heating oil is fixed, the price of bread is fixed. Is this in line, I ask Lorenzo, with the spirit of *Liberazione*? And paying at the till I ask the pretty Cinzia if the price of *brioches* is fixed too, since I notice they always cost the same everywhere. 'Not officially,' she smiles, and is careful to give me my receipt.

Returning to Via Colombare, it's to find Lucilla and Vittorina sitting on their backsides in the middle of the lawn, legs stretched wide apart in dark old wool skirts. Vittorina has her big straw hat against a sun that's getting perceptibly stronger every day. Each woman holds a knife and they have an old shopping basket between them. They thrust their knives into the lawn, wiggle them vigorously about and pull out the fresh young dandelion plants. The roots are cut off and tossed away and the leaves dropped into the shopping basket to be washed for salad or boiled like spinach. They chatter and sing as they work. I have never seen them so happy. Lucilla has put on a green kerchief, peasant fashion. When they've exhausted the garden, they say, they'll go off to the orchard and vineyard fields to try there. And indeed, walking about the countryside in spring, the meadows are full of crouched figures with plastic bags or shopping baskets, gathering dandelion and other leaves.

Giampaolo comes out to discuss lawnmowing rotas and they give him some of their harvest. *Vado Matto*, he grins, I'm crazy for them. We accept too, although I can't say I'm wildly enthusiastic. The locals have a taste for such rough, bitter salads: leaves with the texture of a cat's tongue and the taste of herb medicine. Terribly good for her constipation, Lucilla confides. To me it seems the kind of taste one could only have developed in darkest wartime.

Old Lovato watches us all from over the fence, wondering what we'll do with the garden this year, how much our hedge will grow and steal his light. Behind him, and stinking with fertiliser, his peas are already rising thick as Persian spears at Thermopylae. Meantime, with Vittorina not being able to do much after her stroke, Giampaolo's encyclopaedic, ecological approach has got us no further than a few weedy rows of snail-ridden spinach and salad. The sun may well follow its dazzling trajectory above Via Colombare, the railings and cement, vines and cypresses may drip and drip with light, but somehow that dank little patch below the old cinema wall and Negretti's terrace is always in the dark.

Incredibly, in May – but as a *dipendente* Giampaolo seems born to bad luck – the weather breaks again right on the new moon. Once more it seems the combination of rising pressure and waxing moon is to elude us. The brilliant Mediterranean sky is suddenly replaced by the kind of cloud you expect to find over Halifax or Slough. The rain is desperately heavy. Via Colombare is not cambered and surface water gurgles about looking for a gutter. Lovato stands at the window, staring at his peas, willing them to stand firm. Our lady of the twig broom cycles by under an umbrella, climbs off at her house and, despite the torrent, kicks a cigarette stub away from her gate. Old Signora Marini is another one pedalling under an umbrella. Lack of wind makes this possible as it would not be somewhere else I know. On the third day of uninterrupted rain, I even spy one-armed Negretti, his good hand on the right handlebar, his new dog Ursa tied to the left, and a red umbrella tucked under his stump.

Montecchio being on the water table for countless kilometres of limestone hills above, the ditches are soon full to overflowing. Even the emergency ditches begin to fill, something that happens only once or twice a year. The water is a muddy brown flecked with white as it bears away the heaps of litter people have thrown there. Before the week is out, water floods the section of road by the Cassa di Risparmio di Verona, Vicenza e Belluno, the village's one bank. The Communist Party is quick to get out posters complaining that, while the council has plenty of money to spend for all sorts of other projects, it has never solved this simple drainage problem. The head of the local Christian Democratic Party ducks (as it were) the question at a meeting held in the local library which is temporarily closed for book borrowing because the librarian is away for his military service. Finally, the rain becomes so violent that it fills the emergency ditch to the brim, bursting the stout wall that protects the main road and covering it with water and broken masonry.

How can we possibly bottle *prosecco* in this, Giampaolo complains. He taps his barometer. I've never seen it so low. We watch an evening's TV together over the last of the previous year's bottles. On one of the smaller channels there are frequent ads for talismans (by post) and the services of local astrologers, but nothing on how to get the right combination of atmospherics and lunar cycle for our sixty litres of bubbly. The news quotes the huge sum the government has already promised in compensation to keep the farmers sweet. Should we, perhaps, prepare a claim for our possibly ruined *prosecco*?

Then the miracle happens. The weather clears two days before the weathermen said it would. The pressure is suddenly rising. Giving us a twelve-hour window to do our stuff before the full moon.

31
L'imbottigliamento

Amidst ancient accountancy reviews and stacks of *Nuova Alta Tensione* in Patuzzi's cellar, stand about a hundred cobweb-ridden wine bottles. Giampaolo inspects them, turning them over in his hands, looking inside, putting his nose to the neck. There's a grave expression on his face. It's Friday night. Saturday is our last day for the waxing moon. His own bottles stand in sparkling ranks by his cellar door, each with a square of snap-wrap on top to keep out the dust. Clearly we should have thought of this problem before.

Our neighbour goes away and returns with a bottle full of metal shot and a big cast-iron tub. His instructions are precise. We boil the bottles ten at a time in the tub and for at least five minutes; we then half fill each bottle with the metal shot and, thumb over the top, shake vigorously, up and down and round and round. The shot must be rinsed between each bottle. After which the bottles can be washed in normal fashion, rinsed three or four times to remove the soap, and placed in a position where they can drain off thoroughly before tomorrow morning. Already I'm beginning to wonder if we mightn't perhaps have stuck with supermarket bubbly.

Rubber gloves are required. And infinite patience. But the radio has just the thing for us. As we work late into the evening there's a quiz show which involves people answering questions about intricacies of bureaucratic red tape: 'In what situation might you be asked for a document of *esistenza in vita*?' 'Should an application for a no parking sign for your garage or gate be made on plain paper, or stamped paper (and, if the latter, how much does the stamp cost?)' 'How many years less does a woman teacher have to work for her pension if she has three children?' 'When selling a second-hand car, is it sufficient for just one spouse to take an oath before the solicitor, or do both spouses have to go?' 'When given a prescription for an X-ray, for how long is it valid?' The respondents are quick on their buzzers. We try not to slosh too loudly because the answers are frequently surprising. Actually, it's a pretty useful programme.

Then Saturday morning early, a blond thumbprint of moon only a sliver away from being full, it's straight down to Giampaolo's cellar to do the deed. Like his mind, this tiny space of four or five square metres is admirably tidy and well ordered. There are two shelves of wine bottles, all carefully hand-labelled: the type of grape, the area they come from, the harvest year, the date of bottling: *Cabernet*

–Friuli – vendemmia 1981, imbottigliato il 2 Maggio, 1982;
Traminer – Alto Adige – vendemmia 1982, imbottigliato il 15
Aprile 1983 . . . On the shelves below are boxes and
cabinets full of tools, hardware supplies and the like. Again
there are painstakingly prepared labels: 2 cm anchor nails,
1 cm self-tapping screws, 5 mm rawplugs . . . The air
rarely moves down here. Along the top shelf are hundreds
of editions of the topical magazine, *Panorama* (which may
be worth something one day), plus twenty or so volumes of
a now outdated but still formidable encyclopaedia. Almost
at once I feel I'll have to be on my best behaviour.

Out comes the equipment, handled with the special care
of the fetishistic object. A clear plastic siphon with a tap,
lengthily boiled and rinsed the evening before. There's
something disturbingly surgical about it. A corking tripod
with handpumplike lever. As you bring this down the fat
cork is squeezed pencil thin and forced into the top of the
bottle. *Molto valido*, this piece of equipment, and a bargain
at 50,000 Lire from a friend. The action is *discreto*. Although
of course the quality of any corker is *relativo*, since what
counts above all is the quality of your cork.

And we swing into a long lecture on the various corks the
market offers. Giampaolo has purchased different kinds
for the different wines he is planning to bottle, although
there is also an element of experiment, he explains. He is
eager to see how much effect different corks will have on
the same wine bottled the same day from the same
demijohn. He has corks made from a single piece of quality
cork; these are the most expensive, since they retain their
springiness and breathe well. Careful to wash your hands
before touching them. Then there are some cheaper corks
made from putting together pieces of cork in layers. These

are OK as long as you're not planning to keep your bottle too long; they'll do for the *prosecco*, which will last a max of a year, but not for the Cabernet he's got which should improve with age. And, finally, he has a bag full of plastic stoppers, which have the advantage of being very cheap: you can insert them by hand and remove them by hand, but of course they don't breathe. It will be interesting to see if this makes any difference to the *prosecco*.

He's also going to do five corker of each wine he's got in clear rather than green glass, to check how far the light factor affects the quality. I point out that to do this he will have to open two bottles at once, otherwise he won't be able to make a direct comparison. But he's aware of that. When the in-laws come to lunch, it won't matter if one bottle is not quite up to scratch. Apparently, the tight space of the cellar is breeding a sense of complicity.

We lift the first demijohn on to a chair to get the height required for siphoning. This has to be done with immense delicacy so as not to disturb the sediment at the bottom. Bent over, muscles tense, it is as if we were shifting a tactical nuclear warhead. Then with the Murphy's-law cussedness which upsets even the best-laid plans, the chair turns out to be rickety, or the floor uneven, and the big jar tips perilously from side to side doubtless displacing clouds of sediment inside, like mud in a pond. There's a hunt for pieces of paper and cardboard to slip under the chairlegs, but the damage is done now and we will have to wait at least half an hour for the sediment to settle. In the meantime, we siphon off half a jugful, examine it for cloudiness, then pour a little in and out of our first ten bottles (dark green) to rinse and prime them. Immediately the dankish air down in the cellar takes on a very heady smell indeed.

We line up the bottles ready for action stations. There's a pleasantly conspiratorial feel to mucking about in a cellar that stinks of drink. We are beginning to enjoy ourselves, and at last the siphon is gently lowered into the demijohn. Giampaolo kneels on the cleanswept cement, head down low, to suck the precious liquor through.

At which precise moment, with a great banging of brooms, mops and buckets (the doors are iron down here and resound tremendously), fat Lucilla appears. And announces that she had planned to do the garage spring-clean today. There are a lot of tyremarks on the floor and one or two drops of oil. A rather shell-shocked, but determined Vittorina appears behind her, thinning hair tucked into a kerchief. They stand there in the doorway looking at us. Orietta has also been informed and press-ganged. Rita has pleaded the excuse of pregnancy. That is, having observed Lucilla's cleaning methods, she is concerned about exposure to noxious fumes.

So, at this extremely delicate and exciting moment, Giampaolo and I are obliged to go and move our cars out of the garage, where, hairy upper lip working nervously, Vittorina (despite all doctor's orders not to exert herself) is already sploshing detergent on orange bricks. Lucilla is strewing handfuls of sawdust. Orietta has a grim look. For the first time I notice a Sacred Heart above the four electricity meters. Cars removed, we excuse ourselves hurriedly.

Bottling turns out to be both boring and demanding. The siphon nozzle goes down into the first of a hundred and more bottles. The wine flows slowly, but you have to keep an eye on it so as to stop it at three or four centimetres from the top. Meantime, you're checking that the next bottle has been primed, or, once the process is underway, trying to cork the bottles you've already filled. With a dipstick, Giampaolo examines the wine in the other demijohns and tells bottling stories. How the year before last, for example, all but two of the *prosecco* bottles came out flat and were more or less undrinkable. Although he'd had excellent atmospheric and lunar co-operation. This is just one of those imponderables that make it so exciting.

I ask him why the *prosecco* I buy from the supermarket, admittedly at three times the price, is never flat, despite the fact that the bottling factory can hardly be observing the moon and the barometer. Additives, he says contemptuously. Sugar, fizzing agents. Give you a hangover. That's why shop-bought *prosecco* can never equal the perfect home-bottled variety, just as Bepi's vegetables are never at the same level as those grown in the garden without any pesticides.

Although this particular choice of comparison hardly seems to warrant the gleam of faith and enthusiasm now shining in Giampaolo's eyes, the delicious fumes are sufficient to quell any further objections and keep me more or less merrily at work for the rest of the morning. At least, I reflect, we have escaped the assault on the garage, which we might otherwise have been expected to get involved in. Leaving the cellar in a daze towards lunchtime, we find Lucilla shovelling up bleach-sodden sawdust in an atmosphere suggesting chemical warfare. The ferocious vapours cut right through our tipsiness, would quite probably clear the nose of a man long after he had ceased to be eligible for a certificate of *esistenza in vita*. 'Signor Giampaolo, Signor Tino!' the old woman calls to us. 'See, all the tyremarks and oil stains are gone!' Likewise gone is

Vittorina who apparently felt faint. Orietta has her kerchief round her mouth, her eyes streaming.

32
Fiaccolata

Is it a complete coincidence that the *fiaccolata* occurs toward the end of May, only a few days before tax declarations are due? 'The financial administration', says the form in front of me on the kitchen table, 'has tried to streamline and simplify the contributor's obligations . . .' There follow sixty-four pages of instructions on how I am to fill in my income-tax return, not many of them easily comprehensible, some referring me to paragraphs and articles of laws which I should apparently somehow procure and study. So that I am just reflecting that I will, after all, have to go to an accountant, when a faint murmur of '*Ave, Ave Maria,*' takes me out on to my balcony.

It's a balmy, almost summery evening. The cherry blossom has long gone. The foliage is thick on everything

281

but vines and fig trees. Winter's dry sticks are no longer in evidence; new ivies twine the fences, smothering sharpness and starkness under soft leaves. And all the street's roses have flowered at once, small bright blossoms climbing up stuccoed walls. But not up the railings. Good iron railings must be kept clear. Our cat, who goes by the name of Toro, is scratching at Marini's cypress tree. The swallows whirl about the rooftops in a hurry to catch their supper before retiring. And Simone's car has just drawn up in the street below, when, from round the corner into the curdling twilight, turn the first of a candlelit procession, the *fiaccolata*.

They are coming from the village end of the street, the derelict factory end, led by Don Guido and chanting *Ave Maria*. They are enjoying holding their candles. Among them, as they approach our house, are most of the people I regularly see in the street: Mario, the insurance salesman and his *zitella* sister; old Marini, the Lovatos, man and wife, daughter and son-in-law; the salmon-faced mechanic; the wife and children of the man with the Alfa 75, although not the busy *imprenditore* himself; the elderly, bent, straw-hatted fellow who the mongol-looking woman plants on a chair outside her front door of a morning; Lara with various youths usually to be seen straddling their mopeds, bags of crisps in hand; the woman with the twig broom, of course.

With others from the village, there are perhaps a hundred people altogether, walking rather self-consciously along Via Colombare through the gathering dark towards the Madonnina at the far end. The patient little statue has been freshly painted and a small electric light adds to the halo effect. A bunch of spring flowers has been placed on the ledge below.

Vittorina goes down to join the chanters. Lucilla does not. She comes out on to her balcony for a moment to nod to everybody, then goes back inside where the business of entertaining ex-*carabiniere* Simone is doubtless a demanding one. The dirge grows louder and, as always at this hour, bats begin to flit back and forth, taking over the warm skies from the swallows in a peculiarly appropriate changing of the guard. They swoop below the eaves filling the darkness above the procession's slow candles with quick, demonic life.

Disappointingly, just as the picture is at its most evocative, the street lights go on, reducing the candles to pinpoints. And, immediately afterwards, any mystery that might have persisted is promptly dispelled when, having reached the Madonnina, an amplifier and microphone appear from somewhere for Don Guido to speak into. His uninspiring voice thus has a loud electronic ring to it, with now and then a whine of feedback. And he speaks for almost twenty minutes. What he actually says I don't know, for the words are as distorted as they are loud and uninflected and, after a few moments, I cease to pay attention. In any event, it seems unlikely he will have any useful advice on how I'm to fill in my tax forms. Nor do I imagine that my joining in the ceremony will afford me any particular protection against eventual errors I might make. And I go back inside to wade through the sixty-four pages of instructions.

The alignment of social forces *vis-à-vis* the payment of taxes is not quite perhaps what one would have imagined. Of course, the radio news has been reminding us with some insistency these last few days of our forthcoming civic duty as *contribuenti*. But not so the calendar of the *frate indovino*, who, despite his conservative attitudes on such questions as women and the family, despite his frequent appeals on behalf of all kinds of missions, does not hesitate to tell me at this crucial moment in the financial year that: 'Italy is not, as the Constitution claims, "a Republic founded on labour" (of which there is less every day), but a Republic founded on taxes (of which there are more every day).' Not satisfied with this inflammatory talk, he inserts, only shortly before the declaration deadline, the reflection: 'The criminal is not obliged to testify against himself. The taxpayer is.'

What is the Church's position here? Far from generating a sense of guilt in the would-be evader, the *frate indovino* seems to assume an attitude of solidarity with an oppressed population, as if we were still in the days when spendthrift Bourbon princes sent heavily escorted bailiffs about to wring the last *centesimo* out of a starving peasantry. The complicity will stop when we get back to sex of course, but on questions of rendering unto Caesar what is Caesar's, our Rovigo-based friar has a demagogue's infallible eye for the popular line. 'To make sure that VAT is collected,' he winds up the section entitled 'Predictions', 'the Italian government intends to subject the Italian people to a machine that most nearly approximates a meat mincer.' It's as if, tipping us a wink, he were saying, 'Don't worry folks, do as you feel with your declaration and the Church will be on hand to shrive your peccadilloes afterwards.'

Sometimes, when I pick up my bread of a morning at Bepi's, my friend invites me out for a quick *espresso*, and in these tense days towards the end of May we inevitably find ourselves discussing what is on everybody's mind. 'The government is a thief', he announces almost at once. It's a stock phrase, '*governo ladro*'. You frequently see it sprayed on walls and railway bridges. He shakes his shaggy head as though over an irretrievable and pitiful situation. I make the mistake of remarking a little piously that I do believe in a state where everybody pays what they have to, so that everybody can pay less, and I say I think the Church, with the hold it has over a lot of people, should tell them to cough up rather than conniving with them. Bepi's response is somewhere between the incredulous and the irate. Am I mad? His head-shaking speeds up. His scorn is all too apparent. But then it occurs to him that this is merely my Englishness talking – of course, I'm from a different world, I don't understand – and now he becomes concerned, his big forehead creases up, concerned that I may be about to make a big mistake and declare more than I need. He leans over the table, his voice urgent and conspiratorial: 'What you have to remember' – there's a bright light of conviction in his green eyes – 'what you have to remember is that they are attacking and you are defending. It's naked aggression. And self-defence is always legitimate.'

'The balance of indirect to direct taxation is fairly *valido*,' pronounces Giampaolo more reasonably that evening. He is weighing his words carefully in this sad period when last year's *prosecco* is already finished and the stuff we bottled last week isn't ready yet. 'Then the level of fiscal pressure has been established *discretamente bene*; but all this is rendered *relativo* by the fact that the government makes no serious attempt to collect. Except from *dipendenti*.'

And indeed the *dipendenti* have announced a protest to coincide with the tax-declaration deadline. They will be marching on the parliament in Rome, to demand draconian measures against the demonic *autonomi* who aren't paying their fair share. To hot things up, the newspapers amuse themselves by publishing figures indicating the average level of earnings as declared by various categories of *autonomi* the previous year. Your average jeweller claimed he earned just five thousand pounds, the average doctor even less, the average lawyer not much more, etc. etc. It's ludicrous. But everybody has their justification for behaving as they do, and the *dipendenti*'s protest is quickly followed by a series of articles showing how the government only wastes what it receives anyway, is generally corrupt and inefficient and always will be until Italy is more or less taken over by the European Community.

In the event, the administration of this year's income-tax collection does little to improve the government's image for fairness or efficiency. As May progresses and people go from one tobacconist's to another in search of the appropriate forms, it becomes clear that not enough have been printed. Or perhaps they have been printed, but they are certainly not being distributed. Then to make matters worse, somebody discovers that an important mistake has been made on one of the pages. We will have to return to the tobacconist's to buy a revised form. So that as well as reminding us of our civic duty, the radio is also talking about the possibility of a two-week postponement of the deadline for filing our returns. Indeed, this now seems more or less certain, the newscaster tells us, with a noticeably congratulatory tone to his voice. Just three days before we are supposed to pay, the Minister of Finance is interviewed and says that there will be no postponement, he has never mentioned such a thing, nor does he see why he should be obliged to deny any old rumour as soon as it starts circulating, even if it has been given credence by the public broadcasting network. People should never imagine anything has changed until he personally announces it has. And it hasn't. There will be absolutely no concessions to anybody, and people who don't file their returns inside the deadline will be fined in the regular fashion.

My accountant is thus in a state of desperation when I finally see him at nine in the evening the very day of the deadline. Out come all the invoices, the registers. His fingers incessantly tap the three-zeros button that distinguishes Italian calculators. As usual, I understand little of what he is saying about the various deductions available to me. I notice in my instruction book that if my wife was dependent on me I could reduce my taxable income by a splendid 120,000 Lire, or sixty pounds, and when I have a child I will be able to reduce it by a whole 48,000 Lire, twenty-four pounds.

Yet despite this evident meanness (there is no child benefit here), I am always surprised at how little I have to pay. 'First,' the accountant says briskly, 'we reduce your income by 14 per cent. Now, let's see.' Fourteen per cent! Why? 'Because in the category you fall into, or rather that we have chosen to put you into, taxable income is reduced by 14 per cent, which is considered to be your expenses. If the category were different, the reduction would be different. As would the percentage of national insurance you have to pay, and so on.'

When finally we get to the end of the whole business, it turns out the government actually owes me money. Which I can expect to be refunded in about four to five years' time, the accountant remarks. 'But you definitely will be re-funded. With a modest interest. And it's always welcome when it comes, isn't it?' We finish towards eleven. The accountant has a whole stack of completed forms to be delivered to an office at the station which remains open until midnight the day of the deadline.

Then the following week the Minister of Finance calmly announces that, although he didn't postpone the deadline for filing returns, there will now be an amnesty for those who didn't get them in on time. They have until 14 June. Another two weeks. Perhaps the *fiaccolata* and the power of prayer are not entirely to be overlooked.

33
Mamma!!!

Given their enthusiasm for children, it will at first seem curious that Italians produce so few of them. Lara is an only child. Marta, the daughter of the mongol-looking cleaning woman is an only child. The woman with the twig broom has a little nephew who visits and at age six rushes up and down Via Colombare on a tiny motorbike with two-stroke engine making an awful racket. He is an only child. Many of my adult students have just one child. If they have any at all. The population is expected to fall by two or three million before the end of the millenium. Only in the house next to the cadaverous old lady does a very jolly *signora* have three children, all daughters. 'How many girls', claims an article in the newspaper, 'owe their existence to the elusive quest for a male child!'

It's interesting that those who prefer vegetable gardens to dwarf cypresses and do not clean too obsessionally, or have their blood pressure checked with fanatical regularity, tend to be those who produce more than one child. Again much seems to depend on the family's relationship to the rural past, the extent to which they are influenced by the general clamouring for security. For children are so expensive. They must be provided for from start to finish. First a gynaecologist *di fiducia* must be found, and then a paediatrician *di fiducia*. The little ones must spend their summers in *pensioni* or second homes by the sea to breathe the iodine, in winter they must go to the mountains to escape the fog. Very probably they will have to attend a Church rather than a state nursery, paying more. Then perhaps a private school, of which there are many. Everything they have must be new. Who would buy a second-hand pram or cot for their dear little child? Who would buy anything but the most expensive leather shoes for their toddler? And it will be a costly business sending heir or heiress to university, for this takes an absolute minimum of four years, usually much much longer, and there are no grants. Anyway the child will have a *fidanzata* or *fidanzato* by then, and very probably the family will have to buy them a flat, since they can't marry before they have been bought a flat, can they? And all the furniture. And all the appliances. Nor would it be wise for them to marry until family contacts, or personal prowess, have secured them a steady job. In the local area. It's a major undertaking.

'We didn't have another child', Orietta tells a rather bitter Lara, 'because it wouldn't have been fair to you. How could we have given you everything you need?'

Mamma!!!

A certain Antonio and Sabrina come to talk to Lucilla about the possibility of buying our flat. Their voices boom in the hallway. They now have jobs in the Banca Popolare di Verona in town. But they can't get married until they have bought a flat. And when they buy a flat it must be within walking distance of his parents. They have been looking for more than a year. Via Colombare would be ideal. Antonio's father is with them. A gruff dialect voice. Money isn't a problem, he says, and promises 'all in cash'.

The Veronese don't usually look for cheap 'first homes' as the English do. Indeed, the very notion of first and second is in naked contradiction to the word home, isn't it? Because a home is for always, for keeps. Looking for a 'first home' would thus be as absurd as looking for a 'first wife'. And while one might eventually fall out with one's wife and desire to change her, it's extremely unlikely that one would ever want to change one's home. Only a bomb could shift the people in Via Colombare from theirs. No, you protect your home with iron railings, remote-controlled gates, shock-resistant glass, armoured doors and locking shutters. It's your palace, your bunker, your life sentence. Even the modern Giampaolo will never leave Via Colombare, although his company has offered him positions in Rome and New York. For where would Orietta be without the marble and ceramics she has polished so often? The carefully chosen bathroom porcelain. '*Aggràppati al mattone*,' says a character in Natalia Ginzburg's, *La casa e la città*, when her brother announces he intends to sell his flat: 'Cling on to the bricks.'

The upshot is that most of the people buying in Montecchio are youngsters being eased (regretfully) out of the old nest (to a place not too far down the road).

Antonio's gruff father will pay a fortune to sort out his child. While he himself lives in a decrepit cave of a place off the main square. Because this is what parents must do for their children.

Understandably then, the people at the prenatal course we go to in town are all at their first child. And their last, is the general consensus. For the most part they are reserved and serious. Veronese. A poster shows a pregnant beauty in flimsy, fashionable nightdress looking out of a window into some spiritual distance of motherhood and self-realisation, the faintest smile on her face. On the wall opposite, a smaller photograph shows the blood and gore of birth itself. There is a crucifix of course, although I haven't spied a Madonna yet, which is odd.

An attractive woman social worker arrives and, sitting on a stool, discusses at length all the clothes we must prepare for the *esserino* when he arrives. She smiles constantly as she talks and a relentless use of diminutives generates a warm, cosy feeling in her audience. It's something I'm going to have to get used to over the next few years: *la gambina, la testina, il braccino, il piedino, le manine, i ditini, la boccucia, le spallucce, i ginocchietti, il nasino, il sederino*; and then the clothes: *la tutina, le scarpine, il vestitino, i guantini, il maglioncino, il giubbottino, i pantaloncini* . . . Together they create an overwhelming impression of lovable tininess to be cuddled and coddled and kissed and tweeked and generally thoroughly and triumphantly spoilt.

The previous evening we had seen a news programme showing Italian sailors setting off for their UN mission to Beirut. The camera zoomed in on a young southern boy weeping his heart out at the rail as his ship pulled away.

And it didn't take a lip reader to hear what he was screaming to that crowd on the dock. '*Mammaaaaa! Mammaaaaa!*' His face was broken up with fierce emotion. '*Mammina!*' In a way it's wonderful, this lack of shame.

And when we come out of the prenatal course at nine o'clock, full of warm feelings about our child to be, there are young conscript soldiers everywhere, monopolising the phones in the main square in an attempt to get a call through to *Mamma* before they have to return to their barracks. Verona is a big army town with two major barracks. One of these is out on the road to Montecchio, so that our bus going home is packed despite the hour. And the same boys who, five minutes ago, were desperately trying to get through to their mums are now rowdy and rough, jostling the one or two Montecchio girls on the bus, hoping perhaps to find the future mamma of their own only child. But the girls won't answer back. There seems to be a kind of rule that the locals will have nothing to do with the soldiers.

'Signor Tino, Signora Rita!' As our key clunks, Lucilla emerges from her door in a state of some excitement. She's in the pink brushed nylon dressing-gown, her television grinding out its variety show behind her. Do we know, she shouts, can we for one moment imagine, what Signora Marta has just done? Obviously we cannot. Do we know what she had the brazen cheek to do this very afternoon? No, it's beyond us. She telephoned, she telephoned to suggest that they both give up the court case, sell the flat and go halves on the money.

'*O Dio!*' Rita says coolly. I close my eyes. This is it. Eviction.

'It means she's guilty!' Lucilla is winding herself up into

her usual semi-hysteria. 'Guilty, guilty, guilty! It means she knows she can never win in court. Because the flat is mine. It's mine. It was built with my money and the *professore* left it to me, if only they hadn't destroyed his will. *È mio, mio, mio!*'

If she switched some of the time and resources presently allocated to cleaning to dental care, it would be much easier to talk to Lucilla at moments like this.

'So what did you do?' Rita asks.

I hold my breath.

'*Le ho detto mai* – never. *Mai mai mai mai*. Because she is evil. *Maligna! Una carogna!*'

And we are safe again. You can rely on Lucilla.

Upstairs my *frate indovino* tells me that I must be 'parsimonious with hatred', as hatred nourishes itself with my blood, my hopes , my life. I also notice that every single page of the calendar carries an ad for a book called '*Cara Mamma . . .*' written by none other than the *frate indovino* himself. On the page for May it says:

'Looking for a present for your sweetheart and mother-to-be . . . why not give her the fantastic, CARA MAMMA . . . It's worth more than any gold ring . . . and it costs much less.'

34
Giugno

The month of June is breathtaking, mainly because of the poppies. The corn stands thick in the broad fields of the *pianura*, or bristles in undulating strips between rows of cherry trees and vines up on the hills. It is light green at first, turning a duller, denser colour through May as it grows. Until, with the first truly hot days around the beginning of June, the green is suddenly transformed into a sizzling carpet of red, laid by some magical hand (while you were having your siesta it seems) to usher in the summer. It's quite overwhelming. We walk for hours up the valley to absorb field after field of it. Or we cycle southwards into the plain. The dazzling, dazzling red stretches majestically away, waving above the corn, miragelike, desperately intense, seductive, screaming life as colours will.

Giuliano and Girolamo are not impressed. It's a great pity these scientists haven't found a good spray to get the poppies without damaging the corn, they say. Or I think they say. I can never be 100 per cent sure I have understood these two old farmers. We find them up on the hill with their tractor, dousing the cherry trees one last time before harvest. The marginally younger Girolamo is at the wheel, steering between the terraces; bent forward at 45°, Giuliano stumbles along beside him. From a tank trailed behind the tractor, clouds of filthy-smelling chemicals steam up into thick foliage where here and there ripe cherries peep. I ask Girolamo how he measures the dosages he's giving. He shrugs his shoulders. He just sprays a lot, he says. They need a lot of spray to keep the maggots out. He comes down with us to mix the next tankload in the farmyard and it's clear he does so *ad occhio*, by guesswork. I remind myself I must tell the ecological Giampaolo just to see him shake his head. Giampaolo has now collected a huge number of snails from our sad lettuce patch and imprisoned them in a bucket with a pane of glass on top, but can't decide if it's worth the effort to wash and eat them.

Ciliegge avelenate – Poisoned Cherries – proclaim crudely daubed notices in all the orchards from Montecchio to Mizzole, trying to scare off scavengers by warning of noxious spraying. From the sound of giggling children in the leaves, the ruse would appear to be no more effective than the empty tin cans and strips of plastic strung up against the birds. *Ciliegge avelenate* – when Rita points it out, I am delighted to notice that the dialect-speaking locals have no better grasp of the use of double letters than I do. It should be, *ciliege avvelenate*.

Bepi doesn't stock cherries in his shop, because everybody, he says, either has a tree in their garden or steals
from the orchards. As usual, his reflection comes complete
with a tone and expression which suggest his disillusionment at the local situation (beneath contempt) and his
confidence that he is smart enough to keep a step ahead all
the same. Indeed, very few of the shops sell cherries. The
farmers, it seems, mostly export their fruit to Austria and
Germany. They have quotas to meet and the harvest was
bad this year, thanks to that late flurry of snow. With the
result that, despite all these hills upon hills of orchards, I
personally end up eating very few cherries indeed. There
are none at Via Colombare 10 of course, because fruit trees
are very much a peasant thing, not part of a city person's
garden . . .

'How long is it now?' the woman with the twig broom
rushes out to ask, as we return from a shopping expedition. Everyone wants to talk to Rita. There is a ground swell
of solidarity which rises with the curve of her belly. We are
just a few yards from where the Madonnina is clutching
her own son. Beside the statue, a notice has gone up to tell
us the name of the builder who will be converting the
orchard behind into terraced housing. Like all notices in
Italy it gives the reference number, section and paragraph
of whatever law it is sanctions whatever is being
announced.

'Another two weeks,' Rita says. 'Election day more or
less.'

This stout *zitella*'s brow knits as she thinks and calcu-
lates. 'The full moon won't be until a week after that. The
third I think.'

I smile politely.

Lucilla and Vittorina are disappointed because they are going to be away. Their annual holiday. They have us over to say goodbye and show us photographs of a multi-storied modern hotel on the Adriatic coast north of Venice where they go every year. No more those magnificent adventures – Vienna, Prague – with *il professore*. Lucilla's wistful face is clownish this evening behind approximate make-up. The photo shows miles of beach and the usual evenly spaced rows of brilliant sunshades, ten deep, all the same green and purple pattern, like soldiers on parade. 'The sea air is so good for one's pressure,' Lucilla is confiding to Rita. 'That's why we go.' Vittorina, with her rather dazed post-ictus expression and ever thinning hair, manages a faint, squeaky laugh, twisting her mouth. 'Lucilla only goes for the men,' she croaks. 'Sitting in the bar chatting up men in the evening. And wearing her bikini on the beach naturally.' The image is so bizarre one would like to ask for confirmation. But how? Far from chiding her sister-in-law, Lucilla grins a grin of unqualified self-satisfaction. She has invested a lot in this image of herself as *femme fatale*. She and Vittorina are a good act.

But on popping downstairs to enquire of Giampaolo whether I can start opening my *prosecco* bottles yet, it is to find the Visentinis seriously concerned. And precisely about the question of Lucilla and Vittorina's holiday. Because, yes, sea air is good for high blood pressure, since the atmospherics tend to lower it, so the sea suits Lucilla and always has, but it is most definitely *controindicato*, i.e., a bad idea, for low blood pressure, which is Vittorina's more serious problem. Vittorina should really go to the mountains, since atmospherics there tend to raise pressure. Orietta can't understand why the doctor, who came today, hasn't explained this to them. There is general agreement that the man just takes his money and runs.

For a while voices are urgent and low. Giampaolo and Orietta see the situation as posing a real moral dilemma. Ought they to go and enlighten the two women, encourage them to change destination, at the risk of merely making Vittorina anxious without actually convincing Lucilla, who always has the last word and is very eager to go to the sea and talk volubly to bronzed widowers on deckchairs? Or should they leave be and let the women have their fun, despite concern that the climate could bring on the notoriously fatal second stroke? Really, it was up to the doctor to talk to them about this . . .

Forgetting my *prosecco*, I get drawn into a discussion about the Visentini's own holiday, still to be settled. And, like every Montecchio conversation on the subject, it soon develops into a rehearsal of the pros and cons of the invigorating mountains, the enervating sea. For any other destination is just too hot in holidaytime when factories and offices close. Only a foreigner, for example, would visit Florence or Rome in August, or embark on some walking tour of Tuscany.

Giampaolo declares himself for the mountains, the cool air, the great unspoilt panoramas, the brisk walks, the modern man's righteous ecological pride when he doesn't throw away a sandwich wrapper but tucks it back in his knapsack. Orietta is for the sea and lazy days under a sunshade which will never bring on her heart murmur, copies of her favourite women's magazines, evening barbecues with other members of the holiday village, in Puglia, Calabria, beneath palm trees. Lara just begs and begs to be sent somewhere else, anywhere, on some camp or something, it doesn't matter, so long as she can go on holiday without the family. But Orietta would worry too much.

In the end, as it turns out, Orietta will get her way on all fronts. Giampaolo will go to the travel agency at the last minute in a calculated piece of brinkmanship, hoping to pick up a cut-price place in an undersubscribed holiday village, a cancellation with any luck. Then, doing everything at the same time as they always do, he and twenty million other Italians will load the car in early August to face a seven-hundred kilometre drive in blazing sunshine with miles of tailbacks at every toll booth. But at least the expedition will justify the twin carburettor . . .

Bepi scorns them all, these provincials. For his first holiday since he set up shop, he goes off to the Seychelles. Where he meets more Italian greengrocers than he does at the market of a morning. Paradoxically, he seems quite pleased about this. He has made some useful contacts. New suppliers. Sheep's cheese from a distributor in Lessinia. And, on returning, he asks me to translate a letter for a friend he made there who wants to get in touch with a native girl he fell in love with. The letter is touchingly ingenuous, swearing the writer's determination to go back next year. Bepi seems very eager for me to finish it. His big burly presence and bright green eyes are extraordinary somehow against the funereal backdrop of Patuzzi's bookcase. I tap it out for him: the girl's beauty, their unending love. He watches the letters appear in sickly yellow on my processor screen. Is English the language he will have to learn to speak to girls? Somehow I already know he will not go back.

And, no, you can't open those bottles yet, Giampaolo

says, when I go down to ask him again. Not for another three weeks. There is an element of masochism about it, a casting about for virtue and self-esteem. His *dipendente*'s long-suffering life. If he just bought the stuff from the shop, he wouldn't have to survive this two-month period without. But having decided to bottle his own – because then it's the real thing, alive, not pasteurized and dead on a supermarket shelf – he will never go out and buy a case or so to tide him over. It's a point of honour. And he's rather disappointed when I do. Only to savour the difference when ours is ready, I tell him.

35
Elezioni

It is as summer gets into full swing that you are reminded you are living in a foreign country. A strange breed of wasps, more than an inch long, have made their nest in the eaves above our balcony and will occasionally whirr into the flat causing intense alarm. Opposite the church we see a snake, head held high, sliding rapidly along the wall of the flood-emergency dike. Typing away on *il professore*'s desk, I become aware that a baby lizard has come in through the french window and is soaking up the sunshine on the tiles by my feet. Outside, freed from their winter covers, lemon and orange trees flourish again in tubs by lowly back doors shrouded with bead curtains against the flies.

Meanwhile, Montecchio is being made ugly by preparations for the forthcoming general and local elections. It even seems possible that our child could be born right on polling day, although what kind of omen this might be I don't know. The local council erects long lines of ramshackle scaffolding outside the church and in the main square. These are then hung with laminated billboards rusting with age, thus giving the political parties free advertising space. At least fifty metres of scaffolding and sheet metal are required just to make sure that every party will get a look in. For, of course, there are many.

It was my first Italian general election and, despite the imminent domestic upheaval, I was eager to get a handle on the political life of my adopted country. I read all the editorials in national and local newspapers, I spoke about it to everybody I knew, I went to meetings in the local library. I thus passed from confusion, to disbelief, to further confusion, and, ultimately, a quiescent state of total disillusionment. Which I have maintained ever since.

Of course, every nation is disillusioned with its politicians. Everybody is half aware that a politician can never represent the people who voted for him, for the simple reason that anybody who stands for election is fundamentally different from the mass of people who don't. And if he isn't when he decides to stand, he most certainly will be once elected. The idea of a representative parliament is a pipedream. However, in the other countries I have lived in, one is at least left with the consolation of choosing between, if not different ideologies, then at least different emphases. This party will spend more, this less, this party believes in social security, this doesn't, etc. etc. So that elections can be expected to focus (reductively perhaps, but usefully) around some issue like, should we give more money to the health service, should we possess nuclear weapons, and so on. There is also the government's record. The governing party has done this, this and this. Do you like it, or don't you? Italian elections have none of this refreshing naïvety.

In the early days – heady May and the first half of June – most comment in the newspapers and on TV seemed to be concentrated on which member of the five-party coalition had been responsible for bringing the government down and provoking these early elections. Given that the public generally perceives elections as a great evil (if only because the squares are cluttered with scaffolding, and the TV monopolised by dull talk shows), this is a matter of some importance. Apportioning blame could prove a potentially effective weapon.

So, were the Socialists right to vote against such and such a clause of such and such a bill (usually something quite obscure)? Were the Christian Democrats right to insist on this clause and make it an issue of confidence when they knew the Socialists would vote against it and the Liberals abstain? Why did the Republican Party minister attack a government policy he had just subscribed to in a cabinet meeting? Why wouldn't the Social Democrats agree with the others as to who should be chairman of some bank or TV network? And so it goes on. Blame is never effectively apportioned. In the eyes of your average Montecchiese they are all responsible. They become responsible the moment they are elected. And anyway it wouldn't have mattered if such and such a clause of such a bill had been passed, since everybody would have ignored it just the same.

'The Socialists, a Modern Party for a Modern Italy' –

Bettino Craxi, their leader, is pictured with somebody behind him working on a computer. Despite the fact that their emblem is a carnation, the Socialists are using green posters this year to steal a march on the Greens. Who have unfortunately split into the Rainbow Greens and the Smiling Sun Greens and are arguing heatedly about who was responsible. 'A New Role for Women in a Fair Society', says the Communists' poster. But will it cut much ice in *la strada delle zitelle*?

All in all, there is a curious lack of imagination about this advertising. Especially given the Italians' usual verve and flare for such things. A weariness. As if none of it really mattered. 'Working toward a United Europe', boasts the Christian Democratic Party. But then so, if we're to take them at their word, are the Social Democrats. The Republicans trumpet their 'Honesty and Integrity', clearly hinting what everybody already knows, that the others have neither. But then do the Republicans? And is it what people want? The Movimento Sociale, inheritors of the fascist tradition, think it is. 'Firm Government and an End to Corruption', they proclaim. Well, it's a step forward from the '*Credere, Ubbidire, Combattere!*' – 'Believe, Obey, Fight!' – of their predecessors, a motto still provocatively visible under a thin coat of whitewash on the town hall of a nearby village. 'The Right Choice', say the Liberals about themselves, feeling that no further explanation is necessary. Or perhaps possible. 'Towards a Real Alternative', plead the Communists, their hammer and sickle reduced to a sixpence. 'Stability, Prosperity', thunder back the Christian Democrats, making much of their own emblem of the Crusader's red cross on a white shield. Well, who would ever argue with stability and prosperity?

In the end you have to turn to the extremist fringes to get any hint of policies. 'Rome = Mafia = Taxes', says the slogan of the separatist Liga Veneta. And another poster warns: 'Bringing Blacks to the Veneto = Slavery'. Obviously somebody has a penchant for perverse equations. At the other extreme, the Democratic Proletarian Party wants 'Nuclear Weapons Out Now'. The Pensioners' Party demands social justice for the elderly. Predictable stuff. The Radical Party, splendidly idealistic as ever, proclaims: 'No to World Famine.'

Responsible modern-man Giampaolo Visentini is thus profoundly depressed. 'They don't even bother trying to hoodwink us any more,' he observes. Bepi just snorts. He won't talk about it. It's too ridiculous. In the *sanitaria*, herbalist Maria Grazia's husband thunders for the Liga, the separatists. There are too many *meridionali* moving into the area. Have I heard that they're setting up yet another cooperative to build houses for themselves in Mizzole? Have I? With that and the new high-security prison going up next to the barracks, we'll have the Mafia here in no time. Amusingly, work on the prison is stopped the following week because it's discovered that the contractors involved paid bribes to politicians to get the job. A student of mine tells me she was a Democratic Proletarian activist once, but then she realised they were just the same as all the others.

Meanwhile, the debate on TV has switched to the technical question of whether parties should declare their allegiances *vis-à-vis* other parties before the election, so that people know what kind of coalition they are voting for. This is an age-old Christian Democrat ploy to have people suspect that the Socialists might desert the present government to form an alliance with the Communists after the election. Which would be the end of everything, of course. The Socialists insist that each party must simply present its policies and that is that. Whereas so far nobody has presented any. The Communists accuse the Church of using the pulpit to encourage people to vote Christian Democrat. The smaller parties try to have us all imagine that behind the scenes Christian Democrats and Communists are planning to get together and change the electoral system in such a way as to exclude all the others. There is an enormous amount of talking, much of it deployed about the furthest outposts of comprehensibility, and absolutely no debate. Nobody mentions interest rates, or inflation, or unemployment, or defence spending, or levels of housebuilding, or anything that might remotely have any bearing on day-to-day life. Nobody presents a programme or manifesto. As for the government's record, it is never considered, since each party in the coalition always claims that the other members were responsible for everything bad. Oddly, there are no opinion polls, no suggestion that things are running one way or another. If I could vote, I reflect, I would have absolutely no idea who to vote for.

Election day finally comes around. The baby is due now, but lying doggo. We wake to a perfect Sunday morning and hear the radio reminding the population that it's not just a right, but a duty to vote. They must get along to their polling station before dashing off to swim at the lake or picnic in the mountains. They mustn't let the election be won by apathy and indifference. 'And if you really can't vote today, remember that you have the right to take time off work to vote tomorrow morning. Up to two o'clock.'

The amount of concern suggests fears of an abysmal turnout. Which I would find only too understandable. We shall see.

Being a dutiful citizen, Rita sets off to vote. Who for, I have no idea. We follow the dusty road over the first and second bridges where people take the corners so courageously. The car park is full for early Mass. Six girls pass us on three bicycles. In each case the passenger stands on the saddle with her hands on the shoulders of the rider. One has an ice-lolly in her mouth, another a cigarette. The vines are stretching their tendrils across the pergola of the Bar Centrale in Piazza Buccari, where Moreno the halfwit, in deerstalker hat despite the heat, is cadging cigarettes and being gently mocked by men reading *La Gazzetta dello Sport*. And it's only half past eight. One learns to rise early here to get the best of the day.

We arrive at the other end of the village where the local school has been closed for the last three days to prepare it as a polling station. Although it's difficult to imagine why so much time was needed. In the main entrance, a computer printout has each person's name and, for some reason, their profession. There is an obsession about categorising people by profession. You then go to vote in one of a variety of classrooms, and in each classroom there are two *scrutatori* or observers. Not surprisingly, these are mainly the children of local bigwigs, glad to pick up the 80,000 Lire they get for their services. In the booth, you put a cross over the emblem of the party you want, and then, if you like, the name of one of the many many people who are standing for that party. Each constituency returns a number of deputies, and each party can offer a whole range of possible choices to fill those positions. Which means you can vote for someone in some particular faction of your chosen party, or for the man who has already done you a favour. Or is going to if he gets in. It makes counting terribly complicated.

Curiously absent from the whole process is any real suspense *vis-à-vis* the result. The evening news offers no 'swingometers', no eager experts discussing marginal states or constituencies, no surveys taken of people leaving polling stations. This is partly because the quite extreme system of proportional representation removes any see-saw effect. A swing of 5 per cent means nothing more than a swing of 5 per cent. Not the difference between one government and another. And anyway no such swings are likely to occur. Perhaps 2 or 3 per cent will leave this party, but only to disperse among five or six others. Perhaps at the end of the day one party will have crept forward the few points required to shout victory. But, in the main, the status quo will be left untouched. For the truth is that, disillusioned as they are, most Italians will always get out there and vote for the same party they always have. The football supporter mentality, Giampaolo calls it: 'You stay with them even when they're losing every game and charging you more to watch every time.'

Thus, despite the carefully deployed anxiety of the public broadcasting service before the event, and despite the fact that so many people hold residency and thus voting rights in cities far away from where they live, the turnout is a huge 90 per cent. This truly amazes me, and I bully everybody I know to try and extort some satisfactory explanation. To no avail. A love of secrecy, writing down the name of a friend of a friend in the polling booth perhaps? A residual concern that not voting might prejudice one's position in some *concorso* to become a teacher, or caretaker (Vittorina and Lucilla were both unaccountably worried about missing the election)? Genuine fear of a Communist government? Or perhaps – and it's the explanation I would plump for – perhaps, despite all disillusionment, a very profound, heartfelt satisfaction with the way things are and a determination that they should remain so. I plump for it because it has the hallmark of that profound schizophrenia, which is also the charm, of all matters Italian: the Pope adored and ignored, the law admired and flouted, politicians despised and re-elected. The gulf between officialdom's façade and private thought could not be greater than it is here. But in the secret of the ballot box that façade is always supported. Nothing changes. Italy, one sometimes thinks, is as if frozen in the high noon of its post-war prosperity.

I played a little game with my students on our last lesson of the year. I suggested they write down who they think their barber/hairdresser votes for and why. Normally responsive and fun to teach, my request left them non-plussed, diffident, reticent. It was as if one had asked some ancient Athenian to explain the Eleusinian mysteries. A completely taboo subject. Montecchio, in the event, returned the Christian Democrats with the usual 70 per cent of the vote, but I have yet to meet anyone here who will speak well of the party. 'The only good thing about elections' – Bepi deigned to mention the subject over an *espresso* with grappa at eight in the morning – 'is that the results are so complicated that for a month and more afterwards there's no government at all. And so for a while, *non possono rompere le palle!*' Which loosely translated means, They can't get on our fannies.

'If the country', comments *il frate indovino*, ear perfectly tuned to the popular mood, 'could buy politicians for what they're really worth and then sell them for what they claim they're worth, it could pay off its deficit in no time at all.'

Doubtless our witty priest votes Christian Democrat.

36
La luna

The baby was late. Rita was finding the heat and summer *afa* oppressive. We bought a fan and she sat at her typewriter in a stream of dusty air. When the Visentini got to know, Orietta felt it her duty to come upstairs and warn us that fans were *controindicati*. You sweated, then sat in the air from the fan, and inevitably caught a cold. She was also worried that we hadn't got rid of our cat. Cats could cause all kinds of diseases when one had a little baby in the house. I often wonder if perhaps Italian houses of the future won't be designed with some sort of disinfectant footbath in the entrance way. We liked our cat.

Meanwhile, whenever I bumped into anyone in Via Colombare an eyebrow would be raised. Any news yet? If there's anything I can do . . . Even the mechanic at the end

312

of the street, smelling strongly of grappa after lunch as always, was in the know. Did I want my car looking over before the all-important trip? The last thing I needed was a breakdown on the way to the hospital . . . I thanked him and got filters, plugs and points changed at a very reasonable price. '*Buon giorno Signor Teem,*' said old Marini's wife 'and how is your *signora* this morning?'

What a far cry from the kind of reception I had been getting a year before! Clearly, I thought, a child is the ultimate passport to society here, a blank cheque to draw against vast reserves of Latin sentiment. Far from having my greetings rejected, I now had the opposite problem of having to discuss the relative merits of the various local hospitals with the vaguely mongol-looking woman, while the woman with the twig broom came to clap me on the back and tell ghastly stories about the gynaecologists at Borgo Roma where her sister-in-law had given birth. '*Macellai*', she insisted. 'Butchers. They jump on your belly to push the child out.' And she asked who would be coming in to look after me while my wife was away at the hospital. I wondered for a moment if I had understood this correctly.

'*Chi ti cucinerà?*'

'Nobody, I can manage myself.'

She shook her head, whether in admiration, or despair at a changing world, I don't know. '*Troppo bravo, troppo bravo*', she said. 'You English are so tough.' And she added by way of valediction: 'The full moon will be the night of the third.'

Inspired by the consultant gynaecologist who gave our prenatal course, we have decided to go to his hospital in the small town of Zevio. He appears to be the only consultant in the Italian state system practising the Leboyer method. Or so he says. Obviously, we've driven over there once or twice to check out the route: fifteen miles of twisting country roads, with the last stretch, unfortunately, being resurfaced and hence bumpy as hell. A useful stimulant perhaps, but also another complicating factor in that delicate equation: when to set off. We time the trip at thirty minutes. Getting out of the car to stretch our legs, we find a sleepy, overgrown village with a truly vast main square, in the middle of which is a villa-cum-castle surrounded by a moat. The rest of this inexplicably huge open area is just a desert of asphalt crisscrossed by fading white lines indicating where five or six roads might intersect. On Sundays, we discovered on our second trip, the space is packed to suffocation point with a bustling provincial market selling cheap clothes, fruit, vegetables, and adventurous underwear of mammoth proportions, presumably for ladies like Lucilla. The traffic was backed up for a kilometre and more. Another factor then, is that one must not go into labour on a Sunday morning.

The hot days drag on. We sit under the pergola at Centro Primo Maggio listening to the accordion. People with houses by the streams hang water-melons in the water to keep them cool. They're too big for the fridge. Despite the predictable election results, the politicians, as Bepi predicted, have so far been unable to come up with a government. Nobody's concerned. The shops begin to close as everybody goes off on holiday. There are the usual scandals about poor old people having to walk miles in suffocating heat to find a grocery open. By law, shops are obliged to run a rota system, but the fines are so small they tend to ignore the problem. You go to the post office and find it closes for the afternoon in July and August. There is alarmist talk about the unavailability of doctors in hospitals. We begin to get nervous.

And then the big day arrives at last. Or rather night. Towards two in the morning the terms of the equation are finally and ruthlessly satisfied: fierce contractions. We bundle into our despised orange car and head south across the *bassa* to Zevio. We're about half-way – San Martino, Campalto, Mambrotta – driving along roads that twist and turn unaccountably through perfectly flat countryside, when, over a distant dike, what should sail up into the sky but the moon, a perfectly round, splendid, shining white moon, full as full can be, and apparently drawing us to Zevio as the natal star to Bethlehem. How infuriating! I can just see the satisfied smirk on the face of our lady of the twig broom. Even Giampaolo will consider it as confirmation of his *prosecco*-bottling technique. Yet one feels strangely satisfied to see it too. *La luna*. So bright! So large! We speed on through field after field of silvery peach orchards under that presageful ghostliness lunar light tends to have, especially at important moments in your life. And it does cross my mind for a moment that perhaps the moon has more influence in Italy than it does back home. This would explain so much.

The Chiarenzi hospital in Zevio has long corridors paved with cheap black stone. The porter gives a direction with his thumb, barely looking away from a TV screen. In a spare room, a nurse with nun's headgear takes down the details. Then more corridors. At the entrance to the maternity ward a little waiting area is heaped with flowers and there is a small white statue of the Madonna. One gets to rely on her after a while: that simple passivity, absorbing all, at crossroads, hospital wards, cemeteries. Although somehow, through her very ubiquitousness, the quiescent figure becomes not so much a protecting presence as a reminder that, whatever happens, all will go on as before. Without her and her crucified son, usually much smaller and hidden away by some dusty central-heating pipe near the ceiling, you might imagine that what was happening to you here and now was unique, and desperately important.

Rather surprisingly, I find myself wondering if the Madonna doesn't have some quality in common with the moon.

In the ward, a bright young nurse speaks to us in dialect and listens to the baby's heartbeat through a wooden trumpet pressed against Rita's belly. Interestingly, she is called Stefania, which is the name we have chosen if the baby is a girl. Which no doubt it will be. I'm pretty well resigned to that now. Not that I in any way mind having a girl. On the contrary. What could be more delightful than a little girl? Just that I had hoped the Via Colombare influence would not be confirmed. I'd far rather have a random world than a determinist one, however benevolent.

We spend the night in a tiny room with Rita in labour and me fighting sleep. Enticingly, there's a *pasticceria* right across the street which will surely open at seven o'clock. Shortly after dawn, while a crow sits on a branch not a yard away, a priest leads four men carrying a rough wooden coffin out of the hospital into the street. I decide not to remark on this to Rita. And when a light goes on in the *pasticceria* around eight o'clock, I selfishly hurry out for a *cappuccino*, only to hear that the bar is closed for holidays. The man has merely come to do some decorating work.

And the *pasticceria* the other side of the village is always closed Monday mornings. A test of the extent of your Italianisation is whether you still grind your teeth when you hear that something is closed.

In the event, the low lights and soft music of the Leboyer method have to be forgotten because that room is already occupied. 'Full moon', explains the nurse. 'Haven't had a birth for a week and then six in a single night.' OK, OK, I give in. But the baby, when it finally shows up, is a big bouncy boy. We are both delighted.

The first duty of an Italian father is to buy a rosette, blue for a boy, pink for a girl, and stick it on some highly visible part of his house. Driving home that day, I found a *tabaccheria* in San Martino that sold me one for what seemed a rather expensive 10,000 Lire. The lady at the till was desperately eager to engage me in conversation about the joys of parenthood: '*Sì, sì, sì*, a great change in your life, you can't even imagine yet,' she says excitedly as I walk out in a daze without my receipt. Back in Via Colombare I taped the thing high on the front door of number 10 and hoped that all the *zitelle* in the street would see it immediately and eat their hearts out.

My second duty was to find two witnesses and take them along to register the birth. Since public offices are only open in the morning, this would have to wait till the following day. Giampaolo and Orietta were more than happy to help me out, and we set off early next morning so he wouldn't be too late for work.

Registration had to be in the village of birth, so it was back along the winding road to Zevio again. The *comune* was a baroque *palazzo* in the huge main square where traffic crisscrossed with impressive confidence across the open asphalt. At the top of flights of eighteenth-century stairs, a huge room with ornate ceiling and a long wooden counter was occupied by just two women toying with computers.

The man who registered births was out for a minute, they said. Could we wait?

I generally accept this kind of thing now. But Giampaolo looked at his watch. 'We'll give him five minutes,' he said ominously. As with his behaviour over Negretti and his dogs, phoning the police at the drop of a hat, I was surprised by his immediately tough, legalistic, although always reasonable approach. 'We have come to a public office', he told the women calmly. 'There is no queue, and hence no reason why we shouldn't be dealt with immediately.' Orietta tugged at his elbow. 'Giampaolo!' she muttered.

But after five minutes Giampaolo again politely demanded to be served. The younger of the women, lavishly if not seductively made up, fashionably if not attractively dressed, said the man couldn't possibly be much longer. Giampaolo asked where he was. The girl flustered. Nobody had registered a birth for a week or so, she said. And then they were so pushed still with the aftermath of the elections. Surely we could understand that? But if we were really in a hurry then she would try to handle the matter herself. Her voice echoed petulantly in the big room, designed, presumably, for nobler purposes. A great chandelier gathered dust above a VDU. The lighting was fluorescent.

We were in a hurry, Giampaolo said. We had come early because he had to get to work. People noticed, he remarked pointedly, when he was absent.

The girl, clearly resentful of the fact that her colleague

hadn't budged, came over to the counter, pulled a huge book out from a drawer beneath and asked us for our documents: Giampaolo's, Orietta's, my own. But when she saw the British passport she shook her head. Was I the father? She couldn't possibly take it upon herself to register a foreigner's birth. And she turned to the older woman: 'Do we have any special conventions with England?' The other didn't know. I suggested that the conventions would be the same as for all EC countries. 'Is England a member of the EC?' the girl asked her colleague. '*Credo di sì,*' came a monotone response. But the girl shook her head all the same. We would just have to wait for *il responsabile*.

'But where is he?' Giampaolo returned to the offensive. 'We have no intention of waiting here all morning.'

The girl looked to the woman behind for support. This dusty creature said sourly: 'Running an errand at the hospital.' And she wouldn't look up from her keyboard.

'Ring him up.'

My neighbour, I was discovering, had the disturbingly professional belligerence of somebody who not only knows when to pick a fight but is also perfectly confident of how he is going to go about winning it.

The two hesitated.

Giampaolo announced: 'This is a public service. The office is obliged to have somebody present who can register births. It is now officially open. You have admitted the man is not ill. At this point I am left with no alternative but to *sporgere una denuncia*' (i.e., report the matter to the police).

We had only been waiting ten minutes. It seemed perfectly normal to me.

'Giampaolo!' Orietta protested *sotto voce*.

Turning to us, the usually wooden Giampaolo grinned broadly and whispered: 'The man's in the bar. You'll see. He's having his breakfast.'

At the word '*denuncia*' the two women, rather than protesting or growing more hostile, had begun to confabulate quite urgently under the cover of their computer printer. After a moment they pulled out the phone book and began to leaf quickly through.

'They'd have the number to the hospital written down', Giampaolo whispered. I was all admiration.

The girl picked up the phone, dialled, asked if Lucio was there, hung on. And then the obvious occurred to me. 'It's because the *pasticceria* at this side of the village is closed. He's had to go to the one opposite the hospital and it's taking him longer than it usually does.'

And, indeed, just five minutes later Lucio could be heard hurrying up the stairs, icing sugar on the bristles of a fine moustache. '*Bene, Signori, vediamo.*' He smiled broadly, rubbed his hands together, and scribbled down my passport number as if he saw a dozen a day. To my relief the delay was not mentioned. Everybody was extremely polite and friendly and we all wished each other *buon giorno*. But Giampaolo, walking down to the car, was gloating. If there's one thing an impotent *dipendente* can do, it's demand his rights from a *statale*. Such was the world into which my child had now been officially introduced.

37
Manifesti funebri

So much gets said about the inefficiency of Italian public services that I feel it my duty toward the end of this book to remark on how extraordinarily fast, even in the holiday season, the Gas, Water and Cemeteries Board (AGSM) will authorise a death notice. On every wall or space where ads and announcements are pasted up in the villages of the Veneto – behind the bus-stop, or higgledy-piggledy on a wall at a crossroads – you always find a couple of these simple *manifesti funebri*, giving their sad news. And from time to time, while picking up your newspaper or going for a haircut, you will turn a corner and see a familiar name. You know in Montecchio when your neighbours die. The cemetery encroaches on the shopping streets. Rightly so perhaps. And, while birth may be a frilly silk-blue or pink,

321

death has no sex and, of course, only one colour. So you quickly learn to recognise the black borders and Christ's upturned face with crown of thorns at the top in the centre. Across the middle of the poster there will be a name in large letters, and perhaps a nickname too, since nicknames are common in Italy (Dino Chiericatti, and beneath, '*detto, il capitano*'). The age is placed in brackets, likewise the married woman's maiden name. There is the time and date of the funeral, gratitude in advance for those who attend. And a brief comment such as: 'mourned by all her loved ones', or 'lost to the affection of family and friends' – some appropriate, conventional formula, nothing fanciful. 'Authorised by AGSM', they have stamped askew in the bottom left-hand corner. The very day after Vittorina died the posters were already up all over the village.

Rita returned from the hospital just two days after Michele's birth. In the meantime the old women had come back triumphantly sunburnt from their holiday and were fussing and clucking to see the child. We had barely laid the carrycot on the table before they were knocking on the door, bringing gifts in extravagant packages. They peeked under the covers, went into ecstasies: the first male child born on Via Colombare for heaven knows how long! A jinx had been broken! And again Lucilla made herself cry by recounting the story of her own little boy: the fever in the night, the hot poultices applied to *quel povero corpicino*. Again we said we were sure she had done everything that reasonably could be done. And I glanced up to check that I had written our paediatrician's number on the board by the phone.

Giampaolo came upstairs. He didn't want to disturb us. They would see the baby when we had all had time to settle down. He just wanted to let me know that I was released from my duties of watering and mowing the lawn for a little while. Then whenever we felt ready, we could pop the first of those bottles of *prosecco* together. He now had three in the back of the fridge.

The following afternoon, a day of stifling *afa*, Vittorina did not wake up from her siesta. Lucilla's yells brought me running. Leone and Marisa were visiting and the three of them had discovered the corpse together. When I got downstairs, Lucilla had already recovered sufficiently to start pulling open drawers and thumbing through papers. It was intriguing that, for all the closeness of their friendship, Vittorina had never told her where she kept the will.

Leone lowered the shutters. Marisa lit a candle each side of the bed. I withdrew. On the threshold of her spick-and-span flat, its millimetrically positioned lithographs, and carefully dusted knick-knacks, Orietta had tears in her eyes. That low pressure at the seaside had been a terrible, terrible mistake. Criminal, on the doctor's part. At which the culprit himself drew up in the road outside, a practised smile on his face as he stepped out of his Porsche. *Troppo, ma troppo gentile*, sobbed Lucilla. It occurred to me I had better remove the blue rosette from the door.

Today was Friday and the funeral couldn't be arranged until Monday. With Giampaolo still at work, Orietta came upstairs around fivish to say she was worried about the possible smell. No, the undertakers didn't take away the body here. The relatives had to pray over it until the funeral. They would put her in her coffin tomorrow, but the body would still be lying there until Monday and with this weather . . . Mightn't it cause some kind of disease?

After all, *la poveretta* was only just the other side of the wall from their own bed.

And the *cassonetto* with its rubbish was only the other side of the street.

Rita was trying to breastfeed the little baby. I couldn't imagine there was any serious health risk, I said. But it wasn't my field. Orietta, it appeared, had already consulted Giampaolo's encyclopaedia. And now she stayed in our flat to phone various offices of the health service. There was a corpse just the other side of her bedroom wall. Could it cause disease? Their reassuring answers didn't convince her. She would keep her windows tightly closed, however hot it got.

All Saturday and Sunday the people of Via Colombare trickled by to pay their respects to the deceased and offer *condoglianze*. Lucilla managed to be overdressed in mourning, bursting with energy and self-commiseration, playing the protagonist's part. '*Gradirebbe un gingerino, Signora Rosa, una tazza di tè?*' And yes, Vittorina had left the flat to her, although she didn't want to talk about that kind of thing now. Word spread like wildfire. Bankworkers Antonio and Sabrina stopped by with Antonio's father, all in black, although they had never known Vittorina.

It occurred to me that, with the flat downstairs to dispose of, the heat was probably off as far as we were concerned. And a baby is such an attraction.

Then on the Monday, perhaps a year and a month after we had arrived, I got to see another of Lucilla's balcony performances. About twenty or thirty of us had gathered in the street, trying to keep out of the mud a bulldozer had left, for they had just begun to plough down the cherry trees behind the Madonnina. More work for our lady of the twig broom. Perhaps because of the heat, people were not overly formal. Only Lovato, who had presided so long over Vittorina's gardening, had a suit and tie. Giampaolo had taken time off work and was smartly, although casually dressed. Faces were waxy with sweat. Don Guido arrived in his battered Renault, dents front, back and sides. There was subdued chatter, the bright whistle of a blind blackbird in the dusty morning air. Old Signora Marini whispered to me that we could come and get some figs when they were ripe. Black or green. She knew my wife liked figs. How was little Michele? Weight? Sleeping habits? *Che caro!*

The hearse turned the corner from the derelict factory end, its polished grey flanks bearing the sublimely comforting announcement: *Azienda Municipale Servizi Funebri* – another branch of AGSM. Men dressed in blue overalls went in beneath the Californian eaves of number 10 and lifted the coffin in the shuttered, candlelit room. They were careful with their feet on the polished marble. The ailing tropical plants were moved aside. Then out they came between the two dwarf cypresses that guarded the bourgeois spirit of the glass front door. In the street, one or two people stepped forward to place flowers on top but, as Vittorina had not been a Montecchiese by birth, it was not a big funeral. The hearse had long side windows cut specially low to make an elegant display of the polished wood. Don Guido had to slam his damaged car door twice.

And then, just as the hearse got into gear, just as the crowd was preparing to follow, Lucilla, with a perfect sense of timing, burst forth on her terrace balcony and began to shriek and tear her hair. She had been betrayed, betrayed, betrayed! By life, by death. Her only treasure had been taken from her. The only companion of her old age.

'Vittorina, Vittorina, *tesoro, cara*, how could you? How could you die on me? *Maria Santissima, oh Gesù, perchè, perchè*?' Curiously, there was at least as much anger as sorrow in the performance, as if her sister-in-law's death wasn't so very different from having been cheated out of *il professore*'s flat. Another loss, another encroachment. She bared her crooked teeth and howled, she pulled at her hair. Truly grief-stricken, and truly theatrical. She railed against God and spat. But this time one didn't feel inclined to find anything cartoonlike or caricaturish about it, as one had a year ago. One was part of the crowd now, and one watched and listened respectfully, offering the tubby woman the audience she needed. One reflected that there would always be occasions, many occasions, even in the modern, high-tech, all-problems-solved world Giampaolo yearned for, when appearance on one's balcony and a wild raw wail in stifling heat before a gathered crowd would be both understandable and appropriate.

Late that evening, we opened the first bottles of *prosecco* with the Visentini and wondered who our new neighbours would be. One bottle was flat. The second frothed splendidly. There was just no telling why. The moon, the pressure? '*Salute*! Health!' Orietta was quick to say, clinking glasses. '*Molto valido*,' I said taking my first sip. '*Discreto*,' Giampaolo nodded, not wanting to go overboard. 'But *relativo*,' Rita added, 'if only one bottle out of two is good.' Sharp young Lara giggled.

Afterword

Some four or five years after I arrived in Italy, in a moment of nostalgia for milk-floats and the busy racial mix of Acton High Street, I reread Browning's, *Oh to be in England*. It wasn't April and there are no melon flowers in Montecchio; nor, if there were, would I find them gaudy, for nothing pleases me more than bright colours. Then the things Browning remembered about England are not the things I remember. I go for the back seat up top of a Victoria-bound bus, or gusting wind on the upper Edgware Road. The orchard bough, the swallows, the thrush, are not part of my memories of home. And anyway, all these things can be found in abundance in both Tuscany and the Veneto. There is no need to feel nostalgic for what is all around you. So that perhaps, rather than making any real comparison between the two countries, all Browning was saying, in his very beautiful way, was that he was homesick. And also, by curious implication, that he was not coming home. For anyone whose homesickness can be so exquisitely relished, so effectively deployed, has long passed the point of no return. Browning remembers England the way a happily married man, surprised by a scent some warm spring evening, might remember an earlier girlfriend: with thanks, with pleasure, even a ghost of regret, but no real urgency. If this book is anything, I hope it suggests how I passed that point of no return. Which is a process of immersion in details, whether they be pleasant or unpleasant. For details are sticky as spider's silk; you are very soon caught. And rather than a travel book, perhaps if there were such a category in the libraries, I should call this an arrival book. For by the end, this small square handkerchief of Italy I live in has become home for me. Hopefully, for just a moment, the reader will have been able to feel at home here too.

Critical acclaim for Tim Parks' novels

GOODNESS

'Thrusting software executive George Crawley hauls himself up by his bootstraps to escape from his Methodist upbringing, but finds his faltering marriage further threatened by the birth of a handicapped child. A taut fable about the conflicting claims of religion and common sense, Goodness negotiates the highwire between tragedy and farce with unerring dexterity.'

Independent on Sunday

'The overriding impression is of a brutal but beautiful book.'

Sunday Times

FAMILY PLANNING

'At the end of *Family Planning* the hulking schizophrenic Raymond, whose disposal has been exhaustively argued in family letters and councils of war, is writing to the Court of Human Rights to reveal that his mother, who has been certified after attacking him with a cake knife for butchering the cat, his loyal sister Lorna, and his younger twin brothers, the hopelessly adrift Garry and the self righteous Graham, have all been taken over by alien beings . . .

The novel brilliantly prospects the family's predicament for the best and worst in individuals . . .'

Guardian

'Like a collaboration between Kafka and Aykbourn, *Family Planning* is below the belt writing of the most arresting kind.'

Daily Telegraph

TONGUES OF FLAME

'Touched by undercurrents they do not understand, innocents in an environment of religious fanaticism, the Bowens become the focus and sacrifice of a frenzied envangelical movement: the cost of winning over the soul and saving the body is sometimes the heart. Merging structural simplicity with emotional complexity, Tim Parks has written a novel of extraordinary balance and grace.'

Books & Bookmen

'Not since *The Catcher in the Rye* has there been such a believable portrayal of male puberty. The quality of the story telling and the cadences of the prose have a piercing authenticity.'

Catholic Herald

LOVING ROGER

'Tight and disturbing, *Loving Roger* begins with a dead body and a chilling question. Why has nice, ordinary affectionate Anna picked up her kitchen knife and murdered the man she insists she loves? . . . This brief novel is a mordantly illuminating essay on the way love contains the seeds of vindictiveness and hatred.'

Observer

'Every aspect of this novel is beautifully realized . . . It is compulsive reading and I highly recommend it.'

Illustrated London News

HOME THOUGHTS

'For such a short book, Parks presents an impressive number of characters in full dress. There are well over a dozen, set in a plot of such convoluted intricacy it could fuel a soap opera for years . . . This is a startlingly sharp and impressive piece of work.'

New York Times

'No reader will feel short changed by Parks . . . Between the orderly lines there are passions, betrayals, violent deaths – more surprises and revelations than one narrative could normally contain.'

Hilary Mantel, *Books*

Tim Parks has also written a crime thriller, *Cara Massimina*, under the pseudonym John MacDowell. Set in Verona, it was described by Julian Symons in The *Independent* as, 'an unusually classy thriller, true to life and not to be missed'.